New Perspectives on Sport Volunteerism

The book highlights 'new perspectives' on volunteerism in sport, covering frameworks, methods, context and variables on several levels from community sport clubs to international events. In analysing the processes of control within voluntary sport clubs, a new theoretical framework – critical realism (CR) – challenges how we think about theory and how scientific inquiry should proceed. Further themes raised are: Should sports clubs be viewed as a crossing between a traditional volunteer culture dominated by collective solidarity, and a modern volunteer culture focused on the individual benefits? Are former athletes a new group of possible volunteers? Can personal narratives of experiences of being a volunteer in a big international event provide us with new insight that has not previously been considered?

Identity is suggested as a motive for understanding volunteers at sporting events. Two new theoretical models are presented, one on the development of volunteer commitment and the other on a framework that incorporates both individual- and institutional-level variables. All chapters have recommendations for future research. The testing of these theories and influencing factors will provide new directions in the research of sport volunteerism.

This book was originally published as a special issue of *European Sport Management Quarterly*.

Berit Skirstad is an Associate Professor at the Norwegian School of Sport Sciences, Oslo, Norway.

Alison Doherty is a Professor of Sport Management in the School of Kinesiology, Western University, Canada.

Vassil Girginov is a Reader in Sport Management/Development in the Department of Life Sciences, Brunel University, London, UK.

New Perspectives on Sport Volunteerism

Edited by
**Berit Skirstad, Alison Doherty and
Vassil Girginov**

LONDON AND NEW YORK

First published 2015 by Routledge

2 Park Square, Milton Park, Abingdon, Oxon OX14 4RN
711 Third Avenue, New York, NY 10017, USA

Routledge is an imprint of the Taylor & Francis Group, an informa business

First issued in paperback 2017

Notice:
Product or corporate names may be trademarks or registered trademarks,
and are used only for identification and explanation without intent to infringe.

British Library Cataloguing in Publication Data
A catalogue record for this book is available from the British Library

ISBN 13: 978-1-138-85642-4 (hbk)
ISBN 13: 978-1-138-05899-6 (pbk)

Typeset in Times New Roman
by RefineCatch Limited, Bungay, Suffolk

Publisher's Note
The publisher accepts responsibility for any inconsistencies that may have
arisen during the conversion of this book from journal articles to book chapters,
namely the possible inclusion of journal terminology.

Disclaimer
Every effort has been made to contact copyright holders for their permission to
reprint material in this book. The publishers would be grateful to hear from any
copyright holder who is not here acknowledged and will undertake to rectify
any errors or omissions in future editions of this book.

Contents

Citation Information

The chapters in this book were originally published in *European Sport Management Quarterly*, volume 13, issue 1 (February 2013). When citing this material, please use the original page numbering for each article, as follows:

Chapter 1
Introduction to special issue
Berit Skirstad, Alison Doherty and Vassil Girginov
European Sport Management Quarterly, volume 13, issue 1 (February 2013) pp. 1–4

Chapter 2
Using critical realism: a new perspective on control of volunteers in sport clubs
Terri Byers
European Sport Management Quarterly, volume 13, issue 1 (February 2013) pp. 5–31

Chapter 3
'Continue or terminate?' Determinants of long-term volunteering in sports clubs
Torsten Schlesinger, Benjamin Egli and Siegfried Nagel
European Sport Management Quarterly, volume 13, issue 1 (February 2013) pp. 32–53

Chapter 4
Changing roles: applying continuity theory to understanding the transition from playing to volunteering in community sport
Graham Cuskelly and Wendy O'Brien
European Sport Management Quarterly, volume 13, issue 1 (February 2013) pp. 54–75

Chapter 5
Front line insight: an autoethnography of the Vancouver 2010 volunteer experience
Erin Kodama, Alison Doherty and Megan Popovic
European Sport Management Quarterly, volume 13, issue 1 (February 2013) pp. 76–93

Chapter 6
Development of a hierarchical model of sport volunteers' organizational commitment
Se-Hyuk Park and May Kim
European Sport Management Quarterly, volume 13, issue 1 (February 2013) pp. 94–109

Chapter 7

A multi-level framework for investigating the engagement of sport volunteers
Pamela Wicker and Kirstin Hallmann
European Sport Management Quarterly, volume 13, issue 1 (February 2013) pp. 110–139

Please direct any queries you may have about the citations to
clsuk.permissions@cengage.com

Notes on Contributors

Terri Byers, Faculty of Kinesiology, University of New Brunswick, Canada.

Graham Cuskelly, Griffith Business School, Griffith University, Southport, Queensland, Australia.

Alison Doherty, School of Kinesiology, Western University, London, Ontario, Canada.

Benjamin Egli, Institute of Sport Science, University of Bern, Switzerland.

Vassil Girginov, Department of Life Sciences, Brunel University, London, UK.

Kirstin Hallmann, Department of Sport Economics and Sport Management, German Sport University, Cologne, Germany.

May Kim, Department of Physical Education, College of Education, Korea University, Seoul, South Korea.

Erin Kodama, School of Kinesiology, Western University, London, Ontario Canada.

Siegfried Nagel, Institute of Sport Science, University of Bern, Switzerland.

Wendy O'Brien, Department of Tourism, Leisure, Hotel and Sport Management, Griffith University, Southport, Queensland, Australia.

Se-Hyuk Park, Department of Sports Sciences, Seoul National University of Science & Technology, Seoul, South Korea.

Megan Popovic, School of Kinesiology, Western University, London, Ontario, Canada.

Torsten Schlesinger, Institute of Sport Science, University of Bern, Switzerland.

Berit Skirstad, Norwegian School of Sport Sciences, Oslo, Norway.

Pamela Wicker, Department of Sport Economics and Sport Management, German Sport University, Cologne, Germany.

Introduction

The purpose of this special issue is to bring together knowledge of new perspectives on sport volunteerism that is connected to various levels of sport, from community to engagement with international events. The special issue arises from the workshop on 'New Perspectives on Sport Volunteerism' held at the 19th EASM Conference in Madrid in 2011. The papers came from the workshop participants as well as other scholars. The special issue attracted 22 submissions, and after a robust reviewing process six articles were accepted for publication. The contributions in this collection are by authors from six different countries (Australia, Canada, Germany, the Republic of Korea, Switzerland and the UK) and represent a diverse range of sport voluntary traditions.

Previously, special issues on sport volunteerism have been published in the *European Journal for Sport Management* (1999), *Sport Management Review* (2006) and more recently in the *International Journal of Sport Policy and Politics* (2012) providing a forum for empirical and conceptual work on sport volunteerism and a platform for further studies. Given the rapidly expanding body of research since those publications it was deemed timely to provide a forum for research that is addressing new perspectives on this topic. Wilson (2012) notes that research on volunteerism in general has evolved considerably, particularly from a focus mainly on the individual to a consideration of the organisation as well. Research on sport volunteerism has also evolved, and the papers in this special issue are reflective of at least some of that shift in focus and approach.

The purpose of presenting new perspectives is to challenge our thinking, broaden our horizons and enrich our understanding of phenomena. Hustinx, Cnaan and Handy (2010) note that the dominant theories represent only one view of volunteerism and should be challenged, and perhaps complemented, by alternative perspectives. DiMaggio (1995) argues that 'good theory' is multidimensional, and the best ones are hybrids that come about through different perspectives and approach to research.

The special issue highlights 'new perspectives' in frameworks, methods, context and variables. The collection starts with Byers who uses critical realism (CR) to analyse the processes of control within voluntary sport clubs. It is a new theoretical framework that has not been used to any great extent in sport management, but has been adopted widely in other fields such as economics, sociology, criminology, geography and management (Easton, 2010) to mention a few. This framework allows conjunctional forms of explanation, challenges the way we think about our theory and also challenges how scientific inquiry should proceed. Using an ethnographic approach, Byers examines control as a dynamic combination of explicit management controls and socially negotiated implicit processes. Her study covers a four-year

1

period which allows for better capturing the processes of forming different control mechanisms and their relationships so that various conjunctional forms within the club become apparent. Byer also acknowledges the methodological challenges of the use of ethnographic content analysis, which is based on constructivist assumptions of reality, within a CR framework. CR and constructivism disagree in one important aspect: while the former focuses 'on the contingent relationships between phenomena and structures, they still subscribe to the realist notion that the inherent order of things is "mind-independent"', the latter attributes 'structures not to a mind-independent reality, but rather to the generative (and therefore constructive) act of researchers and theorists' (Mir & Watson, 2001, p. 1169).

The second paper, by Schlesinger, Egli and Nagel, presents the findings of a study that examined new perspectives to explain volunteer commitment, and specifically in community sports clubs. Volunteers' satisfaction with the working conditions and their personal orientation to the collective were considered, providing insight into the relative strength of both aspects as factors in the volunteers' intention to remain with their club. The findings highlight the relative importance of collective solidarity to volunteer commitment, and the authors note that one's attachment and obligation to the group is likely to override dissatisfaction with working conditions. Nonetheless, the new insight into the links between these two perspectives of volunteer commitment leads Schlesinger et al. to suggest that sports clubs should be viewed as a cross between a traditional volunteer culture dominated by collective solidarity and a modern volunteer culture where volunteers have expectations and evaluations towards working conditions.

Next, Cuskelly and O'Brien use continuity theory (Atchley, 1993) and a transition-extension hypothesis to examine the phenomenon of athletes transitioning from playing roles to key non-playing roles such as administration and coaching in sport clubs. Former players may be a particularly valuable source of (new) volunteers who are so critical to club functioning. Twelve volunteers with an average of 30 years of involvement in a sport club located in the area of Brisbane City Council were interviewed. The study examined whether the social relationships and sense of belonging the volunteers developed as players explained their original and ongoing involvement as club volunteers. The authors concluded that while continuity theory was useful to understand the ongoing commitment of volunteers in known roles and settings, it may have limited application in understanding such a significant change as from player to volunteer. Longitudinal data collected at the point of transition and then at various points after transition would more fully explore the complexity of ongoing involvement. The authors conclude that further research is needed to more fully test both continuity theory and the notion of transition-extension in explaining the factors that influence ongoing involvement as a volunteer in sport and other settings.

The fourth paper, by Kodama, Doherty and Popovic, uses autoethnography to uncover the nuances and complex experience of volunteering at large sport events such as the 2010 Winter Olympic Games in Vancouver. By using this approach they allowed new knowledge and new perspectives to be explored in ways that have seldom been done before in the field of sport management. The presentation of and reflection on personal narratives that are based on the first author's direct experience enriches and draws attention to new insights that have not been previously considered. The findings highlight how knowledge from personal experience can complement, nuance or contradict quantitative research. The manuscript identifies a few gaps in the research (e.g. understanding the difficult recruitment process) and emerging themes for future research (e.g. leisure time of volunteers when not 'working'). In addition, the authors recommend the consideration of identity as a mechanism for understanding the potentially wide range of more specific sport event volunteer motives than have been considered previously in the literature.

The special issue concludes with two articles that present new theoretical models of sport volunteerism. Park and Kim's paper proposes a theoretical model that applies Kohlberg's (1986) theory of moral development to the study of volunteers' commitment to their organisation from a developmental perspective. Specifically, they extend Allen and Meyer's (1990) classic three-component model of commitment by proposing five hierarchical stages that explain the development of volunteer commitment, namely, primitive, continuance, external, normative and affective commitments. Primitive and external commitments are the two new concepts that are gained from this exercise. The authors provide recommendations and direction for future research that include empirically testing the model and determining unique characteristics of each sport volunteer commitment stage.

Finally, Wicker and Hallmann's contribution advances research by proposing a framework that incorporates both individual- and institutional-level variables. 'Volunteers are nested within sport institutions' (Wicker & Hallmann, p. tbd), and thus it is critical to consider both individual and institutional factors to understand their engagement there. The multilevel framework is consistent with a heterodox approach that acknowledges the utility in integrating a potentially wide set of theoretical principles, such as economic, sociological and psychological, rather than a single or at least narrow perspective to explain a phenomenon. The authors note that research to date on sport volunteer engagement has focused predominantly on individual factors (micro-level) or institutional factors (macro-level), with very few studies considering their combined, and relative, effect within in a single investigation or analysis. They provide a comprehensive listing of the existing research in Tables 1 and 2 in the paper. The framework comprises individual economic, demographic, social and psychological indicators of involvement in volunteering, as well as institutional characteristics that should be taken into account. Further, the authors recommend the use of hierarchical linear modelling as an appropriate means of statistically analysing this multilevel data. They outline several recommendations for future research utilising this more sophisticated framework.

The new perspectives on sport volunteerism presented in this special issue introduce a number of considerations for the examination of this phenomenon, such as the multiple realities associated with sport volunteering, the use of ethnography and autoethnography as beneficial methodologies, and the consideration of the institutional level in the examination of volunteerism in this context. We are pleased to present this collection of diverse works and trust they will enhance understanding of sport volunteerism along a number of lines, and will open gates and provide new directions for continued research in this critical area.

References

Allen, N.J., & Meyer, J.P. (1990). The measurement and antecedents of affective, continuance, and normative commitment to the organization. *Journal of Occupational Psychology, 63*, 1–8.

Atchley, R.C. (1993). Continuity theory and the evolution of activity in later life. In J. Kelly (Ed.), *Activity and ageing: Staying involved in later life* (pp. 5–16). Newbury Park, CA: Sage.

DiMaggio, P. (1995). Comments on "What theory is not?" *Administrative Science Quarterly, 40*, 391–397.

Easton, G. (2010). Critical realism in case study research. *Industrial Marketing Management, 39*, 118–128. doi:10.1016/j.indmarman.2008.06.004

Hustinx, L., Cnaan, R.A., & Handy, F. (2010). Navigating theories of volunteering: A hybrid map for a complex phenomenon. *Journal for the Theory of Social Behaviour, 40*, 410–434.

Kohlberg, L. (1986). *The philosophy of moral development.* San Francisco: Harper and Row.

Mir, R., & Watson, A. (2001). Critical realism and constructivism in strategy research: Towards a synthesis. *Strategic Management Journal, 22*, 1169–1173. doi:10.1002/smj.200

Wicker, P., & Hallmann, K. (2013). A multi-level framework for investigating the engagement of volunteers. *European Sport Management Quarterly, 13*, 110–139.

Wilson, J. (2012). Volunteerism research: A review essay. *Non-profit and Voluntary Sector Quarterly, 41*(2), 176–212.

Berit Skirstad
Norwegian School of Sport Sciences, Oslo, Norway

Alison Doherty
Western University, London, ON, Canada

Vassil Girginov
Brunel University, London, UK

Using critical realism: a new perspective on control of volunteers in sport clubs

Terri Byers

Faculty of Business, Environment and Society, Coventry University, William Morris Building, Coventry, UK

The purpose of this paper is to demonstrate the theoretical and practical application of Critical Realism (CR) as a new methodological perspective in research on sport volunteering. To date, much of the sport volunteering research has been underpinned by a polarity of positivist and interpretivist methodologies which has contributed to narrow ontological perspectives of the sport volunteering phenomenon. Data from a 3-year multiple case study of three equestrian sport clubs are used to illustrate how CR provides a new perspective of control in this context. To complement the CR philosophy, Altheide's Ethnographic Content Analysis (ECA) was employed in data analysis. Using the CR ontology of multiple realities and ECA, control in sport clubs is theorised as complex, dynamic and contextually sensitive. The results of this analysis reveal the objective, observable elements of control, the subjective interpretations of control and the underlying generative mechanisms which are thought to have given rise to the forms of control and how they are used within the clubs in this dataset. Building on Downward's introduction of CR to research on Sport Tourism, this paper contributes to the literature on sport volunteerism by offering a more extensive discussion of CR as a new methodological perspective worthy of further application across a range of issues related to sport volunteerism.

Introduction

Critical Realism (CR) takes elements from both positivism and interpretivism and is therefore an appropriate tool to provide a new perspective on sport volunteerism. CR advocates a unique ontological stance that has significant implications for what and how we can learn about the world. It is a philosophy of science that encourages systematic retroductive analysis in an attempt to identify underlying factors which explain the existence of a phenomenon (Reed, 2005). This perspective has yet to be explored within the sport volunteerism literature or in the wider field of sport management. Research on sport volunteerism has taken a positivist (e.g. Kim, Zhang, & Connaughton, 2010) or interpretivist (e.g. Seippel, 2004) stance. Both of these approaches have provided valuable contributions to the literature. Positivist approaches have provided statistical evidence of key macro issues such as the size and scope of the sport volunteering sector (Taylor et al., 2003), the demographics (Nichols & Shepherd, 2006) and motivations of volunteers (Pauline & Pauline, 2009).

Interpretivist research has provided more sensitive, subjective accounts of, for example, sport volunteering (Adams & Deane, 2009), sport event volunteers (Nichols & Ojala, 2009) and the experiences of older volunteers (Misener, Doherty, & Hamm-Kerwin, 2010). Mixed methods studies have also contributed to more robust, validated (through triangulation of data) accounts of sport volunteering (e.g. Kay & Bradbury, 2009; Vos, Breesch, & Sheerder, 2011), but the ontological span of these studies remains narrow.

This paper contributes to the literature on sport volunteering by demonstrating the application of CR to understanding control of volunteers in the context of voluntary sport clubs (building on the work of Downward, 2005), giving a new perspective of volunteering that accommodates elements of positivism and interpretivism. This paper is also significant to the wider field of sport management as it is the first to fully explore CR and present the application of this methodology in research on the management of sport. The remainder of this paper is structured as follows. A brief literature review relevant to understanding control of volunteers in sport clubs is provided. The methods associated with the study are then discussed and the key principles and tenets of CR are explored. Second, further evidence from previously published data (see Byers, Henry, & Slack, 2007) is provided showing the practical implications of employing a CR perspective, followed by a discussion of the challenges associated with CR and its implementation. Finally, suggestions for future applications of CR to understanding control of volunteers are articulated.

Literature review

There is over 100 years of research on organisation control (e.g. Blau & Scott, 1962; Byers et al., 2007; Daft, 2009; Delbridge & Ezzamel, 2005; Ferner, 2000; Glover & Coleman, 1937; Green & Welsh, 1988; Meira, Kartalis, Tamenyi, & Cullen, 2010; Styre, 2008; Taylor, 1906). This literature review provides a concise overview of important developments in the understanding of organisation control and as such includes some 'classic' sources as well as more recent studies of control. It is worth noting that studies on control since 2005 have been sparse (Delbridge & Ezzamel, 2005). The concept of control is highly regarded as 'an essential and central process of management yet it is strangely neglected by many writers on organization' (Child, 2005, p. 111).

Research on control in organisations has tended to focus on either administrative control mechanisms such as operating procedures, job descriptions or disciplinary policy (see, e.g. Agarwal, 1999; Anthony, Dearden, & Bedford, 1989; Fortado, 1994; Kirsch, 2004), management control as a function of an organisation (see Anthony & Young, 1988) or contextual controls such as structure, size and the external environment (see Burns & Stalker, 1961; Khandwalla, 1977; Lawrence & Lorsch, 1967; Pugh et al., 1963; Slack, 1997). These mechanisms as objects of analysis are directly observable and tangible to a researcher and are of course attractive to those employing a positivistic investigation. Focusing on tangible controls, these positivistic approaches do little to consider the different types of controls (i.e. intangible controls such as emotion, ideology or culture) that are employed by different stakeholders such as customers or organisational members (see Barker, 1993; Hopwood, 1974; Perrow, 1995). Yet research has recognised that subordinates as well as managers attempt to control the actions and values of others (Ashforth & Saks, 2000; Oliga, 1989), and 'control' may not always be attempted or achieved to accomplish organisational goals. Therefore, a more appropriate view of control is as an 'holistic phenomenon', conceptualised as a dynamic combination of explicit 'management' controls and socially negotiated, implicit processes. These two types of control are not mutually exclusive, but they operate and influence one another throughout organisational life.

For several decades control has been analysed as an external phenomenon, a function of management that is employed through organisational systems (see Gupta & Govindarajan, 1991; Ouchi, 1977; Tankersley, 2000; Tosi, 1983). Much of this understanding of organisational control is based upon research conducted in the commercial sector, and public organisational contexts (see e.g. Agarwal, 1999; Ferner, 2000; Gupta & Govindarajan, 1991; Tankersley, 2000). It has long been recognised that the environment and context of an organisation has a considerable effect on its operations (Burns & Stalker, 1961; Lawrence & Lorsch, 1967), with some research specifically noting the key influence of contextual variables upon the methods of control adopted in organisations (Anthony & Young, 1988; Johnson & Gill, 1993; Maguire, 1999).

The term context refers to 'the circumstances relevant to something under consideration' (Thompson, 1995, p. 288). Contextual features which have been shown to impact on the function of organisations include structure, size and the external environment (see Burns & Stalker, 1961; Lawrence & Lorsch, 1967). Researchers such as Johnson and Gill (1993) and Maguire (1999) have specifically noted the key influence of contextual variables upon the methods of control adopted in organisations. They argue that important to understanding control is the structure, cultures and social/political/economic (external) environment of organisa- tions, and that these variables can influence control processes in a wide variety of ways. Specifically, the authors note the impact of size, geographical dispersion, technological complexity and environmental stability on the mechanisms and process of control adopted in an organisation.

Little attention has been paid to control in the voluntary organisational context. This is unfortunate for several reasons. The voluntary sector makes a considerable contribution both socially and economically in the UK (Kendall, 2003). These organisations are known to be sociologically complex and tend to be lacking in formal structures as seen in many commercial firms and government bureaucracies (Pearson, 1982). Sport clubs represent an interesting context within voluntary organisations in which to study control. The contextual features of sport clubs which may influence the study of control within these organisations are evident in several studies. The structures and practices within local sport clubs are heavily influenced by the individual values of the voluntary staff (Kirk & MacPhail, 2003; Pearce, 1993). There is a tendency in small clubs for the majority of work to be performed by a few individuals (Shibli, Taylor, Nichols, Gratton, & Kokolakakis, 1999), hence, these individuals would have considerable influence over club operations. Many clubs have also been noted for their informal, social nature as opposed to being bureaucratic with extensive use of rules or formal operating procedures (Friederici & Heinemann, 2007).

Voluntary sport clubs are under pressure to professionalise their operations and focus on improving their service delivery, in line with standards experienced in the private sector (Nichols & Shepherd, 2006; Nichols et al., 2005; Papadimitriou, 2002). There is some suggestion that voluntary sport clubs are not effective enough in delivering government objectives such as increasing sports participation, and there have been calls for a 'more systematic and structured development of sports clubs across the country' (DCMS, 2002, p. 40).

Taking the external pressures of voluntary sport organisations into consideration, it could be argued that formal mechanisms of control related to structures and systems will be important in understanding what control mechanisms operate and why these exist. However, literature highlighting the features of the internal environment of sport clubs would seem to suggest these organisations have strong ideas related to the existing modes of operation which are unlikely to include formal mechanisms of control. Perhaps it is more important to examine the relationship between mechanisms and how mechanisms are changing over time. The diversity in individual values and strong social emphasis in club histories is in opposition with societal and government pressures to formalise and professionalise club operations. This conflict is part of the contextual environment within which clubs operate and is likely to have an influence on the control and operations of clubs.

Other characteristics of sport clubs which may have an impact on the nature of control are related to the motivations and characteristics of the volunteers. Sport clubs rely primarily on voluntary labour with no economic necessity to participate in the organisation. Many sport club volunteers do so to help meet their own needs, but there is also some degree of altruistic motivation whereby volunteers want to help other people or improve a club (Shibli et al., 1999) Clubs are often individually weak and limited in capacity due to limited finances, facilities and expertise (Collins & Kay, 2003; Garrett, 2004). Research from Denmark (Pfister, 2006), Norway (Seippel, 2004, 2005), Canada (Inglis, 1997) and the UK (Nichols & Padmore, 2005; Shibli et al., 1999) suggested that there is a higher proportion of male volunteers in sport clubs, particularly in leadership positions. Sport England (2003) described the profile of adult volunteers as 40% of people between the ages of 35–39 with twice as many male volunteers as female. Shibli et al. (1999) noted that volunteers tend to be well educated, and club officers are often employed in some professional capacity.

A framework to guide the study of control in voluntary sport clubs needs to take these contextual attributes into consideration. One such framework is the categorisation of control mechanisms presented by Hopwood (1974).

Theoretical framework

Hopwood (1974) identified three categories of control within organisations: administrative, social and self-control mechanisms. Hopwood described administrative controls as formal rules and standard procedures, found in, for example, plans, budgets, standards, operating manuals, formal patterns of organisational relationships and recruitment policies. Granted, these controls are open to the interpretation of organisational members and therefore may not always achieve desired results. Rules, procedures and other similar mechanisms are therefore a 'necessary means to a wider end' but their intended effect depends considerably upon the social pressures and personal motivations/desires that exist among employers and employees simultaneously (Hopwood, 1974, p. 21).

Social controls are the shared values, norms and commitments of organisational actors developed through formal, planned strategies designed by management to 'regulate systems of beliefs and meaning' (administrative control) and/or through spontaneous social interaction (Johnson & Gill, 1993, p. 30). Bourdieu's (1985) notion of capital is useful here and suggests an individuals' position within a social structure may be important in understanding the operation and control of voluntary sport clubs. Various forms of capital (e.g. cultural, social, economic and physical) may have different levels of importance within the organizations under investigation. Capital can be a resource itself, used consciously by individuals (e.g. networking as a form of social capital) or serve to influence a group more generally (e.g. lack of economic capital of a club limits the development options for the club).

Self-controls constitute the personal motives of individual members. Hopwood (1974) suggested that in order for administrative and social controls to be effective, they must operate as 'self-controls' suggesting the importance of the internalisation (directly or indirectly) of the norms embodied in the social and administrative controls. Conformity to social and administrative controls can occur through internalisation or 'identification' in which an individual feels emotional gratification and attachment to 'significant' organisational members (Kelman, 1961). Actors may be heavily influenced by social interaction with certain individuals and/or groups, which they consider significant (Johnson & Gill, 1993) whereby that individual or group may serve as a 'reference' (and acts as a control) for what constitutes appropriate behaviour.

A central premise of Hopwoods' conceptualisation of control is that administrative, social and self-controls do not act independently, suggesting that control is 'a much more complex and subtle process than the limitation of behaviour by administrative devices' (Hopwood, 1974, p. 27). Management controls alone cannot significantly influence employee behaviour, if the employees do not internalise or identify with the values and norms advocated by the external control mechanisms (Manz & Simms, 1989). Attention to the individual members of an organisation is therefore essential to understanding control as it is these individuals who create administrative mechanisms resist forms of control with which they do not identify and attempt to create or recreate control mechanisms which fit with their own values, needs or expectations of what is appropriate.

The Hopwood conceptualisation provides a useful framework for examining control more holistically. However, given the difficulty in applying structural controls in voluntary organisations (Johnson & Gill, 1993) and the different contextual demands placed upon the voluntary sector, it is possible that the more subtle forms of control (social and self) play a more pivotal role in the control process. The increasing pressure, and consequent compliance, to adopt professional (and perhaps administrative) modes of operation in voluntary organisations (Cunningham, 2000; Saeki, 1994) also suggests support for the notion that there is a strong tendency for social and self-controls to be prevalent in these organisations. The next section introduces the critical realist perspective as suitable for examining control in the context of voluntary sport clubs.

CR methodology and methods

CR methodology

If we consider a continuum of research perspectives ranging from positivism on the left to interpretivism on the right, CR can be located in the centre. CR takes elements from the positivistic school of thought and elements from the interpretivist school to offer a more balanced research perspective.

According to CR, the social world is comprised of four levels of reality: material, ideal, artefactual and social. This is a key and unique feature of CR that multiple realities exist for all phenomenon under investigation. The levels of reality correspond to the depth of reality being considered ranging from the superficial material reality to the deeply embedded social reality. The CR perspective suggests that accurate understanding of a phenomenon can only be obtained through considering all levels of reality. Figure 1 shows the different layers of CR ontology with examples. The figure is adapted from Tsoukas (1994) who used the CR perspective to contemplate the meaning of 'management'. In a similar fashion, the examples given in Figure 1 relate to the concept of control rather than management.

Marsh's (1999) six major assumptions of CR are useful to demonstrate the applicability of this methodology to understanding control in voluntary sport clubs. The six assumptions are:

(1) There is a reality external to individuals
(2) Reality consists of superficial and deep structures
(3) Objects and structures have causal power
(4) Actors' discursive knowledge regarding 'reality' has a construction effect on the outcomes of social interrelations
(5) Structures such as cultures, ideologies, and institutional practices enable and constrain everyday social activities rather than *determine* outcomes
(6) Social science involves the study of reflexive agents who may construct, deconstruct and reconstruct structures

Applying CR to understand control

Taking these assumptions into account, we can see that any attempt to understand the control of volunteers is incomplete without some understanding of the social structural context that impacts upon people in these organizstions. For instance, the critical realist ontology accepts that there is a 'reality' external to individuals (assumption 1) that contains both superficial structures and deep structures that are

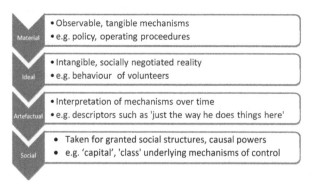

Figure 1.   Critical realism: levels of reality
Source: Adapted from Tsoukas (1993, p. 296).

not easily and/or directly observable (assumption 2). Furthermore, an individual's knowledge of any 'reality', including structures, is limited by the individual's background and education.

The third assumption suggests that if there is necessity in the world, objects and structures therefore have causal power indicating a need to make causal statements. However, actors' discursive knowledge regarding 'reality' has a construction effect on the outcomes of social interrelations (assumption 4). This perhaps suggests that objects and structures, more accurately, can have causal power. Furthermore, structures such as cultures, ideologies, and institutional practises enable and constrain everyday social activities rather than determine outcomes (assumption 5). They may enable, for example, the dominant class and constrain a lower class or vice versa. Taking assumptions 3–5 into consideration, the reality of the concept of control mechanisms can be directly illustrated by formal procedures and policies within an organisation, but also by job descriptions, reporting templates and hierarchical reporting relationships. At first glance these superficial 'structures' may appear to 'control' members' behaviour by indicating the appropriate way in which to perform their job roles. However, the deep structures that underlie organisation members' acceptance and utilisation of these control mechanisms may be underpinned by more latent constructs, such as emotion, values, norms and/or identification. Therefore, as social science involves the study of reflexive agents who may construct, deconstruct and reconstruct structures (assumption 6) to understand the deep, subtle forms of organisation control, the researcher only partially relies on organisation members' perceptions and discursive constructs to understand what control mechanisms exist, how they operate and why they influence members' behaviour.

Importance of CR to agent-structure debate

CR also suggests a unique relationship between structures and agents when seeking to understand multi-realities which Reed (1997) has argued offer a robust framework to understand and explain the interplay between structures and agents. The agency/ structure debate is one that has been of concern to researchers in organisation studies for many years and continues to occupy debates. The agency/structure debate raises significant questions about the nature of social reality in organisations and has consequences for how we can learn about that reality. Agents produce and reproduce the structures which constrain and enable their action. But agents are not without power to resist pressures from the structures they created and therefore the psychological dimension of agent action has been the predominant focus of organiation studies attempting to understand the behaviour of agents (Llewellyn, 2007). Structures are the 'relatively enduring institutionalized relationships between social positions and practices located at different levels of analysis that constrain actors capacities to 'make a difference'" (Reed, 1997, p. 25).

The critical realist perspective views structures and agents as factors that in combination determine the outcomes of social phenomena. That is, a phenomenon such as control cannot be understood by examining structures alone. Nor can an understanding be obtained through reliance solely on agents. Rather the agents, located within a social-political context (Marsh, 1999), interpret their surroundings and these interpretations influence their behaviour. Therefore, structures alone do not constitute control in an organisation, be they administrative control mechanisms (i.e. job description, policy) or social/self-control mechanisms (i.e. emotion, identification). It is the relationship between the actors and these mechanisms, notably the interpretation by actors of their environment and of each other's behaviour. However, relationships and social phenomena cannot be always understood by causal statements and the researcher must also interpret the social structural context that underpins and shapes the control mechanisms active in the organisations under investigation. Marsh and Smith (2001) suggest this involves considering beyond appearances, such as what people say and do, and questioning the underlying reasons of motive and actor assumptions.

Methods: data collection and analysis

Data collection

The data reported in this paper were recorded over a period of 4 years through participant observation, interviews and historical documentation (newsletters, past minutes of meetings, newspaper articles, etc.). The study focused on three small equestrian clubs in the South of England, and participant observation focused on the committees and organised activities (meetings, competitions, club events) of the clubs. All members of each committee read and signed an informed consent and confidentiality statement. Participation in the clubs increased gradually, and relationships and roles/responsibilities were unique to each individual club. For purposes of anonymity original names of clubs and people have been changed and those names that appear in this document are pseudonyms.

Within the committees investigated for this study, administrative control mechanisms examined included meeting agendas, minutes of meetings, club constitutions and governing body rule books (i.e. policy on organising competitions, club operations). Garfinkel (1967) and later Holy (1984) suggested that validity of research data from fieldwork is attained by getting sufficiently closely involved in the research setting so as to be able to 'describe the world as they [subjects] see it' (Fortado, 1994, p. 255). However, even once the formal field work was complete, due to the relationships and involvement with the clubs, contact with individuals continued and therefore insight into the club and individuals within the committee continued to develop for approximately one year. Historical material was also obtained such as past minutes and newsletters, histories of clubs and past versions of club constitutions. Any formal written document designed to direct the clubs' operations or indicate how the club currently operated was collected as evidence of administrative control mechanisms. Unfortunately availability of documents varied between clubs. For example, while all clubs had some minutes and newsletters, the filing and storage of these documents were not centrally controlled or monitored. From one club, research identified a founding member of the club who held a scrap book, and early records of accounts, newsletters and minutes were obtained and this member was interviewed. However, even these items were not systematically or rigorously archived and some information was missing. In total, data consisted of 23 interviews, 176 documents (newsletters, minutes of meetings, constitutions, financial records, letters, policies and scrapbook), 80 pages of field notes, 40 pages of reflective diary and 57 committee meeting/minutes/observations.

The concept of social control and self-controls, intangible in comparison to administrative controls, was more difficult to operationalise. While it was essential to consider the existing literature, and observe for social (e.g. use of emotions by committee members) and self (e.g. self-identity matching organisation identity) control mechanisms, indicators of the concepts were not definitively derived from the literature. Rather, the researcher chose to enter the research setting with some knowledge and allow for the concept to develop within the context of the organisations under analysis. This was important because the research focused on small voluntary organisations largely because little is known about control in this type of context. It was important therefore not to simply draw on indicators derived from the general literature on control in organisations.

Table 1 outlines some indicators of social and self-control mechanisms that were used in this study. The table also provides examples of the indicators to demonstrate how each could be recognised in a data set, with these definitions being based upon secondary literature, listed in the last column of the table. The development continued throughout data collection and other concepts emerged as possible control mechanisms, which are identified and discussed in the Results and Discussion section of this paper. Therefore Table 1 is the version of indicators used at the start of the data collection and analysis. The operationalisation of concepts is important within the CR framework to enable retroductive analysis, a process by which conceptual abstraction and interpretation occurs from a systematic account of concrete events and phenomenon (Reed, 2009).

Data analysis

Data were analysed in accordance with the principles of Altheide's (1996) Ethnographic Content Analysis (ECA) which requires concepts to be derived from the data as well as looking for evidence of the anticipated effects of structures (as defined in the literature) in the data. ECA is based upon three main assumptions. First, this approach considers that analysis of text should take into consideration the environment which the person speaking or writing the text has experienced. Thus, it is important to the interpretation of meaning to understand, for example, a persons' educational and ideological background, experiences in life generally, work related or professional influences, given the potential influence of such factors on an individuals' world view.

Second, this communicative process breaks the distinction between subject and object, joining them in the reality that is experienced but often taken for granted. Through an individual communicative discourse regarding self and others, organisa-tion and control, mechanisms can be identified. Additionally, an individual's activities as part of the social world may be reflexive, whereby they refer to past experiences or stories about the past which suggest relevant action in the present. The researcher must try to take account of the process by also being reflexive of the overall process or of theoretical foundations, including assumptions about social science and order.

The third assumption of Altheide's (1996) ECA places great importance on the notion of process, given that everything is socially constructed, including morals, values and personal commitment. In trying to understand any given social situation, it is as important to recognise the process by which morals, values or behaviour are

Table 1.   Examples of indicators of control mechanisms.

Concept (type of control)	Indicators	Authors
1 Administrative control mechanisms	*1.1. Rules/operating procedures* e.g. club Constitutions, governing body guidelines on running competitions, written rules for club members	Johnson and Gill (1993) and Hopwood (1974)
	or formal (written) planned strategies to 'regulate systems of beliefs and meanings'	Johnson and Gill (1993, p. 30)
	or training manuals, recruitment policy, formal communication channels e.g. agenda used to guide committee meetings, by whom	Hopwood (1974)
	1.2. Contracts – formal agreements to clarify responsibilities	Johnson and Gill (1993)
2. Social control mechanisms	Social control mechanisms (also referred to as 'normative' controls (Das & Teng, 1998) produce desirable behaviour without explicit rewards and/or punishments	Maguire, Phillips, and Hardy (2001)
	2.1. Emotion Multidimensional systems that include many components including cognitive, behavioural, expressive and psychological changes	Fineman (1999, 2000) and Tiedens (2000)
	2.2. Language/discourse – control by having the key terminology, concepts, linguistic etiquette (e.g. how to propose a motion, how to defeat opposing ideas)	Boden (1994)
	2.3. Identity Actors may constitute themselves in ways which render them more subject to those mechanisms which confirm their individual sense of self	Coombs, Knights, and Wilmott (1992)
	2.4. Organisational socialisation (social processes and structures which influence the prevention of deviance from organisational norms) (trust)	Hollinger and Clark (1982), Van Maanen and Schein (1979) and Tiedens (2000)
	2.5. Social hierarchy (negotiated order) Social hierarchy is defined as the 'status and power' that individuals experience at different 'levels' in an organisation as a result of social negotiation and may be dependent on, for example, capital	Bourdieu (1989)

Table 1 (*Continued*)

Concept (type of control)	Indicators	Authors
3. Self-control mechanisms	*3.1. Identity* An actor's sense of self and the meanings they attach to the social categories in which they place themselves e.g. a committee member consciously/unconsciously behaves in a certain way which reinforces their perceived personal characteristics	Coombs et al. (1992) and Maguire et al. (2001)
	3.2. Emotion Actors may either consciously control their emotions within a situation to behave in line with norms and expectations	Fineman (1999)

deemed acceptable as it is to identify what those morals, values and behaviours actually are. Thus, a research investigation is also socially constructed in that research methods are formed from a theoretical position about what constitutes reality, knowledge of which is impacted by social context. This highlights the importance of recognising how context and perception influence the individual behaviour of actors (including the researcher) but also important may be notions of faith and beliefs in seeking knowledge which shape both the process by which taken-for-granted-assumptions are formed and by which they become routine to an organisation, actor or researcher.

Documents used in this research include, as defined by Altheide (1996), primary (interview transcripts, field notes) and secondary sources (past newsletters, minutes, club histories) as well as some auxiliary documents as they became available (emails, notes about interviewees' dress, etc.). A variety of documents thus may be used to enable what Altheide (1996) called an 'emergence of meaning', in which he refers to the gradual shaping of meaning through the interpretation of documents. This occurred after each interview when the interview schedule would change slightly, adding questions/themes to use in subsequent interviews as a result of new ideas suggested by the interviewee. This was, in part, practised under the assumption that meaning or patterns in the data would appear over time and not all at once. This method of analysis allows for reflexive movement between concept development, document sampling, data collection, coding and analysis/interpretation required in retroductive analysis with a focus on actors' perceptions within the constraints of their own context and structures (reality as defined within CR).

Results

The results of a critical realist analysis of control in voluntary sport organisations are presented here within the four levels of reality proposed by the CR framework.

The CR framework encourages examination of phenomenon over time (i.e. change in control) and attention to context (Table 2). Results indicated here reflect how control developed in each of the three clubs. In this respect, four key findings are offered:

(1) Contextually, the three clubs showed variations and there were significant similarities and differences in how control was enacted in each club (corresponds to material reality).

The variations in contextual elements are shown in Table 3. Generally, these clubs were of a similar size, structure and purpose, but a closer examination of contextual features reveals important differences. This corresponds to some important similarities and differences noted regarding control in these clubs, illustrated in Table 4.

(2) All clubs exhibited Hopwood's (1974) administrative, social and self-control mechanisms, but each club tended to rely more heavily on a different category, which changed over time (corresponds to ideal reality).

An abundance of control mechanisms from across all categories of the Hopwood (1974) framework was found in each club. Volunteers employed a mechanism 'reactively' as a control tactic or employed a mechanism more 'strategically' when there was greater, direct long-term implications to their action/decision.

Table 2.   Results summary: multiple realities of control per club.

	Club A	Club B	Club C
Material reality (observable tangible elements of control)	Constitution, agenda/minutes and organisation structure	Constitution, agenda/minutes and organisation structure	Constitution, agenda/minutes, organisation structure, role descriptors and operating manual
Ideal reality (socially negotiated forms of control)	Predominant founding values 'social' Social and self control mechanisms	Predominant founding values 'administrative' and 'social'	Predominant founding values 'administrative'
Social reality (interpretation of control over time)	Predominant values changed to 'administrative' during fieldwork	Predominant values changed to 'social' during field work	Predominant values changed to 'administrative' and 'social' during field work
Artefactual reality (taken for granted social structures, underlying mechanisms of control)	'Systemic' mechanisms served to control without volunteers knowledge	'Systemic' mechanisms served to control without volunteers knowledge	'Systemic' mechanisms served to control without volunteers knowledge

Table 3. Contextual features of clubs.

Contextual elements (relevant to control) and authors	Club 1: CWRC	Club 2: WRC	Club 3: WHRC
External environmental dynamism and complexity (see Burns & Stalker, 1961; Duncan, 1972; Thompson, 1967)	Relatively stable; mainly unaffected by foot and mouth due to local nature of club; regulation of national governing body mainly stable; 'suppliers' (i.e. venues) fluctuate	Relatively stable; affected by foot and mouth but not affiliated to NGB (not linked with national structure of rules and competitions)	Diverse and complex; high diversity and the number of activities organised, external environment (rules and regulations, 'customer needs', sponsors) also medium/highly diverse and complex
Task and technological complexity (see Perrow, 1967; Woodward, 1965)	Co-Chairs (one of which also Team Manager), Secretary, Treasurer, Newsletter, Web-site, Points, Social, PR & Marketing, general members	Chair (later made honorary President), Vice-Chair, Secretary, Treasurer, Show sub-committee, general members	Chair, Secretary, Treasurer, Membership Secretary, Team Manager, Newsletter
Organisation size (Child, 1975)	Committee of 9–12 people; club membership 50–60 people Turnover: approx. £5000	Committee of 10; club membership 70–80 people Turnover: approx. £10,000	Committee of 10–12; club membership approximately 100 (plus a waiting list) Turnover: approx. £36,000
Diversity of activities (Stopford & Wells, 1972)	Held two shows (30–40 competitors), three dressage competitions (15–20 competitors) and one social event per year (80 people)	Held three shows (50–70 competitors), several social events, three Show Jumping Competitions per year (30–40 competitors)	Held numerous events in dressage, show jumping, hunter trials, showing, roads and tracks, sponsored rides, training and social events
Existence of employee expectations regarding autonomy and self-control (Lorsch & Morse, 1974)	'Medium' – expected great amount of input/idea generation; wanted autonomy in event management with support	'High' – expected complete autonomy and little resistance to ideas	'Low' – established rules for new members, input encouraged and discussed, support provided to new members

Tables 5–7 contain evidence from each club which illustrates the existence of these mechanisms. Given the large amount of data, it is not possible to provide tables that are directly comparable with evidence of all control mechanisms within each category. Therefore each table provides a sample of different mechanisms and their mode of operation. Results are more fully explained in the following section devoted to discussion of control using the CR methodology.

Table 4. Key similarities and differences in control.

Similarities	Differences
All categories and mechanisms found to operate across the three clubs	Development of mechanisms over time
Differences in use of mechanisms related to individual employing/affected by the mechanisms	Founding values and control mechanisms different in each club
Differences in what mechanisms most prominent in the organisation related to type and level of conflict in club	Nature of leadership in each club
Each mechanism could exist in three different ways: a tactic or strategy employed or a systemic mechanism	Use of mechanisms by individuals
	Contextual features of each organisation differed slightly

(3) Differences in control can be attributed to the historical development of control mechanisms over time, individual use of control mechanisms, the level of conflict in each club and the nature of leadership in each club (corresponds to social reality).

The social structural context (individuals, their relationships) was unique to each club, and individuals served to reinforce the existing mechanisms, challenge the existing mechanisms and create change in mechanisms on a regular basis throughout field work.

(4) Control and the differences in control can be attributed to differences in social class and accumulated capital (corresponds to artefactual reality).

Discussion

Results suggest that a CR view of control in voluntary sport clubs has identified a complex array of mechanisms which operate and change continuously over time. This reinforces the notion that control is a dynamic combination of the interaction between agents and structures. Within these clubs, the agents (i.e. volunteers) operated within social structures (e.g. history, values and norms of the club) that they may have contributed to creating. New members were not part of that creation and so challenged the existing structures and attempted to create new modes of operation, norms and values which they identified with more strongly than the existing structures. This was particularly evident in one club where five new committee members were elected at the club Annual General Meeting (AGM). The Chairwoman reacted to this by using her position of authority to change from a club which valued and operated with primarily social control to one where administrative mechanisms (e.g. agendas, rules) were strictly enforced (by the Chair herself) as essential to club operations.

As shown in Tables 5–7, each club used all categories of mechanisms, and these could operate as a reactive tactic, a more thoughtful and proactive strategy or not

Table 5. Club A (CWRC) sample evidence of control mechanisms and mode of operation.

Hopwood (1974) categories/control mechanisms	Tactical	Strategic	Systemic/structures
Administrative			
Agenda	Can we get back to this – hello, we shouldn't be talking about that til later anyway' (field notes CWRC, 08/10/01)	This is the agenda and it is specific for every meeting – you can only talk about something when it comes up on the agenda or we'll be here all night.!. (field notes CWRC, 07/01/02)	[over time, became routine to use agenda and refer to agenda of last meeting]
Structure: Rules (NGB or other), formalisation and centralisation	N/A	Right, a new rule – if you miss more than 3 committee meetings and don't have a good reason, didn't let me know, then you won't be on the committee. (field notes CWRC, 07/01/02)	...we're small and that limits how much we can do. (interview Ellen, 10/10/02) other clubs have one person to do one little things but we have to multi-task a lot! (field notes CWRC, 06/05/02) [common to dwell on limitations]
Social			
Emotion	... I said something that wasn't too tactful and made her burst into tears and leave. (interview Lisa, 03/04/03)	Well, if everyone is having a good time and enjoying themselves that's enough for me and that will make people want to be part of the club... (interview Al, 09/01/03)	[Cultural rules regarding appropriate display of emotion]
History		I just think, once you've done something once, next time you know exactly how to do it, you learn from your pitfalls all the time... (interview Al, 09/01/03)	...we've tried that and it just didn't work, nobody wanted it... (interview Al, 09/01/03) [a common reference]
Cultural capital	I could do that, I do web site stuff at work so I know how to do it ... (field notes CWRC, 07/10/02)	Well I don't really want him doing that job – you need experience in the show ring to assist the judge properly. (interview Al, 09/01/03)	also my Dad, he's done a lot on committees and I'm just like him really. (field notes CWRC, 24/09/01)
Self			
Emotion	N/A	...I don't feel welcome by the committee... decided to resign. (field notes CWRC, 04/03/02)	...I feel too guilty not to do [it] really. (interview Al, 09/01/03)

Table 5 (*Continued*)

Hopwood (1974) categories/control mechanisms	Tactical	Strategic	Systemic/structures
Avoidance	...oh well, we don't need to discuss it anymore, I think enough people agree...(field notes CWRC, 05/08/02)	...I just don't get involved in that side of things now cause of I do I'll want to take over...(interview Lisa, 03/04/03)	N/A
Cultural Capital	N/A	'Yeah, I did lots of different jobs, just helping out to start with and gradually 'worked my up' [laughing] to Chair! But I've say on committees at work, professionally and they are different but basically I know how committees should work. (interview Al, 09/01/03)	...ultimately as the Treasurer I know we have got X amount of money and perhaps we'll spend out.. and I'll have a word with [Chairperson] and she'll probably put it to the committee...ask any of them how much money we've got and they don't know...they don't care what's spent. (interview Lisa, 03/04/03)

used by an individual but affect individuals in a systemic manner whereby they were not necessarily aware of the controlling influence of that mechanism. Club A (CWRC), as illustrated in Table 5, predominantly exhibited social control mechanisms but throughout field work made a change to an emphasis on administrative mechanisms. Club B (WRC), as illustrated in Table 6, was founded on administrative and social control mechanisms but due to the high level of conflict and lack of leadership in this club, there was a continuous struggle to establish the values of the club as being either social or administrative. Club C (WHRC), as illustrated in Table 7, was founded on administrative controls and values, and these continued to be important to the club as they also developed more social and self-controls in line with those administrative values. This club was the only club in the dataset to have developed control consistent with Hopwood's (1974) suggestion that to be effective, administrative controls should develop into social and ideally self-control mechanisms.

The nature of conflict also differed in each club and had an effect on how control was exerted within the clubs. In CWRC and WRC, both organisational and interpersonal conflict was observed at committee meetings and events, whereas there were much lower levels of observable conflict within WHRC. Through factors such as a successful history of competition and the reputation of the club as well organised, a new leader and an influx of new committee members coupled with the Chairwoman's avoidance of emotionality, a very powerful systemic mechanism of control operated whereby the history of the club was a source of pride for committee

Table 6. Club B (WRC) sample evidence of control mechanisms and mode of operation.

Hopwood (1974) categories/control mechanisms	Tactical	Strategic	Systemic/structures
Administrative			
Agenda	Can we please stick to the agenda!?... hello?...we are supposed to talk about that now. (field notes WRC, 07/05/02)	N/A	Was not evidently routine to use an agenda
Minutes	N/A (only produced once during field work)	[Minutes were not standardised in format and were produced, once to the knowledge of the researcher, like a script indicating a conversation rather than a summary of key points of the meeting]	Minutes not produced regularly (only once during field work, resembling a 'conversational script')
Social			
Emotion	...people were afraid to say anything, but I don't think they are now. (interview Edward, 23/04/03)	...they are badgered into doing it. He just keeps on at you, makes you feel whatever until you agree. (interview Edward, 23/04/03)	Social/cultural rules about emotion display
Social hierarchy	N/A	N/A	[long-standing members and new members unquestioned belief that each were more valuable in their contribution to the club]
Economic capital	I don't see why he should give up his whole day, for nothing!! I paid them – they do a good job and I paid them to make sure it got done. (interview William, 13/06/03)	...well we can have shows at different venues now because people have better horses and almost everyone has a trailer or some transport. (interview Gill, 19/03/03)	N/A
Self			
Identification	It seems to me some people think they ARE WRC! (field notes WRC, 16/07/02)	I love this club and I would never profit from it – I did those jobs for my costs. (interview Gill, 19/03/03)	I've always been associated with it...it's like my baby, I was there when it was born. (interview Gill, 19/03/03)

Table 6 (*Continued*)

Hopwood (1974) categories/control mechanisms	Tactical	Strategic	Systemic/structures
History	Well we've always had a show committee – it was not just for the July show. (interview Gill, 19/03/03)	I do try to make them remember what the club is supposed to be about – what it was founded on – every chance I get. (interview Edward, 23/04/03)	She always does the Secretary tent at shows – always has and there's no way she'll let you help. (interview Margaret, 30/06/03)
Personal identity	N/A	Because that's me you see, I just can't bear to see a job done poorly. (interview Gill, 19/03/03)	N/A

members, who worked to continue the successful past documented by the club. WHRC was in a more stable environment and developmental stage than the other two committees/clubs who were experiencing high levels of change (and conflict).

The importance of a temporal perspective in organisation control research has been articulated by Cardinal, Sitkin, and Long (2004) who attempted to extend control theory by studying the creation and development of control systems during a company's first 10 years of operation, suggesting that the balance between formal and informal controls is dynamic and that organisations must find a balance where multiple forms of control are used in harmony. The three clubs analysed in this data indicate that control is not only dynamic in the founding years but continues to evolve and change in response to changes in the internal environment of the organisation. CWRC became more effective and efficient in its operations as reported by the respondents when the Chair made a successful effort to increase the importance of administrative mechanisms to balance the overuse of social mechanisms of control that had dominated club operations for a considerable period. WRC, being in a continuous state of conflict, demonstrated a significant imbalance in use of control mechanisms with very little agreement or acceptance of administrative mechanisms. WHRC seemed to have a good balance between formal (administrative) mechanisms such as their internal rule book ('the Bible'), agendas/minutes, NGB rules and informal (social and self) control mechanisms such as the use of various forms of capital, avoidance, emotion and identification. There was little overt conflict within this group and the committee organised a significant number of events for its membership each year and appeared to operate smoothly. A few months after the field work for this research finished, there was a change in leadership in WHRC, with the Chairwoman Patricia Drysdale resigning after four years' service. An email from her indicated that the change may lead to conflict within the committee when she stated:

> Well, we had the AGM and I resigned, as I said I would. The new committee have their first meeting soon and yes, feathers will fly! There will be lots to sort out – lots of shouting I think!. (Email Patricia, 14 November 20004)

Table 7. Club C (WHRC) sample evidence of control mechanisms and mode of operation.

Hopwood (1974) categories/control mechanisms	Tactical	Strategic	Systemic/Structures
Administrative			
Structure: Rules (NGB or other), formalisation and centralisation	I'll have to check the Governing Body rules to see about horse/rider eligibility. (field notes WHRC, 09/07/02)	I created our rule book – and called it the 'Bible' so we can learn from things that are really good or really bad. (interview Patricia, 14/06/03)	[traditional committee structure adopted]
Social			
Avoidance	At the time I thought, 'what do I do' but I decided to just leave it, deal with it later, after I had a chance to think about it. (interview Patricia, 14/06/03)	I won't react, I will often just back off and think about it for a while, ask some opinions and then decide what to do. (interview Patricia, 09/09/03)	[Avoidance not a routinely utilised mechanism. Rather, discussion and open debate encouraged]
Social capital	I'll deal with it – I know her so I'll just call and find out what is going on. (field notes WHRC, 24/11/03)	I make a point of introducing people, knowing people – I think you've got to get the club to gel – I think I've done that. (interview Patricia, 14/06/03)	Oh, we all sort of know each other from having horses anyway... (interview Jennifer, 06/03/02)
Cultural capital	'When we had our first meeting I admitted that I would need them to tell me how to do things – I don't know all this etiquette and things! So I just 'this is what I think, what do you think?'...(interview Patricia, 14/06/03)	We really relied on them to tell us how things work – none of us [new members] had done it before. (interview Jennifer, 10/10/03)	[knowledge of committee operation and structure or of equestrian event planning, etc]
Self			
Avoidance	I may not discuss it in committee first but ring a few people and ask what they think first. (interview Patricia, 09/09/03)	She doesn't come too often, if she can get away with it – she avoids having to answer whether she' s done the things she is supposed to! (interview Patricia, 14/06/03)	N/A

Table 7 (*Continued*)

Hopwood (1974) categories/control mechanisms	Tactical	Strategic	Systemic/Structures
Cultural capital	N/A	I think I learned through my childhood to be a bit tough, it is just the way I am . . . you know I don't take any . . . (interview Patricia, 09/09/03)	. . . interact with one another in a professional manner, discuss issues openly . . . (field notes WHRC, 09/07/02)
Social capital	N/A	N/A	Well, I came on the committee because Alison said she was doing it and it was only a meeting every once in a while – yeah so we joined together. (interview Jennifer, 06/03/02)

Control mechanisms, such as emotion and identification, could overlap when exercised as self control. Emotion has been acknowledged as pivotal in the achievement of organisation control (e.g. Fineman, 1993). While emotion work has traditionally been viewed as conducted for organisational purposes and by the direction of management (Hochschild, 1979, 1983), Callahan (2000) realised that it is also possible for individuals to control their emotions for personal reasons or in response to commitment to the organisation rather than simply at the command of management. Similarly, emotion has been linked to identity in organisations by Albert, Ashforth, and Dutton (2000) who suggested that identity is crucial in determining how and what an individual thinks and feels although they have also indicated that the relationship is ill understood. Drawing upon the work of Simon (1945), Tompkins and Cheney (1985), cited in Barker, 1993) noted the effect of identification in organisations to limit the range of alternatives considered in decision-making, highlighting 'organisational identity' as a mechanism of control which serves to limit the perspective of agents.

This notion that identification with an organisation controls/limits an actor's perception and therefore range of actions from which they may choose is evident within each of the case studies in this research. However, in contribution to the literature on the role of identification in organisation control, this study highlights the diversity of this mechanism. While Alvesson and Willmott (2002) focused on how identity is formed, revealing the importance of discourse to identity regulation and control, they also concentrate on managements' intentional attempt to influence this process in describing organisation control. Within the committees in this study, identity was mainly used as a self-control mechanism and served to influence individuals both tactically and strategically. It can also be argued that personal identity and identification with the club could serve as systemic mechanisms of control as the individual, or contribution of the individual, gradually became part of the history of the club. In WHRC, personal identities consistent with identification with the organisation, consistent over time served to provide a strong systemic mechanism of control which suggested the character of the club, committee and its serving members.

Identification with an organisation can also have negative consequences, leading to conflict and difficulties in controlling and co-ordinating organisation activities. In WRC, founding and long-standing members strongly identified with 'their' club. The remaining committee members did not identify with the same image of the club that the long-standing members held. This caused considerable friction between the two groups, and many conflicts could be traced to this significant difference in identification. For example, Margaret suggested that the long-standing members constantly referred to the founding principles of the club and stated in interview:

> They are always banging on 'have you read your Constitution!?' – well, no I haven't! [laughing] - so what! They really hold the club back, they don't want to try anything new or different or do anything other than the way it used to be. (Interview Margaret, 30/06/03)

Similar to CWRC, Patricia created administrative mechanisms to provide guidance and control within the group. However, whereas Al (CWRC) created the agenda mechanism to enforce her authority to direct the club, Patricia created mechanisms which took the emphasis of control away from her. For example, in creating the 'Bible', it was possible for her to refer to this document when making decisions which enabled her to avoid responsibility for difficult decisions. When the potential club member who presented a case for not helping at events was refused membership, it was Patricia's insistence that the rule must be upheld at all times and that it is in 'the Bible' as good practice.

Members of WHRC held considerable autonomy and authority in organising events, and this was perhaps a reason for the lack of (observable) conflict within the committee. Individuals were inherently reliant upon each other to perform their jobs but each person held relatively equal amounts of resources to complete their tasks. Therefore, there was little competition over resources and no [obvious] use of social capital (as there was in the previous two clubs) to secure support/resources. Members of WHRC were relatively equally endowed with cultural capital in that they were from an affluent geographical area, all professionally employed, retired or students (university education).

Leca and Naccache (2006, p. 627) point to a body of research in institutional analysis (e.g. DiMaggio, 1988; Hoffman & Ventresca, 2002; Lounsbury, 2003) that has sought to break from traditional institutional theory and provide 'deeper explanations of institutional reproduction and change, power mechanisms and actors' capacities to develop strategies and shape institutions'. Through the critical theory lens, the powerful influence of institutional practices are acknowledged, but CR also provides some initial evidence for how these practices are developed over time – through individual's reproduction of their structural context, influenced strongly by their cultural capital and current demands of the organisation's internal and external environments.

The post-structuralist view of control highlighted by CR demonstrates the importance of context, particularly issues of language, identity and/or resistance in organisations (Delbridge & Ezzamel, 2005). The constructive role of language highlighted by discourse analysis rejects the duality of structure and agency, and suggests that reality is shaped by actor's discourse. This perspective has been widely supported (e.g. Alvesson & Karreman, 2004; Chia, 2000; Phillips, Lawrence, & Hardy, 2004) and fundamentally suggests that reality is not in existence independent of an actor's knowledge of it. Therefore, reality is 'constantly negotiated' (Torfing, 1999, p. 85) and emergent as discourses are developed. This view has been criticised, however, for its ignorance of the socio-political context in which organisations operate (Delbridge & Ezzamel, 2005) and its over reliance on 'texts' as a sole source of data (Said, 1994). Without considering the social and historical context in which the organisations in this study operate, suggestions on how and why control mechanisms have come into existence within the organisations would be limited. The description of control provided in this paper and the complexity of how control mechanisms operate contribute to the recent body of knowledge surrounding organisation control which call to develop more dynamic theories of control in organisations. This dynamism can only be realised through the study of control over extended periods of time.

Conclusions

Results of this critical realist view of control suggest that it is very difficult to provide generalisations about the control of voluntary sport clubs. This has significant implications for policy makers who have indicated an important role for sport clubs in the implementation of national sport policy in the UK. Even within clubs of a similar size, structure and sport/purpose as is evident in this dataset, there were considerable variations in operations and control of volunteers. It is plausible that extending this study to consider other sports would reveal even greater variety in operating procedures and control of the volunteers in those specific contexts. To expect all sports to implement public policy in a consistent and effective manner without consideration of how their differences may impact on this implementation is cause for concern.

The CR framework requires extensive resources to implement given its emphasis on seeking an understanding of multiple realities and the interpretation of the combination of those realities rather than a focus on only one reality. Considerable time is needed to operationalise concepts under investigation and to systematically explore these in the data. Underlying mechanisms which serve to reproduce social structure can be difficult to identify through interviews alone and so some participant observation seems necessary to provide the researcher with the level of experience and interaction needed to yield this information. This can also be sought through triangulation of interview data. Through interviews, a CR framework requires the researcher to explore what may be sensitive information about participants' education, background and class. Given these challenges of CR, it may not be possible to employ the methodology in all instances, but the framework does reveal a more comprehensive and deeper understanding of concepts that a sole focus on observable or interpretive elements of volunteering. It offers a research perspective that enables more critical investigation of the volunteering phenomenon.

This paper has made a contribution to the literature on sport volunteering by demonstrating how the critical realist methodology can be applied to understand control of volunteers in voluntary sport clubs. The results provide interesting evidence for how these volunteers continuously challenge club norms and operations and how widely variable clubs can be, even within the same sport. Future research needs to explore these variations in greater detail in order to provide policy makers with a clearer picture of how sport clubs may be able to participate in policy implementation and the limitations they face in attempting to do so.

References

Adams, A., & Deane, J. (2009). Exploring formal and informal dimensions of sports volunteering in England. *European Sport Management Quarterly, 9*(2), 119–140.

Agarwal, S. (1999). Impact of job formalization and administrative controls on attitudes of industrial salespersons. *Industrial Marketing Management, 28*(4), 359–368.

Albert, S., Ashforth, B.E., & Dutton, J.E. (2000). Organizational identity and identification: Charting new waters and building new bridges. *Academy of Management Review, 25*(1), 13–17.

Altheide, D.L. (1996). *Qualitative media analysis.* London: Sage.

Alvesson, M., & Karreman, D. (2004). Interfaces of control: Technocratic socio-ideological control in a global management consultancy firm. *Accounting Organizations and Society, 29*(3–4), 423–444.

Alvesson, M., & Willmott, H. (2002). Identity regulation as organisation control: Producing the appropriate individual. *Journal of Management Studies, 39*(5), 619–644.

Anthony, R.N., Dearden, J., & Bedford, N. (1989). *Management control systems* (5th ed.). Homewood, IL: Irwin.

Anthony, R., & Young, D. (1988). *Management control in non-profit organizations* (4th ed.). Homewood, IL: Irwin.

Ashforth, B.E., & Saks, A.M. (2000). Personal control in organisations: A longitudinal investigation with newcomers. *Human Relations, 53*(3), 311–339.

Barker, J.R. (1993). Tightening the iron cage: Concertive control in self-managing teams. *Administrative Science Quarterly, 38*, 408–437.

Blau, P.M., & Scott, W.R. (1962). *Formal organizations: A comparative approach.* San Francisco, CA: Chandler.

Boden, C. (1994). *The business of talk.* Oxford: Polity Press, Blackwell Publishers.

Bourdieu, P. (1989). *Distinction. A social critique of the judgement of taste.* London: Routledge.

Bourdieu, P. (1985). The social space and the genesis of groups. *Theory and Society, 14*, 723–744.

Burns, T., & Stalker, G.M. (1961). *The management of innovation.* London: Tavistock.

Byers, T., Henry, I., & Slack, T. (2007). Understanding control in voluntary sport organisations. In M.M. Parent & T. Slack (Eds.), *International perspectives on the management of sport* (pp. 269–286). London: Elsevier.

Callahan, J. (2000). Emotion management and organizational functions: A case study of patterns in a not-for-profit organization. *Human Resource Development Quarterly, 11*(3), 245–267.

Cardinal, L.B., Sitkin, S.B., & Long, C.P. (2004). Balancing and rebalancing in the creation and evolution of organizational control. *Organization Science, 15*(4), 411–431.

Chia, R. (2000). Discourse analysis as organizational analysis. *Organization, 7*(3), 513–518.

Child, J. (1975). Managerial and organisational factors associated with company performance – part II, a contingency analysis. *Journal of Management Studies, 7*, 12–27.

Child, J. (2005). *Organization: Contemporary principles and practice.* Oxford: Blackwell.

Collins, M.F., & Kay, T. (2003). *Sport and social exclusion.* London: Routledge.

Coombs, R., Knights, D., & Wilmott, H.C. (1992). Culture, control and competition: Towards a conceptual framework for the study of information technology in organizations. *Organization Studies, 13*(1), 51–72.

Cunningham, I. (2000). Managing employee commitment in the UK voluntary sector: A frontier for further research. *Management Research News, 23*(9/10/11), 45–47.

Daft, R.L. (2009). *Organization theory and design.* Mason, OH: Southwestern College Learning.

Das, T.K., & Teng, B.S. (1998). Between trust and control: Developing confidence in partner cooperation in alliances. *Academy of Management Review, 23*(3), 491–512.

DCMS (2002). Department for culture media and sport annual report. Retrieved from http://www.culture.gov.uk/Reference_library/Annual_Reports/ar_2002.htm

Delbridge, R., & Ezzamel, M. (2005). The strength of difference: Contemporary conceptions of control. *Organization, 12*(5), 603–618.

DiMaggio, P.J. (1988). Interest and agency in institutional theory. In L. Zucker (Ed.), *Research on institutional patterns and organizations: Culture and environment* (pp. 3–22). Cambridge, MA: Ballinger.

Downward, P. (2005). Critical (realist) reflection on policy and management research in Sport, Tourism and Sports Tourism. *European Sport Management Quarterly, 5*(3), 303–320.

Duncan, R. (1972). Characteristics of organisational environments and perceived uncertainty. *Administrative Science Quarterly, 17*, 3–27.

Ferner, A. (2000). The underpinnings of 'bureaucratic' control systems: HRM in European multi-nationals. *Journal of Management Studies, 37*(4), 521–539.

Fineman, S. (1993). *Emotion in organizations.* London: Sage.

Fineman, S. (1999). Emotion and organizing. In S. Clegg, C. Hardy, & W.R. Nord (Eds.), *Handbook of organization studies* (pp. 543–564). London: Sage.

Fineman, S. (Ed.). (2000). *Emotion in organizations.* London: Sage.

Fortado, B. (1994). Informal supervisory social control strategies. *Journal of Management Studies, 31*(2), 251–274.

Friederici, M.R., & Heinemann, K. (2007). Sport clubs – Computer usage – Emotions. In M. Parent and Slack (Eds.), *International perspectives on the management of sport* (pp. 287–315). London: Elsevier.

Garfinkel, E. (1967). *Studies in ethnomethodology.* Englewood Cliffs, NJ: Prentice Hall.

Garrett, R. (2004). The response of voluntary sport clubs to Sport England's Lottery funding: Cases of compliance, change and resistance. *Managing Leisure, 9*, 13–29.

Glover, J.G., & Coleman, L.M. (1937). *Managerial control.* New York, NY: Ronald.

Green, S.G., & Welsh, M.A. (1988). Cybernetics and dependence: Reframing the concept of control. *Academy of Management Review, 13*(2), 287–301.

Gupta, A.K., & Govindarajan, V. (1991). Knowledge flows and the structure of control within multi-national corporations. *Academy of Management Review, 16*(4), 768–792.

Hochschild, A.R. (1979). The sociology of feelings and emotions: Selected possibilities. In M. Millman & R. Kanter (Eds.), *Another voice* (pp. 280–307). Garden City: Anchor.

Hochschild, A.R. (1983). *The managed heart: Commercialization of human feeling.* London: University of California Press.

Hoffman, A., & Ventresca, M. (2002). Introduction. In A. Hoffman & M. Ventresca (Eds.), *Organizations, policy and the natural environment: Institutional and strategic perspectives* (pp. 1–38). Stanford, CA: Stanford University Press.

Hollinger, R.C., & Clark, J.P. (1982). Formal and informal social controls of employee deviance. *Sociological Quarterly, 23*, 33–43.

Holy, L. (1984). Theory, methodology and the research process. In R.F. Ellen (Ed.), *Ethnographic research: A guide to general conduct* (pp. 13–24). London: Academic Press.

Hopwood, A. (1974). *Accounting and human behaviour.* London: Prentice Hall.

Inglis, S. (1997). Roles of the board in amateur sport organizations. *Journal of Sport Management, 11*(2), 160–176.

Johnson, P., & Gill, J. (1993). *Management control and organizational behaviour.* London: Paul Chapman.

Kay, T., & Bradbury, S. (2009). Youth sport volunteering: Developing social capital? *Sport, Education and Society, 14*(1), 121–140.

Kelman, H. (1961). The processes of opinion change. *Public Opinion, 25*, 57–78.

Kendall, J. (2003). *The voluntary sector.* London: Routledge.

Khandwalla, P.N. (1977). *The design of organizations.* New York, NY: Harcourt Brace Jovanovich.

Kim, M., Zhang, J.J., & Connaughton, D.P. (2010). Comparison of volunteer motivations in different youth sport organizations. *European Sport Management Quarterly, 10*(3), 343–366.

Kirk, D., & MacPhail, A. (2003). Social positioning and the construction of a youth sport club. *International Review for the Sociology of Sport, 38*(1), 23–24.

Kirsch, L.J. (2004). Deploying common systems globally: The dynamics of control. *Information Systems Research, 15*(4), 374–395.

Lawrence, P.R., & Lorsch, J.W. (1967). *Organization and environment: Managing differentiation and integration.* Boston, MA: Harvard University Press.

Leca, B., & Naccache, P. (2006). A critical realist approach to institutional entrepreneurship. *Organization, 13*(5), 627–651.

Llewellyn, S. (2007). Introducing the agents. *Organization Studies, 28*(2), 133–153.

Lorsch, J.W., & Morse, J.J. (1974). *Organisations and their members: A contingency approach.* New York, NY: Harper & Row.

Lounsbury, M. (2003). The problem of order revisited: Toward a more critical institutional perspective. In R. Westwood & S. Clegg (Eds.), *Debating organizations* (pp. 210–219). Oxford: Blackwell.

Maguire, S. (1999). The discourse of control. *Journal of Business Ethics, 19*, 109–114.

Maguire, S., Phillips, N., & Hardy, C. (2001). When 'silence = death', keep talking: Trust, control and the discursive construction of identity in the Canadian HIV/AIDS treatment domain. *Organization Studies, 22*(2), 285–310.

Manz, C.C., & Simms, H.P. (1989). *Super leadership: Leading others to lead themselves.* Berkeley, CA: Prentice-Hall.

Marsh, D. (1999). *Post War British politics in perspective.* London: Polity Press.

Marsh, D., & Smith, M.J. (2001). There is more than one way to do political science: On different ways to study policy networks. *Political Studies, 49*(3), 528–541.

Meira, J., Kartalis, N.D., Tamenyi, M., & Cullen, J. (2010). Management controls and inter-firm relationships: A review. *Journal of Accounting & Organizational Change, 6*(1), 149–169.

Misener, K., Doherty, A., & Hamm-Kerwin, S. (2010). Learning from the experiences of older adult volunteers in sport: A serious leisure perspective. *Journal of Leisure Research, 42*, 267–290.

Nichols, G., & Ojala, E. (2009). Understanding the management of sports events volunteers through psychological contract theory. *VOLUNTAS: International Journal of Voluntary and Nonprofit Organizations, 20*(4), 369–387.

Nichols, G., & Padmore, J. (2005). Who are the volunteers in sports clubs? Sheffield University Management School, working paper.

Nichols, G., & Shepherd, M. (2006). Volunteering in sport: The use of ratio analysis to analyse volunteering and participation. *Managing Leisure, 11*, 205–216.

Nichols, G., Taylor, P., James, M., Holmes, K., King, L., & Garrett, R. (2005). Pressures on the UK voluntary sport sector. *International Journal of Voluntary and Nonprofit Organizations, 16*(1), 33–50.

Oliga, J.C. (1989). *Power, ideology and control.* London: Plenum Press.

Ouchi, W.G. (1977). The relationship between organizational structure and organizational control. *Administrative Science Quarterly, 22*, 95–112.

Papadimitriou, D. (2002). Amateur structures and their effect on performance: The case of Greek voluntary sport clubs. *Managing Leisure, 7*(4), 205–219.

Pauline, G., & Pauline, J.S. (2009). Volunteer motivation and demographic influences at a professional tennis event. *Team Performance Management, 15*(3/4), 172–184.

Pearce, J. (1993). *Volunteers: The organizational behavior of unpaid workers.* London: Routledge.

Pearson, K. (1982). Conflicting interests in organizational goals in voluntary associations. *Sportwissenscaft, 11*, 169–182.

Perrow, C.A. (1967). A framework for the comparative analysis of organizations. *American Sociological Review, 32*, 194–208.

Perrow, C. (1995). Why bureaucracy? In S.R. Corman, S.P. Banks, C.R. Bantz & M.E. Mayer (Eds.), *Foundations of organizational communication: A reader* (pp. 28–50). White Plains, NY: Longmans.

Pfister, G. (2006). Gender issues in Danish sports organizations: Experiences, attitudes and evaluations. *Nordic Journal of Women's Studies, 14*(1), 27–40.

Phillips, N., Lawrence, T.B., & Hardy, C. (2004). Discourse and institutions. *Academy of Management Review, 29,* 635–652.

Pugh, D.S., Hickson, D.J., Hinings, C.R., Macdonald, K.M., Turner, C., & Lupton, T. (1963). A conceptual scheme for organizational analysis. *Administrative Science Quarterly, 8*(3), 289–315.

Reed, M.I. (1997). In praise of duality and dualism: Rethinking agency and structure in organizational analysis. *Organization Studies, 18*(1), 21–42.

Reed, M. (2005). Doing the loco-motion: Response to Contu and Wilmott's commentary on 'The Realist turn in organization and management studies'. *Journal of Management Studies, 42*(8), 1663–1673.

Reed, M. (2009). Critical realism: Philosophy, method, or philosophy in search of a method? In D.A. Buchanan & A. Bryman (Eds.), *The Sage handbook of organizational research methods.* London: Sage.

Saeki, T. (1994). The conflict between tradition and modernization in a sport organization: A sociological study of issues surrounding the organizational reformation of the all Japan Judo Federation. *International Review for the Sociology of Sport, 29*(3), 301.

Said, E.W. (1994). *Culture and imperialism.* New York, NY: Vintage Books.

Seippel, Ø. (2004). The world according to voluntary sport organizations: Voluntarism, economy and facilities. *International Review for the Sociology of Sport, 39*(2), 223–232.

Seippel, Ø. (2005). Sport, civil society and social integration. *Journal of Civil Society, 1*(3), 65–78.

Shibli, S., Taylor, P., Nichols, G., Gratton, C., & Kokolakakis, T. (1999). The characteristics of volunteers in UK sports clubs. *European Journal for Sport Management, 6*(special issue), 10–27.

Simon, H. (1945). *Administrative behavior: A study of decision-making processes in administrative organization* (1st ed.). New York, NY: Macmillan.

Slack, T. (1997). *Understanding sport organizations.* Champaign, IL: Human Kinetics.

Sport England. (2003). *Sports volunteering in England in 2002: A summary report.* London: Sport England.

Stopford, J.M., & Wells, L.T. (1972). *Managing the multinational enterprise.* London: Longman.

Styre, A. (2008). Management control in bureaucratic and postbureaucratic organizations: A lacanian perspective. *Group and Organization Management, 33*(6), 635–656.

Tankersley, W.B. (2000). The impact of external control arrangements on organizational performance. *Administration and Society, 32*(3), 282–304.

Taylor, F.W. (1906). On the art of cutting metals, paper no. 1119. *Transactions (American Society of Mechanical Engineers), 27,* 31–350.

Taylor, P., Nichols, G., Holmes, K., James, M., Gratton, C., Garrett, R., …, King, L. (2003). *Sports volunteering in England: A report for Sport England.* Sheffield: Leisure Industries Research Centre.

Thompson, J.D. (1967). *Organizations in action.* Maidenhead: McGraw Hill.

Thompson, D. (Ed.). (1995). *The concise oxford dictionary of current English.* Oxford: Clarendon Press.

Tiedens, L.Z. (2000). Powerful emotions: The vicious cycle of social status positions and emotions. In N.M. Ashkanasy, C.E.J. Hartel, & W.J. Zerbe (Eds.), *Emotions in the workplace: Research: Theory and practice* (pp. 71–81). Westport, CT: Quorum Books.

Torfing, J. (1999). *New theories of discourse.* Oxford: Blackwell.

Tosi, H. (1983). The organizational control structure. *Journal of Business Research, 11*(3), 271–279.

Tsoukas, H. (1993). Analogical reasoning and knowledge generation in organisation theory. *Organization Studies, 14*(3), 323–346.

Tsoukas, H. (1994). What is management? An outline of a metatheory. *British Journal of Management, 5,* 289–301.

Van Maanen, J., & Schein, E.H. (1979). Towards a theory of organisational socialisation. In B.M. Straw (Ed.), *Research in organizational behaviour* (Vol. 1, pp. 209–264.). Greenwich, CT: JAI Press.

Vos, S., Breesch, D., & Sheerder, J. (2011). Undeclared work in non-profit sports clubs: A mixed methods approach for assessing the size and motives. *VOLUNTAS: International Journal of Voluntary and Non-Profit Organizations, 23*(4), 846–869. Retrieved from http://dx. doi.org/10.1007/s11266-011-9232-2

Woodward, J. (1965). *Industrial organisation, theory and practise.* London: Oxford University Press.

'Continue or terminate?' Determinants of long-term volunteering in sports clubs

Torsten Schlesinger, Benjamin Egli and Siegfried Nagel

Institute of Sport Science, University of Bern, Berne, Switzerland

This study analyzed the determinants underlying sports club volunteers' tendencies to continue or terminate their long-term commitment to volunteering in order to help sports clubs improve their volunteer management. Their risk of terminating was viewed in terms of subjective expectations and evaluations (satisfaction) regarding club-related working conditions and normative commitments (solidarity) to the sports club. These relationships were tested empirically with an online questionnaire of 441 sports club volunteers in a selection of 45 Swiss sports clubs. Results showed that the constructs orientation toward collective solidarity and volunteer job satisfaction correlated positively with long-term volunteering commitment. The effect of the former was stronger than that of the latter. Volunteers with a higher orientation toward collective solidarity were unlikely to terminate their voluntary engagement in their club. The discussion presents recommendations to help clubs retain volunteers.

Volunteers continue to be the most important resource in noncommercial sports clubs, because producing and delivering affordable sports services requires large numbers of committed individuals. Indeed, without the support of volunteers, most sports clubs could no longer survive (e.g., Wicker & Breuer, 2011). However, there are continuous complaints about increasing difficulties in getting members to volunteer. Although many people do volunteer in sports clubs, it is particularly the long-term voluntary commitment to formal positions (e.g., as coach, secretary) that can no longer simply be taken for granted. A recent report on sports clubs in Switzerland confirms that recruiting and retaining volunteers who are prepared to make a long-term commitment is now a major problem for about 40% of all Swiss sports clubs; and for 10%, it is even a threat to their continued existence (Lamprecht, Fischer, & Stamm, 2011). Similar problems can also be observed in other countries such as Australia (Cuskelly, 2005), Belgium (Scheerder & Vos, 2009), Germany (Breuer, 2011), or Great Britain (Nichols et al., 2005; Taylor et al., 2003).

Discussions on this decline in volunteering trace it back to two contributory factors: a lower recruitment of new volunteers and a higher termination by existing volunteers. The main focus of this paper is on the latter: the risk of termination in sports clubs; in other words, whether volunteers decide to terminate or continue volunteering. How to retain volunteers in sports clubs more effectively is becoming an increasingly important management issue. Because many of the individual variables determining volunteering cannot be modified by managers of sports clubs, it is particularly important to identify those determinants that are accessible to change. A clear understanding of what triggers and sustains long-term voluntary commitment would help sports clubs to tackle this problem more effectively. Hence, the importance of volunteers as a basic resource in producing sports club services combined with the increasing problems in achieving long-term voluntary commit-ment in Swiss sports clubs clearly indicate the potential benefits of taking a closer look at the question: *Which determinants influence the tendency to continue or to terminate long-term commitment to volunteering?*

This paper addresses this question by discussing various approaches to explaining characteristics of voluntary engagement on the one side and decreasing long-term commitment to volunteering on the other side. It will then take a theoretical approach and conceptualize the central parameters for long-term volunteering in sports clubs, and derive hypotheses and questions guiding research for the further empirical analysis.

Literature review

A review of the literature reveals several studies that have analyzed the characteristics of individuals who engage in voluntary work in sports clubs. The most frequently analyzed sociodemographic variables in this context are gender and age. Various studies have confirmed a significant gender effect (men engage in more voluntary work) (e.g., Braun, 2003, 2011; Cuskelly, 2005; Taylor et al., 2003). Age tends to reveal a curvilinear relation, with the age profiles of volunteers in organizations being concentrated in the middle years, and both younger and older people showing less voluntary engagement (e.g., Braun, 2011; Nichols & Padmore, 2005; Ringuet, Cuskelly, Zakus, & Auld, 2008). Research has shown that economic variables such as workloads, income, and human capital are also decisive for volunteering. Findings on workloads are ambivalent: on the one hand, lower workloads do not necessarily lead to greater voluntary engagement (e.g., Erlinghagen, 2000; Freeman, 1997); on the other hand, higher workloads place constraints on the number of hours committed to volunteering (Burgham & Downward, 2005). The variable income promotes volunteering, and a lot of studies have confirmed that more highly educated people, who thus have more human capital, volunteer more often and also more frequently hold a formal position in sports clubs (e.g., Braun, 2011; Nichols & Padmore, 2005; Ringuet et al., 2008). Furthermore, various studies have applied volunteer motivation (Braun, 2003; Farrell, Johnston, & Twynam, 1998; Strigas & Jackson, 2003) and sport- and member-specific characteristics as explanatory variables. Some evidence indicates that having children who belong to one's sports club impacts positively on volunteer engagement (e.g., Burgham & Downward, 2005; Ringuet et al., 2008). Nichols and Shepherd (2006) have also shown that team sports (e.g., soccer) produce a higher volunteer–member ratio than individual sports (e.g., golf). Furthermore, commitment of the members to their club also has a positive impact on volunteering (e.g., Braun, 2003; Cuskelly & Boag, 2001).These studies refer particularly to the willingness to volunteer. Nonetheless, it is not clear how far these variables also play an important role in the decision to make a long-term voluntary commitment to a sports club.

Several explanations in the volunteer context reveal that the attitudes toward volunteer commitment and engagement are undergoing profound change. They indicate an increasing destabilization of voluntary commitment on different levels and from differing perspectives, which can be systematized as follows. (1) First, microeconomic approaches assume that individuals try to maximize their utility. These explain the willingness to volunteer in terms of the potential returns for volunteering (e.g., Emrich, Pitsch, & Flatau, 2010; Flatau, 2009; Lipford & Yandle, 2009; Ziemek, 2006). If the volunteer experience does not deliver these returns, then individuals are likely to leave in pursuit of more gratifying leisure activities. Therefore, declining voluntary commitment (intention to terminate) can be seen as the result of a negative outcome of cost–utility considerations due to diverging individual expectations and/or organizational incentive structures. (2) Further explanations address the opportunities provided by volunteering. According to Becker's (1965) newer economic household theory, households (individuals) also optimize their behavior in nonmarket- or only partially market-oriented choices such as volunteering by considering the associated direct investments in terms of time and opportunity costs: the higher the income and/or the broader the leisure-time alternatives, the greater the increase in, above all, the opportunity costs of voluntary work (Downward, Dawson, & Dejonghe, 2009; Duncan, 1999). This makes it increasingly less profitable to invest one's limited time in (temporally inflexible) voluntary work. (3) Sociological explanations discuss the increasing instability of voluntary commitment in terms of the erosion of traditional community-related norms and forms of solidarity that is attributed particularly to far-reaching changes in values and an increasing demand for individualistic self-fulfillment (e.g., Hustenix & Lammertyn, 2003; Putnam, 2000). (4) Furthermore, the decline in voluntary commitment is explained as a consequence of organizational changes in sports clubs. In particular, their increasing professionalization and service industry orientation combined with opening their doors to nonmembers is leading to greater divergences between individual and collective interests (e.g., Horch, 1998; Nagel, 2006). This is increasingly eroding the attachment between members and their club, thereby reducing the obligations to solidarity and commitment to the club's interests.

In summary, it would seem to be particularly club-related aspects that play a central role in the individual decision to make a long-term volunteering commitment to one's sports club. On the one hand, individual expectations regarding volunteering conditions and whether they are met are of central importance. On the other hand, volunteering in sports clubs is obviously embedded in emotional commitment and obligations of solidarity. These different aspects will be specified more precisely in the following.

Theoretical framework

Subjective expectations, volunteer job satisfaction, and volunteer commitment

Voluntary work describes an exchange of time and efforts for different rewards compared to those from work (Downward et al., 2009; Emrich et al., 2010). Hence, volunteers also bring their own particular needs and expectations to their volunteer activity. The extent to which members work in their sports club and the stability of their commitment could be influenced by the way the specific working conditions match these subjective expectations and evaluations. Achieving this match is crucial if members are to continue volunteering (e.g., Chelladurai, 2006; Doherty, 2005), because volunteers may well adapt their expectations to the working conditions of the sports club only up to a certain point. Powell and Steinberg (2006) postulated that organizations should adopt retaining practices for volunteers that are unique to the volunteer setting, because volunteers have a different set of expectations than paid employees. The volunteer situation differs from that of paid workers in that volunteers are not remunerated. Volunteering is considered to be a leisure experience in that, consistent with definitions of leisure, it can be seen as a freely chosen activity that individuals find attractive (Stebbins, 1996). Thus, it is also possible to be a member of a sports club and take part in its benefits without directly helping to produce the club goods (for discussions on the free-rider problem in organizations, see Heckathorn, 1989).

In the following, the concept of job satisfaction will be transferred to volunteering in sports clubs. In this context, individual job satisfaction reflects a volunteer's expectations and experiences; and volunteer job satisfaction is an outcome based on the cognitive and emotional evaluation of the relationship of volunteers' expectations and experiences of the work situation and to what the work situation actually provides (e.g., Chelladurai, 2006; Chelladurai & Ogasawara, 2003). Volunteer job satisfaction is realized when the volunteers' expectations are met (e.g., Farrell et al., 1998; Finkelstein, 2008). Conversely, when volunteers face unpleasant working conditions in their sports club, they are more likely to experience lower levels of satisfaction or even dissatisfaction. Findings from research on job satisfaction in different sporting contexts confirm that the degree of job satisfaction correlates negatively with the degree of fluctuation (intention to leave) (e.g., Chelladurai & Ogasawara, 2003; MacIntosh & Doherty, 2010). Such relations have also been confirmed for different volunteer contexts (e.g., Galindo-Kuhn & Guzley, 2001; Green & Chalip, 2004; Kim, Chelladurai, & Trail, 2007; Silverberg, Marshall, & Ellis, 2001). Hence, volunteers who are very satisfied are less often preoccupied with terminating voluntary work in the sports club, whereas dissatisfied volunteers more often think about termination. This leads to the following Hypothesis 1: *The greater the volunteer job satisfaction of sports club volunteers, the lower the risk that they will terminate volunteering.*

There is a consensus in the literature that job satisfaction is a multidimensional construct composed of various facets (e.g., Chelladurai, 2006; Gidron, 1983). This leads to the question, what are the central determinants of satisfaction for volunteers in sports clubs? The strong interest in job satisfaction has led to the development of numerous tools for its measurement in the paid work setting. However, measurement concepts of job satisfaction developed for paid work do not readily transfer to voluntary work satisfaction in sports clubs. Although voluntary work is quite similar to paid work in some respects, it takes place during leisure time. Therefore, several measurement concepts have been developed in volunteer research to assess the determinants of volunteer job satisfaction across a range of nonprofit areas and settings (see, for a summary, Galindo-Kuhn & Guzley, 2001). Different features of work conditions for volunteering in a sports club need to be weighted by their relative importance. The most important incentive for volunteering comes from the special character of the work itself. Work conditions are particularly motivating when volunteers experience a high level of autonomy in doing their work, the work is varied and flexible, and it contributes to self-development (e.g., Chelladurai, 2006; Galindo-Kuhn & Guzley, 2001). The form of voluntary work also plays an important role: providing opportunities for learning new skills or developing new competencies (growth of human capital) (e.g., Doherty, 2005), social relationships (social capital) with other members (e.g., Harvey, Levesque, & Donnelly, 2008), and an appropriate feedback culture from the club management or leadership should all exert a positive influence (Gidron, 1983; Thiel & Meier, 2009). Alongside the organization of working conditions, the incentive structures in sports clubs should also be important. Although financial incentives are generally significant only for paid workers, there may well be other material incentives that are important for volunteers. These are so-called 'fringe benefits' (e.g., reduced membership fees; see Horch, 1987). In the voluntary context, nonmaterial gratification and recognition (e.g., volunteer events, letters of thanks) may be particularly relevant (Frey, 2007; Heinemann, 2004). The analysis of the various facets of volunteering conditions leads to the following research question: *Which aspects play a central role for volunteer job satisfaction in sports clubs?*

It also needs to be considered that individual variables such as age and gender influence the preference structures of volunteers, thus leading to differences in their expectations and evaluations of working conditions. This then also impacts on the level of satisfaction with volunteering (e.g., Kikulis, 1990). Furthermore, many aspects of utility have to be conceived as so-called 'experience' goods that are acquired only after engaging in voluntary activity for some time. Thus, the expectation and evaluation of different working conditions of volunteering can vary depending on how much and how long a person volunteers and which job functions they volunteer for.

Voluntary commitment and the orientation toward collective solidarity

Voluntary sports clubs can be characterized in terms of the specific social structure of the interest community as defined by Coleman (1974). Sports clubs are interest communities with an organizational logic based on self-organization and the pooling of resources (cf. Coleman, 1974; Vanberg, 1978). Their aim is to produce certain club goods (e.g., sports and social services) at a reasonable price with the help of volunteer services and to provide these goods exclusively for the utility and interests of their members. This requires the assumption that club members are prepared to deliver not only financial (membership fees) but also and above all temporal resources (work donations) in order to collectively produce the club goods (Buchanan, 1965; Sandler & Tschirhart, 1980). Hence, the production of the club goods depends on actions based on reciprocity and relations based on solidarity among club members (Schlesinger & Nagel, 2011). This expresses itself in club-specific norms and values including the view that voluntary support of club work is a matter of course and that supporting the work of the club is quite simply part of being a member of this interest community. Such norms and values could be defined as an unwritten contract that involves individual beliefs in reciprocal or solidarity-based obligations between sports clubs and their members. Although this is not a binding contract, the members' interpretation of agreements made with their club may influence perceptions of obligation and loyalty (Engelberg, Zakus, Skinner, & Campell, 2012; Heinemann, 2004). Hence, obligations of solidarity within the club combined with a social and emotional commitment can be viewed as the central basis for volunteering in sports clubs. Because commitment and solidarity do not 'fit' with a consumption-oriented membership or a free-rider mentality, it can be assumed that the (normative) attitude from the perspective of the club member is that the goods and services of the club are only possible when one engages voluntarily in the sense of 'it wouldn't be possible without me!' Examined from the perspective of the sports club, a high proportion of committed volunteers is an indicator for a strong sense of collective solidarity within the club (Nagel, 2006). Hence, it can be assumed that the stability of volunteering depends on the strength of the orientation toward collective solidarity. This leads to Hypothesis 2: *The higher the volunteer's orientation toward collective solidarity with the sports club, the lower the risk that volunteering will be terminated.*

In this context, volunteers may well display differences in the extent of their collective solidarity and their commitment due to club-specific socialization processes (the social process through which individuals gradually acquire club-specific norms and a growing sense of belonging to a sports club) and the duration of volunteering in their sports club (e.g., Flatau, 2009; Schlesinger & Nagel, 2011). Indeed, Braun (2003) has shown that the length of membership in a sports club has a positive influence on the commitment to it. However, Engelberg, Skinner, and Zakus (2006) found that there are no differences in commitment to their organization between older and younger volunteers and between committee members and other volunteers.

Relating volunteer job satisfaction and the orientation toward collective solidarity to the risk of terminating

Up to now, it is still not known how the two constructs orientation toward collective solidarity and volunteer job satisfaction relate to the risk of terminating voluntary engagement. On the one hand, when referring to economic concepts, it can be assumed that volunteers are committed particularly through the utility of volunteering, that is, the specific design of incentive structures and volunteering conditions. In addition, soft incentives such as returns to social recognition are integrated along with other social benefits, and norm-deviating behavior is modeled as costs while retaining the overall mechanism of rational exchange (e.g., Emrich et al., 2010; Flatau, 2009). Nonetheless, when the imbalance between utility and disutility becomes disproportionately high and leads to dissatisfied volunteers, an individual is most likely to terminate voluntary work (e.g., Chelladurai, 2006). On the other hand, observations in sports clubs have shown that voluntary work often becomes habitual. Hence, due to their specific embedment in a sports club, volunteers will not engage continuously in instrumental reflections on their voluntary commitment (Braun, 2003). Moreover, sports clubs in particular reveal one repeatedly occurring phenomenon: when difficulties arise that would have to be considered as utility reducing, they can even have the opposite effect and increase stability and solidarity (voice instead of exit; see Hirschman, 1970). Therefore, it can be assumed that both aspects – individual expectations and evaluation on the one hand and social norms on the other – represent divergent action logics of long-term voluntary commitment,

37

and cannot be merged completely (see Esser, 2009). Consequently, the relationship between the two constructs volunteer orientation toward collective solidarity and volunteer job satisfaction needs to be considered and analyzed more exactly. This leads to the following research question: *How significant are the two constructs for a long-term commitment to volunteering and how do they interrelate?*

Method

Sample and data collection

Case studies were carried out in Swiss sports clubs that were already participating in our research. The clubs asked to participate in this study were selected to represent the different structural types of sports clubs in Switzerland in terms of their number of members, divisions, and types of sport (according to Lamprecht et al., 2011). Data were collected with an online questionnaire from members in 45 sports clubs. The sports clubs sent an e-mail newsletter to all members (> 16 years) with a valid e-mail address. This contained a link to the survey. Interested club members completed a questionnaire containing items on voluntary activity in their sports club. One advantage of an online survey is that it permits the recruitment of a large sample within a very short time period. However, it is only possible to question persons with specific media habits, thereby limiting any control over the selectivity of the sample. Nonetheless, these problems with sample selectivity should tend to be minor for the present analysis, because all volunteers in the sports clubs could be contacted by e-mail. The study sample contained a total of $n = 1528$ participants (club members) after data cleaning. In line with the research question (end or continue long-term voluntary commitment), the following analysis regarded only members holding a formal position (e.g., as coach, treasurer, secretary) in their sports club at that time; this reduced the sample to $n = 441$ participants. Club members who did not perform voluntary work or volunteered only sporadically were excluded.

The sample statistics are presented in Table 1. The majority of respondents (62%) were male. This unequal gender distribution may be due to women still being underrepresented in sports clubs. According to the Swiss sports club report by Lamprecht et al. (2011), approximately 64% of sports club members are male and 36% female. A small percentage (5.6%) were aged less than 20 years, 49.5% were aged between 21 and 40 years, 36.2% were aged between 41 and 60 years, and 8.7% were aged over 60 years. Regarding age, it should be pointed out that although a great number of younger club members do voluntary work in sports clubs, appointment to a formal position is often preceded by a long-term career within the club (e.g., Braun, 2003). As a result, younger volunteers are comparatively underrepresented in formal positions. The majority of the participants (58.1%) volunteered in the sports domain (e.g., coach, referee), 30.1% were in the administrative domain of the club (committee members, e.g., president, treasurer), whereas the remaining participants fulfilled other formal positions in, for example, the technical (e.g., equipment manager) or organizational domain (e.g., organizer of club events or sporting competitions). It needs to be noted that 46.5% of the volunteers held several formal voluntary positions in different areas of their club (accumulation of posts). Most participants (37.5%) had been volunteers for less than 5 years; 22.9%, for 6–10 years; 24.3%, for 11–20 years; and 15.3%, for more than 20 years. Regarding average time volunteered

Table 1.   Random sample differentiated by age, gender, formal position, time volunteered, and length of volunteering.

Criteria	Random sample n%	
Age		
≤ 20 years	23	5.6
21–40 years	205	49.5
41–60 years	150	36.2
> 61 years	36	8.7
Gender		
Female	167	38.0
Male	272	62.0
Job function (main domain of formal position)		
Sports domain	251	58.1
Administrative domain	130	30.1
Technical domain	17	3.9
Organizational domain	34	7.9
Average time volunteered (in hours per month)		
≤ 5 hours	82	20.2
6–10 hours	86	21.2
11–20 hours	111	27.4
> 20 hours	127	31.2
Length of volunteering in years		
≤ 5 years	162	37.5
6–10 years	99	22.9
11–20 years	105	24.3
> 20 years	66	15.3

(hours per month), 20.2% volunteered less than 5 hours for their club; 21.2%, for 6–10 hours; 27.4%, for 11–20 hours; and most respondents (31.2%), more than 20 hours.

Measures

A pool of 34 items addressing different aspects of the work environment in sport clubs was generated on the basis of the theoretical examination of the construct of volunteer job satisfaction. This item pool was pretested ($n = 189$ respondents) for content relevance, comprehensibility, and the avoidance of redundancies. This left a total of 27 items for the main study. Volunteers reported their expectations and needs by rating the importance of these items on a 5-point scale ranging from 1 (*unimportant*) to 5 (*very important*). Subjective satisfaction with the conditions for volunteering in the club was assessed on a further 5-point scale ranging from 1 (*not satisfied*) to 5 (*very satisfied*).

The construct orientation toward collective solidarity was operationalized with an elaborated version of a multidimensional measurement concept designed specifically for sports clubs (see Nagel, 2006). This measurement concept was based on theoretical ideas about aspects of the social and emotional attachment to sports clubs (Cuskelly & Boag, 2001; Engelberg et al., 2006; Green & Chalip, 2004; see, for a basic treatment, Meyer, Allen, & Smith, 1993), aspects of solidarity and collective interests in sports clubs (Braun, 2003), and different frames of sports club culture (Heinemann, 2004). Respondents assessed the single items on a 5-point scale ranging from 1 (*not at all true*) to 5 (*completely true*).

Finally, volunteers were asked to report their intention to terminate volunteering ('How often have you felt like quitting your voluntary engagement for your sports club in the past few months?') on a 5-point scale ranging from 1 (*never*) to 5 (*often*). A total of 48.9% reported *never*; 19.9%, *yes, but only occasionally*; 19.0%, *sometimes*; and 12.2%, *frequently* and *often* combined. Hence, approximately two-thirds of volunteers could be characterized as stable and about one-third as unstable. Although the majority of those thinking about terminating their volunteering may well not actually do so, the risk of no longer volunteering was probably higher among those who had already entered into such a decision-making process.

Data analysis

The aims of this research were threefold. The first aim was to perform a preliminary assessment of the factor structure of the two constructs volunteer job satisfaction and orientation toward collective solidarity in an exploratory factor analysis (EFA) using principal-component analysis with varimax rotation. EFA is an appropriate way to identify key items and eliminate weak factors in the early stages of research. Following the Kaiser criterion, only factors with an eigenvalue > 1 were considered. Items loading 0.50 or higher on a factor and not correlating with any other factor within a range of 0.20 were also retained (Backhaus, Erichson, Plinke, & Weiber, 2008). Sampling adequacy for factor analysis was examined using the Kaiser-Meyer-Olkin test with an acceptable value set at >0.60 (Backhaus et al., 2008). The psychometric properties of the volunteer job satisfaction scale were tested by analyzing its reliability with Cronbach's α and performing scale intercorrelations.

The second aim was to explore whether individual (sociodemographic and work related) variables led to differences among the scale dimensions for the two constructs volunteer job satisfaction and orientation toward collective solidarity. Therefore, descriptive statistics are reported and univariate analyses of these dimensions were computed for both constructs.

The third aim was to test the postulated relationships. The first test analyzed the risk of terminating volunteering as a function of the two constructs volunteering job satisfaction and orientation toward collective solidarity. In addition, the relationship between the two constructs was tested with a bivariate analysis of variance. Finally, linear regression analysis was used to test how far further socioeconomic and volunteering-related variables might influence long-term commitment to volunteering in sports clubs.

Results

Measurement and characteristics of the construct 'volunteer job satisfaction' in sports clubs

Before comparing different aspects of job satisfaction, the measurement properties of the scale were assessed. This was done with the first set of satisfaction measures indicating the importance of various aspects of the work environment. The Kaiser-Meyer-Olkin sampling statistic (KMO $=0.84$) indicated an adequate sample size for conducting an EFA. The factor analysis of the survey data (eigenvalues > 1.0) and further reliability analyses resulted in a 5-factor solution explaining 52.9% of the variance (Table 2). This only considered items with loadings of >0.50. Twenty-one of the original 27 items were retained within the resulting factor structure. The identified five factors were subsequently labeled: *task design* (6 items, $\alpha =0.83$), *material incentives* (4 items, $\alpha =0.75$), *leadership* (5 items, $\alpha =0.70$), *support* (3 items, $\alpha =0.56$), and *recognition* (3 items, $\alpha =0.70$). Results of the reliability analyses of the single dimensions with Cronbach's α (for the factors) and the selectivity coefficients (for the single items) were generally satisfactory. Furthermore, the independence of the different job satisfaction factors was examined with scale intercorrelations. Values ranging from 0.25 to 0.53 indicated no problems with multicollinearity, because scale intercorrelations were well below the cutoff of 0.90 recommended by Backhaus et al. (2008). The aggregated means of each factor were computed from the items assigned to it.

In the next step, univariate tests were computed to evaluate the influence of the person-related determinants gender and age along with the work-related determinants length of volunteering, hours of volunteering, and job functions on each job satisfaction factor (Table 3). Results showed hardly any major differences between women and men regarding their expectations about volunteering conditions. The two factors, support, $t(1, 399) =5.16$, $p =0.02$, and material incentives, $t(1, 405) =5.54$, $p =0.02$, were both significantly more important for women volunteers than for men. Differentiation according to age analyses indicated that material incentives were more important for younger volunteers, $F(3, 390) =3.78$, $p =0.01$, $\eta^2 =0.03$. Results on the intensity of volunteering (average time volunteered) revealed that the more hours volunteers worked in their club, the greater their expectations regarding the conditions of volunteering. There were significant differences for the factors task design, $F(3, 377) =3.47$, $p =0.02$, $\eta^2 =0.03$, leadership, $F(3, 379) =7.07$, $p =0.01$, $\eta^2 =0.05$, and recognition, $F(3, 379) =2.70$, $p =0.04$, $\eta^2 =0.02$. There was also a tendency for the expectations regarding the conditions of volunteering to increase the longer people had been volunteering. This attained significance for the factors task design, $F(3, 393) =3.32$, $p =0.02$, $\eta^2 =0.02$, leadership, $F(3, 397) =2.53$, $p =0.05$, $\eta^2 =0.02$, and recognition, $F(3, 391) =2.80$, $p =0.04$, $\eta^2 =0.02$. Differentiated according to job functions, results showed that material incentives, $F(3, 397) = 10.25$, $p =0.001$, $\eta^2 =0.07$, and an attractive task design, $F(3, 394) =8.43$, $p =0.001$, $\eta^2 =0.06$, were particularly important for volunteers in the sports domain.

Measurement and characteristics of the construct orientation toward collective solidarity in sports clubs

The scale for the construct orientation toward collective solidarity was also subjected to an EFA (principal-component analysis with varimax rotation). Applying the Kaiser criterion, a three-factor solution was extracted that explained 68.4% of variance. All 12 items were retained within the resulting factor structure. The factors of action oriented toward collective solidarity were labeled as follows: social and emotional attachment (5 items, $\alpha =0.85$), collective interest and commitment (3 items, $\alpha =0.65$), and open communication and cooperation (4 items, $\alpha =0.87$).

Table 2. Descriptive statistics, factor loadings, and reliability estimates (Cronbach's α) for factors of volunteer job satisfaction.

Factor	Item	M (SD)	Selectivity coefficients	Factor loadings[a]
Task design (M = 3.98, SD = 0.75, α = 0.83)	Challenging task	3.60 (1.07)	0.62	0.79
	Interesting work/field	4.07 (0.94)	0.72	0.78
	Varied work	3.90 (0.92)	0.67	0.72
	Autonomy when carrying out one's work	4.31 (0.81)	0.56	0.62
	Opportunity to exchange knowledge and experience	3.81 (1.02)	0.59	0.59
	Opportunity to extend and deepen one's own competencies	4.34 (0.79)	0.58	0.54
Material incentives (M = 2.99, SD = 1.17, α = 0.75)	Financial assistance with further training	3.70 (1.21)	0.55	0.76
	Fringe benefits (e.g., reduced membership fees)	2.74 (1.34)	0.59	0.71
	Payment for voluntary work	2.44 (1.25)	0.56	0.65
	Reduced price/free admission to club events	2.71 (1.24)	0.57	0.63
Leadership (M = 4.26, SD = 0.71, α = 0.70)	Constructive feedback from club management	4.23 (0.92)	0.58	0.74
	Information on major club affairs	4.49 (0.75)	0.50	0.67
	Close contact between club management and volunteers	4.20 (0.95)	0.52	0.64
	Information on club policy	4.36 (0.86)	0.47	0.58
	Encouragement from management to engage in further training	3.92 (1.08)	0.41	0.53
Support (M = 4.58, SD = 0.54, α = 0.56)	Problems and concerns of volunteers are taken seriously	4.50 (0.76)	0.44	0.74
	Respectful treatment of volunteers	4.76 (0.51)	0.45	0.61
	Support from other club members	4.30 (0.85)	0.50	0.60
Recognition (M = 3.83, SD = 0.95, α = 0.70)	Appreciation of what one has achieved	4.14 (0.97)	0.53	0.74
	Recognition of one's commitment from other club members	3.68 (1.10)	0.54	0.70
	Acknowledgment of one's services through symbolic recognition	3.41 (1.13)	0.50	0.63

[a]Loadings < 0.50 were suppressed.

Findings on the factor loadings and the reliability of these factors were satisfactory (see Table 4). The scale intercorrelations revealed acceptable values ranging from $r = 0.28$ to 0.64, suggesting no multicollinearity.

In the next step, descriptive and univariate statistics were calculated to evaluate the influence of gender and age along with length of volunteering, hours of volunteering, and job functions on the two factors social and emotional attachment and collective interest and commitment (Table 5). First of all, no gender-specific

Table 3. Volunteer job satisfaction factors differentiated by subgroups.

	Task design M (SD)	Material incentives M (SD)	Leadership M (SD)	Support M (SD)	Recognition M (SD)
Gender					
Female	4.02 (0.66)	3.17 (0.92)	4.19 (0.78)	4.66 (0.50)	3.88 (0.94)
Male	4.04 (0.66)	2.88 (0.99)	4.29 (0.66)	4.53 (0.56)	3.80 (0.95)
t test	1.14	5.54*	1.86	5.16*	0.58
Age					
< 20 years	3.97 (0.61)	3.69 (0.97)	4.14 (0.69)	4.53 (0.67)	3.98 (0.62)
21–40 years	3.99 (0.69)	3.07 (0.80)	4.22 (0.67)	4.56 (0.60)	3.84 (0.70)
41–60 years	3.91 (0.80)	2.80 (0.97)	4.24 (0.78)	4.60 (0.49)	3.80 (0.80)
> 60 years	4.04 (0.89)	2.97 (0.78)	4.54 (0.73)	4.66 (0.42)	4.01 (0.98)
ANOVA *F*	0.46	3.78**	1.80	0.33	0.54
η^2	–	0.03	–	–	–
Average time volunteered (hours per month)					
< 5 hours	3.77 (0.82)	2.75 (1.1)	4.17 (0.77)	4.47 (0.64)	3.63 (0.82)
5–10 hours	3.86 (0.85)	2.87 (0.98)	3.99 (0.88)	4.50 (0.66)	3.77 (0.95)
11–20 hours	4.07 (0.74)	3.09 (0.98)	4.28 (0.67)	4.67 (0.45)	3.79 (0.95)
> 20 hours	4.06 (0.61)	3.10 (1.0)	4.44 (0.49)	4.60 (0.49)	4.02 (0.92)
ANOVA *F*	3.47*	1.99	7.07**	2.36	2.70*
η^2	0.03	–	0.05	–	0.02
Length of volunteering					
< 5 years	3.93 (0.76)	2.93 (0.96)	4.20 (0.69)	4.60 (0.49)	3.67 (0.93)
5–10 years	3.86 (0.84)	3.06 (0.90)	4.49 (0.70)	4.49 (0.61)	3.94 (0.95)
11–20 years	4.02 (0.68)	3.06 (0.98)	4.58 (0.71)	4.59 (0.56)	3.86 (0.93)
> 20 years	4.22 (0.62)	2.91 (1.1)	4.65 (0.71)	4.65 (0.54)	4.03 (0.92)
ANOVA *F*	3.32*	0.48	2.53*	1.24	2.80*
η^2	0.03	–	0.02	–	0.02
Job function					
Administrative domain	3.75 (0.72)	2.57 (0.89)	4.25 (0.64)	4.59 (0.41)	3.75 (0.88)
Sports domain	4.13 (0.66)	3.25 (0.90)	4.26 (0.70)	4.59 (0.54)	3.88 (0.72)
Technical domain	3.63 (0.64)	2.94 (0.89)	4.21 (0.76)	4.47 (0.90)	3.48 (0.95)
Organizational domain	3.83 (0.88)	2.69 (0.95)	4.20 (0.80)	4.53 (0.67)	3.93 (0.91)
ANOVA *F*	8.43***	10.25***	0.08	0.34	1.34
η^2	0.06	0.07	–	–	–

*$p \leq 0.05$, **$p \leq 0.01$, ***$p \leq 0.001$.

differences could be ascertained. However, there were significant age effects: both social and emotional attachment, $F(3, 410) = 2.62$, $p = 0.02$, $\eta^2 = 0.02$, and collective interest and commitment, $F(3, 410) = 4.54$, $p = 0.004$, $\eta^2 = 0.03$, increased with age. With reference to volunteering-related variables, the volunteers with the highest workload in their club possessed a stronger collective interest and commitment, $F(3, 430) = 16.46$, $p = 0.001$, $\eta^2 = 0.11$, and stronger social and emotional attachment to their club, $F(3, 430) = 2.52$, $p = 0.04$, $\eta^2 = 0.02$. Results on the duration of volunteering showed that social and emotional attachment, $F(3, 430) = 2.95$, $p = 0.03$, $\eta^2 = 0.02$, and collective interest and commitment, $F(3, 430) = 6.47$,

Table 4. Descriptive statistics, factor loadings, and reliability estimates (Cronbach's α) for factors of orientation toward collective solidarity.

Factor	Item	M (SD)	Selectivity coefficients	Factor loadings[a]
Social and emotional attachment ($M = 4.08$, SD $= 0.80$, $\alpha = 0.85$)	I feel that I belong to the club	4.47 (0.78)	0.74	0.79
	I am proud to be able to say that I belong to this club	4.39 (0.80)	0.71	0.70
	I enjoy attending our club events	4.18 (0.91)	0.66	0.74
	I like being in our club	4.51 (0.73)	0.65	0.57
	I often discuss club affairs with other members	4.34 (0.84)	0.56	0.63
Collective interest and commitment ($M = 3.27$, SD $= 1.01$, $\alpha = 0.65$)	My private interests are secondary to the collective interests of our club	3.56 (1.02)	0.66	0.80
	I actively take part in making the decisions in our club	4.00 (1.17)	0.56	0.71
	I am happy to help when things need to be done in our club	4.43 (0.76)	0.53	0.64
Open communication and cooperation ($M = 4.16$, SD $= 0.81$, $\alpha = 0.87$)	We openly discuss problems in our sports club	3.91 (0.88)	0.69	0.83
	There is a good atmosphere in our club	4.29 (0.80)	0.78	0.82
	We place great value on working together as a team	4.21 (0.84)	0.73	0.79
	We make sure we deal with each other in a frank and friendly way in our club	4.52 (0.73)	0.73	0.76

[a]Loadings < 0.50 were suppressed.

$p = 0.01$, $\eta^2 = 0.04$, also went hand in hand with long-term volunteering in the club. Differentiated according to different job functions, results showed that it was particularly volunteers in the administrative domain who tended to have a greater collective interest and commitment, $F(3, 410) = 7.06$, $p = 0.001$, $\eta^2 = 0.05$.

Test of the determinants influencing long-term commitment to volunteering

For further analyses, first, the factors representing importance and respective measures of satisfaction were combined into weighted volunteer job satisfaction constructs (e.g., Scharnbacher & Kiefer, 1996). Second, the volunteer job satisfaction

Table 5. Factors of orientation toward collective solidarity differentiated by subgroups.

	Collective interest and commitment M (SD)	Social and emotional attachment M (SD)
Gender		
Female	3.99 (0.77)	4.40 (0.61)
Male	3.99 (0.76)	4.36 (0.66)
t test	0.05	0.34
Age		
< 20 years	3.49 (0.69)	4.19 (0.86)
21–40 years	3.99 (0.71)	4.34 (0.69)
41–60 years	4.06 (0.77)	4.46 (0.53)
> 60 years	4.15 (0.72)	4.53 (0.49)
ANOVA *F*	4.54**	2.62*
η^2	0.03	0.02
Average time volunteered (in hours per month)		
≤ 5 hours	3.65 (0.81)	4.31 (0.65)
6–10 hours	3.86 (0.76)	4.35 (0.57)
11–20 hours	3.99 (0.78)	4.39 (0.65)
> 20 hours	4.34 (0.59)	4.50 (0.57)
ANOVA *F*	16.46***	2.52*
η^2	0.11	0.02
Length of volunteering		
≤ 5 years	3.84 (0.77)	4.31 (0.66)
6–10 years	4.01 (0.72)	4.34 (0.68)
11–20 years	4.04 (0.79)	4.43 (0.58)
> 20 years	4.28 (0.59)	4.56 (0.49)
ANOVA *F*	6.47**	2.95*
η^2	0.04	0.02
Job function		
Administrative domain	4.22 (0.60)	4.47 (0.55)
Sports domain	3.86 (0.71)	4.33 (0.64)
Technical domain	3.88 (0.70)	4.30 (0.70)
Organizational domain	4.06 (0.64)	4.55 (0.61)
ANOVA *F*	7.06***	2.28
η^2	0.05	–

*$p \leq 0.05$, **$p \leq 0.01$, ***$p \leq 0.001$.

and orientation toward collective solidarity constructs were each aggregated. This was done by constructing indices summing up all the relevant factors within a construct (Kromrey, 2002). Discriminant analyses were used to test the significance of the individual factors of volunteer job satisfaction on total satisfaction. Results showed that all five identified factors were relevant, so that these could be summarized into a volunteer job satisfaction index (SAT-IND): the higher the SAT-IND, the more satisfied the individual. The three factors in the construct orientation toward collective solidarity were also summed to one index (SOL-IND): the higher the SOL-IND, the stronger the orientation toward collective solidarity.

The next step was a more detailed analysis of the risk of terminating volunteering as a function of the two central constructs volunteer job satisfaction and orientation toward collective solidarity (Table 6). The indices were used to distinguish between three subgroups reflecting different levels of the independent constructs volunteer job satisfaction ($<15 =$low, 15–$20 =$mid, >20 high) and orientation toward collective solidarity ($<10 =$low, 10–$12 =$mid, >12 strong). The ANOVA confirmed the hypothesized relations for both SAT-IND and SOL-IND (H1 and H2). Volunteers with a strong orientation toward collective solidarity, $F(2, 433) = 12.47, p = 0.001, \eta^2 = 0.06$, and satisfied volunteers, $F(2, 390) = 14.88, p = 0.001, \eta^2 = 0.07$), both had a lower risk of terminating volunteering. The reciprocal relationship of the two constructs to voluntary commitment was assessed with a bivariate analysis of variance (Table 6). This revealed that volunteers with a strong sense of orientation toward collective solidarity showed a lower risk of terminating volunteering ($M = 2.09$) even when their satisfaction was low, $F(2, 390) = 15.89, p = 0.001, \eta^2 = 0.08$. In contrast, the risk of terminating volunteering was higher when SOL-IND values were lower but job satisfaction was high ($M = 2.50$). However, those volunteers in whom a low orientation toward collective solidarity was combined with dissatisfaction toward expected volunteering conditions had the highest risk of terminating volunteering ($M = 3.11$).

Finally, a stepwise linear regression analysis was computed to test which variables also influence long-term volunteering (Table 7). The analysis revealed that the regression model accounted for 23% of the total variance in perceived risk of terminating volunteering. Orientation toward collective solidarity was found to be the most significant predictor of voluntary commitment to the club ($\beta = -0.26$), followed by volunteer job satisfaction ($\beta = -0.18$), and the variable children belonging to the sport club ($\beta = -0.17$). Whereas the length of volunteering tended to have a negative effect ($\beta = 0.13$), the longer volunteers actively volunteered in a club, the greater their risk of terminating. The variables age, gender, education, income, workload, average time volunteered, length of club membership, and job function were not significant predictors, and therefore excluded from the model.

Table 6. Risk of terminating volunteering differentiated for the grouped factors volunteer job satisfaction (SAT-IND) and orientation toward collective solidarity (SOL-IND).

| | Groups SAT-IND | | | | | | | |
| | < 15 | | 15–20 | | > 20 | | Total | |
Groups SOL-IND	n	M	n	M	n	M	n	M
< 10	9	3.11	22	2.41	6	2.50	37	2.59
10–12	13	2.69	42	2.38	27	1.64	82	2.19
> 12	23	2.09	94	1.83	154	1.53	271	1.68
Total	45	2.47	158	2.06	187	1.57	390	1.86

Analysis of variance	df	F	p	η^2
SOL-IND	2	12.47	0.001	0.06
SAT-IND	2	14.88	0.001	0.07
SOL-IND × SAT-IND	2	15.89	0.001	0.08

Table 7.   Estimated linear regression function (stepwise method).

| Variable | Dependent variable: risk of terminating voluntary work | | | | |
| | Nonstandardized coefficients | | Standardized coefficients | | |
	Regression coefficient B	SE	β	t	p
(Constant)	3.910	0.583		6.710	0.001
Orientation toward collective solidarity (SOL-IND)	−0.190	0.038	−0.264	−4.984	0.001
Volunteer job satisfaction (SAT-IND)	−0.055	0.017	−0.177	−3.530	0.001
Child belonging to sports club (dummy: yes = 0)	−0.592	0.155	−0.175	−3.268	0.001
Length of volunteering	0.015	0.006	0.130	2.444	0.015
Excluded variables	Age, gender, education, income, workload, length of membership, average time volunteered, job function (dummies)				
Explained variance	$R^2 = 0.25$ corr. $R^2 = 0.23$				

Discussion

The purpose of the current study was to find out which determinants influence the tendency to continue or to terminate long-term commitment as a volunteer in sports clubs. The commitment of volunteers (risk of termination) was conceptualized as a decision-making act between the tendency either to continue or to terminate volunteering in their sports club. The hypotheses derived from this were confirmed by the present findings. In line with previous research (Green & Chalip, 2004; Kim et al., 2007; Silverberg et al., 2001), more satisfied volunteers exhibited a lower risk of terminating their volunteering. Results also confirmed a positive relation between the orientation toward collective solidarity and commitment to volunteering in sports clubs. Indeed, the construct orientation toward collective solidarity had a stronger influence on commitment to volunteering than the construct volunteer job satisfaction. A stable, long-term voluntary commitment to produce certain club goods is evidently tied to a high orientation toward collective solidarity. The relationship between these two constructs revealed that the influence of lower volunteer job satisfaction on the risk of terminating could be relativized to a certain extent by the strength of the orientation toward collective solidarity. That means, although volunteering is then perceived and experienced as being far from optimal (lower job satisfaction values), to stop volunteering is not an option because of the sense of obligation to solidarity and the specific attachment to the club. The results underline the increasing importance of aspects such as reciprocity or solidarity and emotional attachment when explaining individual social actions such as continuing or terminating volunteering (Engelberg et al., 2012; Schlesinger & Nagel, 2011). Because of their specific attachment and the normatively anchored orientation toward collective solidarity, volunteers are less likely to think about terminating their volunteering, and for some, this is probably even more or less out of the question.

It is far more the case that a destabilization of volunteering and thus an intention to terminate will emerge only when the orientation toward collective solidarity is no longer so unconditional. This may be indicated by a decreasing collective solidarity due to an increasing divergence of interests (indicators can be overt conflicts within the club or a breakdown in club climate). It is also conceivable that the solidarity of other club members is no longer perceived as being so absolute (e.g., problems in filling positions, increasing free-rider mentalities). The results show that the risk of terminating volunteering grew markedly when the orientation toward collective solidarity was low and members were simultaneously dissatisfied with volunteering conditions.

In addition, the linear regression analysis showed that it was exclusively volunteering-related variables that were significant for the long-term commitment to sports clubs, whereas socioeconomic variables (in contrast to the analysis of willingness to volunteer) had no mentionable influence. The two constructs job satisfaction and the orientation toward collective solidarity were the strongest determinants of long-term voluntary commitment. Moreover, having children who belong to the club also had a positive influence on voluntary commitment. This probably relates to the fact that the opportunity costs are lower when one's own children are also actively involved in one's club. In contrast, the length of volunteering had a negative effect on long-term commitment, which may possibly be a sign of saturation.

Furthermore, results suggested that other individual variables influenced the respondents' perceptions of volunteer job satisfaction and the orientation toward collective interest. (1) *Volunteer job satisfaction*: differences in how volunteers perceive their specific working conditions depended on age and experiences in volunteering. It appears that particularly younger volunteers and those volunteering in the sports domain place more value on material incentives (Hustenix & Lammertyn, 2003). This suggests that younger age groups tend to anticipate material rewards for their voluntary engagement. Moreover, the factor material incentives appears to be more important in the sports domain than in other volunteering domains. In addition, the longer the length of volunteering, the higher the expectations tended to be regarding the factors leadership and recognition. (2) *Orientations toward collective interest:* the findings showed further, that the levels of the two factors social and emotional attachment and collective interest and commitment are determined by age and the length and extent of volunteering in the sports club. This indicates that the attachment of volunteers to their club and their increasing familiarization with obligations of solidarity and reciprocity can be interpreted as the outcome of a long-term club-specific socialization process (Braun, 2003; Cuskelly, McIntyre, & Boag, 1998).

Recommendations for volunteer management in sports clubs

The present findings indicate that an orientation toward collective solidarity is essential for the long-term commitment of volunteers. The promotion of obligations of solidarity and reciprocity, a cooperative club atmosphere, and the emotional and social attachment of club members need to be central elements for effectively managing volunteers and retaining them in sports clubs. However, this should not be restricted to single measures, but viewed far more as one element within a broader volunteer management strategy. It is particularly club-specific socialization processes that are important in this context; that is, processes that impart, promote, and cultivate reciprocal obligations and individual beliefs encouraging solidarity. Such socialization processes are formed particularly through the length and intensity of the relationship between club and member. Therefore, both younger and new club members should be acquainted with the values of the club and become aware of the need for collective solidarity. This should be accompanied by gradually familiarizing members with the need for committed volunteering.

Regarding the importance of the construct orientation toward collective solidarity for long-term voluntary commitment, the present study contributes to resolving the controversial discussion over whether today's sports clubs should be characterized as efficiency-oriented service organizations rather than collectives based on solidarity. An increasingly service- and growth-oriented perspective in sports clubs increases the probability of diverging individual and collective interests. This may weaken the ties between members and their sports club even further, and it also erodes obligations of reciprocity and solidarity (Nagel, 2006). Hence, any suggestion that sports clubs would be able to overcome some of their current problems by becoming more efficient and professional like modern service companies must take care to ensure that this does not have a boomerang effect and lead to a further destabilization of long-term voluntary commitment.

We argue that sports clubs should be viewed as meeting place between a traditional volunteer culture dominated by solidarity on the one side and a modern volunteer culture, where volunteers develop real expectations and evaluations toward working conditions in their club on the other. Therefore, it is necessary to provide high volunteer job satisfaction in order to ensure stability among volunteers. If a sports club wants to retain its volunteers, it needs to consider the individual expectations and needs of its club members and design volunteering conditions and incentive schemes that meet these expectations. The results of the study show that volunteer job satisfaction is a multidimensional construct. Concerning volunteer management it is important to develop a socially competent and communicative management style that provides information on important activities and goals of the club and fosters close contacts to members. In addition, the factor support plays a major role in volunteer job satisfaction. Therefore, sports clubs should provide supportive measures and assistance. A differentiated assessment based on further individual parameters also revealed that volunteers may have different expectation structures. This also has to be taken into account in order to align volunteering conditions more specifically with expectations. Particular attention should be given to long-term volunteers here, because these revealed a heightened risk of terminating due to satiation effects. For long-term volunteers, the factor recognition was particularly important. The need for recognition of their volunteering can still be achieved particularly well through (classic) measures such as awarding honors for many years of volunteering or organizing specific volunteer events. Material incentives were particularly important for young volunteers and those in the sports domain. In view of what are mostly limited financial resources in sports clubs (e.g., Wicker & Breuer, 2011), this calls for creativity – only the wealthiest clubs can afford to honor volunteers financially. Hence, a competent and well-planned use of fringe benefits (e.g., regarding the use of sport facilities and services) or reduced member-ship fees should be a central element of every volunteer management concept in sports clubs. Nevertheless, in the volunteer context, material incentives should be administered moderately, because they may well trigger exclusionary effects that can suppress values and norms based on collective solidarity (e.g., Frey, 1997).

Limitations and future research

The present analysis focused solely on the intention to terminate volunteering. Future studies could also ask club members whether they actually have terminated volunteering recently (e.g., in the last 2 years). In addition, there is a need for more precise analyses of not only the decision on whether or not to continue but also the time commitment involved in volunteering.

The conceptualization of the two constructs volunteer job satisfaction and orientation toward collective solidarity in the present study was based on explorative measurement concepts. Further research should specify these measurement concepts further and validate them (e.g., with confirmatory factor analyses). Refining existing measurement models could lead to a more concrete understanding of which determinants can be manipulated.

The present study explained the decision to commit oneself to volunteering on the basis of individual determinants. It neglected the specific structural conditions of a sports club (e.g., club size, incentive structures, etc.) that probably also impact on the decision to make a long-term voluntary commitment. Therefore, future research on decisions to volunteer should link together the individual data from club members with the corresponding structural data on their clubs. Multilevel analyses would be the correct method of analysis for such hierarchical data (members within clubs) (Hox, 2002). However, this method could not be applied to the present database because of insufficient numbers of individual level observations in the analyzed clubs. The usual recommendation for a multilevel analysis is to have at least 25 cases on the highest level (club level) and at least 20 observations on each lower level (the individual level) (e.g., Snijders & Bosker, 1999). Further studies will need to generate correspondingly large case numbers in order to examine in more detail how both the individual and the corresponding structural determinants influence the decision to volunteer.

Finally, the generalizability of finding from our study is limited to the specific understanding and valuation of volunteering in sports clubs varies across different sports systems, and this could have different effects on the individual decision to long-term volunteering in sports clubs. Therefore, it has to be noted that the results generalize only to Swiss sports clubs. Further research in various countries is needed in order to validate the present results and ascertain how far they generalize beyond Swiss sports clubs.

References

Backhaus, K., Erichson, B., Plinke, W., & Weiber, R. (2008). *Multivariate Analysemethoden. Eine anwendungsorientierte Einführung* [Multivariate analysis methods: A practice-oriented introduction] (12th ed.). Berlin: Springer.

Becker, G.S. (1965). A theory of the allocation of time. *Economic Journal, 75,* 493–517.

Braun, S. (2003). Leistungserstellung in freiwilligen Vereinigungen. Über "Gemeinschaftsarbeit" und die "Krise des Ehrenamts" [Delivering services in voluntary associations: Collective work and the volunteer crisis]. In J. Baur & S. Braun (Eds.), *Integrationsleistungen von Sportvereinen als Freiwilligenorganisationen* [Integration efforts of sports clubs as voluntary organizations] (pp. 191–241). Aachen: Meyer & Meyer.

Braun, S. (2011). *Ehrenamtliches Engagement im Sport. Sportbezogene Sonderauswertung der Freiwilligensurveys von 1999, 2004 und 2009* [Voluntary engagement in sport: Special sport-specific analysis of the 1999, 2004, and 2009 volunteer surveys]. Köln: Sportverlag Strauß.

Breuer, C. (Ed.) (2011). *Sportentwicklungsbericht 2009/2010. Analyse zur Situation der Sportvereine in Deutschland* [Report on trends in sport 2009/2010: The situation of sport clubs in Germany]. Köln: Sportverlag Strauß.

Buchanan, J.M. (1965). An economic theory of clubs. *Economica, 32*, 1–14.

Burgham, M., & Downward, P. (2005). Why volunteer, time to volunteer? A case study from swimming. *Managing Leisure, 10*, 79–93.

Chelladurai, P. (2006). *Management of human resources in sport and recreation* (2nd ed.). Champaign, IL: Human Kinetics Publishers.

Chelladurai, P., & Ogasawara, E. (2003). Satisfaction and commitment of American and Japanese collegiate coaches. *Journal of Sport Management, 17*, 63–73.

Coleman, J.S. (1974). *Power and the structure of society*. New York, NY: Norton.

Cuskelly, G. (2005). Volunteer participation trends in Australian sport. In G. Nichols & M. Collins (Eds.), *Volunteers in sports clubs* (pp. 87–104). Eastbourne: Leisure Studies Association Publication.

Cuskelly, G., & Boag, A. (2001). Organizational commitment as a predictor of committee member turnover amongst volunteer sport administrators: Results of a time-lagged study. *Sport Management Review, 4*, 65–86.

Cuskelly, G., McIntyre, M., & Boag, A. (1998). A longitudinal study of the development of organizational commitment amongst volunteer sport administrators. *Journal of Sport Management, 12*, 181–202.

Doherty, A. (2005). *Volunteer management in community sport clubs: A study of volunteers'perception*. Toronto, ON: The Sport Alliance of Ontario.

Downward, P., Dawson, A., & Dejonghe, T. (2009). *Sports economics: Theory, evidence and policy*. Amsterdam: Elsevier.

Duncan, B. (1999). Modeling charitable contributions of time and money. *Journal of Public Economics, 72*, 213–242.

Emrich, E., Pitsch, W., & Flatau, J. (2010). Ehrenamtliche Leistungserbringung zwischen rationalem Kalkül und sozialer Verantwortung [Voluntary services between rational calculation and social responsibility]. *Sozialmanagement, 8*(2), 11–32.

Engelberg, T., Skinner, J.L., & Zakus, D.H. (2006). Exploring the commitment of volunteers in Little Athletics centres. *Australian Journal on Volunteering, 11*(2), 56–66.

Engelberg, T., Zakus, D.H., Skinner, J.L., & Campell, A. (2012). Defining and measuring dimensionality and targets of the commitment of sport volunteers. *Journal of Sport Management, 26*, 192–205.

Erlinghagen, M. (2000). Arbeitslosigkeit und ehrenamtliche Tätigkeit im Zeitverlauf [Temporal trends in unemployment and volunteering]. *Kölner Zeitschrift für Soziologie und Sozialpsychologie, 52*, 291–310.

Esser, H. (2009). Rationality and commitment: The model of frame selection and the explanation of normative action. In M. Cherkaoui & P. Hamilton (Eds.), *Raymond Boudon: A life in sociology*, Vol. 2, Part two: *Toward a general theory of rationality* (pp. 207–230). Oxford: The Bardwell Press.

Farrell, J.M., Johnston, M.E., & Twynam, G.D. (1998). Volunteer motivation, satisfaction, and management at an elite sporting competition. *Journal of Sport Management, 12*, 288–300.

Finkelstein, M.A. (2008). Volunteer satisfaction and volunteer action: A functional approach. *Social Behavior and Personality, 36*, 9–18.

Flatau, J. (2009). Zum Zusammenhang von Sozialisation und ehrenamtliche Mitarbeiter in Sportvereinen – Erste Überlegungen unter Anwendung der Rational-Choice-Theorie [Relation between socialization and volunteers in sports clubs: Preliminary ideas when applying rational choice theory]. *Sport und Gesellschaft, 6*, 259–281.

Freeman, R.B. (1997). Working for nothing: The supply of volunteer labour. *Journal of Labor Economics, 15*, 140–166.

Frey, B.S. (1997). *Markt und Motivation. Wie ökonomische Anreize die (Arbeits-)Moral verdrängen* [Market and motivation: How economic incentives suppress (work) morale]. München: Vahlen.

Frey, B.S. (2007). Awards as compensation. *European Management Review, 4*, 6–14.

Galindo-Kuhn, R., & Guzley, R.M. (2001). The Volunteer Satisfaction Index: Construct definition, measurement, development, and validation. *Journal of Social Service Research, 28*, 45–68.

Gidron, B. (1983). Sources of job satisfaction among service volunteers. *Journal of Voluntary Action Research, 12*, 20–35.

Green, B.C., & Chalip, L. (2004). Paths to volunteer commitment: Lessons from the Sydney Olympic Games. In R.A. Stebbins & M. Graham (Eds.), *Volunteering as leisure/leisure as volunteering: An international assessment* (pp. 49–68). Wallingford: CAB International.

Harvey, J., Levesque, M., & Donnelly, P. (2008). Sport volunteerism and social capital. *Sociology of Sport Journal, 24*, 206–223.

Heckathorn, D.D. (1989). Collective action and the second-order free-rider problem. *Rationality and Society, 1*, 78–100.

Heinemann, K. (2004). *Sportorganisationen: Verstehen und Gestalten* [Understanding and designing sport organizations]. Schorndorf: Hofmann.

Hirschman, A.O. (1970). *Exit, voice, and loyalty: Responses to decline in firms, organizations, and states.* Cambridge, MA: Harvard University Press.

Horch, H.-D. (1987). Personalwirtschaftliche Aspekte ehrenamtlicher Mitarbeit [Human resources aspects of volunteering]. In K. Heinemann (Ed.), *Betriebswirtschaftliche Grundlagen des Sportvereins* [Basics of business management in sports clubs] (pp. 121–141). Schorndorf: Hofmann.

Horch, H.-D. (1998). Self-destroying process of sports clubs in Germany. *European Journal of Sport Management, 5*, 46–58.

Hox, J.J. (2002). *Multilevel analysis: Techniques and applications.* Mahwah, NJ: Erlbaum.

Hustenix, L., & Lammertyn, F. (2003). Collective and reflective styles of volunteering: A sociological modernization perspective. *Voluntas, 14*, 167–187.

Kikulis, L. (1990). Understanding the satisfaction of volunteer sport administrators. *CAHPER Journal, 56*(4), 5–11.

Kim, M., Chelladurai, P., & Trail, G.T. (2007). A model of volunteer retention in youth sport. *Journal of Sport Management, 21*, 151–171.

Kromrey, H. (2002). *Empirische Sozialforschung* [Empirical social research] (10th ed.). Opladen: Leske + Budrich.

Lamprecht, M., Fischer, A., & Stamm, H.-P. (2011). *Sportvereine in der Schweiz* [Sports clubs in Switzerland]. Magglingen: BASPO.

Lipford, J., & Yandle, B. (2009). The determinants of purposeful voluntarism. *The Journal of Socio-Economics, 38*, 72–79.

MacIntosh, E., & Doherty, A. (2010). The influence of organizational culture on job satisfaction and intention to leave. *Sport Management Review, 13*, 106–117.

Meyer, J.P., Allen, N.J., & Smith, C.A. (1993). Commitment to organizations and occupations: Extension and test of a three-component conceptualization. *Journal of Applied Psychology, 78*, 538–551.

Nagel, S. (2006). Mitgliederbindung in Sportvereinen – Ein akteurtheoretisches Modell [Membership retention in sports clubs: An actor theory model]. *Sport und Gesellschaft, 3*, 33–56.

Nichols, G., & Padmore, J. (2005). *Who are the volunteers in sports clubs?* Working paper, Management School University of Sheffield, Sheffield, England.

Nichols, G., & Shepherd, M. (2006). Volunteering in sport: The use of ratio analysis to analyse volunteering and participation. *Managing Leisure, 11*, 205–216.

Nichols, G., Taylor, P., James, M., Garret, R., Holmes, K., & King, L. (2005). Pressures on the UK voluntary sport sector. *Voluntas, 16*, 33–60.

Powell, W.W., & Steinberg, R. (2006). *The nonprofit sector: Research handbook.* Westport, CT: Yale University Press.

Putnam, R. (2000). *Bowling alone: The collapse and revival of American community.* New York, NY: Simon & Schuster.

Ringuet, C., Cuskelly, G., Zakus, D., & Auld, C.J. (2008). *Volunteers in sport: Issues and innovation.* A report on a research-based consultancy project for NSW Sport and Recreation, Griffith University, Brisbane, Australia.

Sandler, T., & Tschirhart, J.T. (1980). The economic theory of clubs: An evaluative survey. *Journal of Economic Literature, 18,* 1481–1521.

Scharnbacher, K., & Kiefer, G. (1996). *Kundenzufriedenheit: Analyse, Messbarkeit und Zertifizierung* [Customer satisfaction: Analyses, measurement and certification]. München: Oldenbourg.

Scheerder, J., & Vos, S. (2009). *Panel van Sportclubs in Vlaanderen anno 2008. Eerste resultaten* [The Flemish sports club panel 2008: First results]. Leuven: K. U. Leuven, Research Unit of Social Kinesiology and Sport Management.

Schlesinger, T., & Nagel, S. (2011). "Freiwilliges Engagement im Sportverein ist Ehrensache!" – Ein Modell zur Analyse der Mitarbeitsentscheidungen in Sportvereinen ["Voluntary commitment to the sports club is a matter of honor!" A model for analyzing decisions to volunteer in sports clubs]. *Sport and Society, 8,* 3–27.

Silverberg, K.E., Marshall, E.K., & Ellis, G.D. (2001). Measuring job satisfaction of volunteers in public parks and recreation. *Journal of Park and Recreation Administration, 19,* 79–92.

Snijders, T., & Bosker, R. (1999). *Multilevel analysis: An introduction to basic and advanced multilevel modeling.* London: Sage.

Stebbins, R.A. (1996). Volunteering: A serious leisure perspective. *Nonprofit and Voluntary Sector Quarterly, 25,* 211–224.

Strigas, A.D., & Jackson, E.N., Jr. (2003). Motivating volunteers to serve and succeed: design and results of a pilot study that explores demographics and motivational factors in sport volunteerism. *International Sport Journal, 7,* 111–123.

Taylor, P., Nichols, G., Holmes, K., James, M., Gratton, C., Garrett, R., & King, K. (2003). *Sports volunteering in England.* London: Sport England.

Thiel, A., & Meier, H. (2009). Besonderheiten der Personalführung im Sportverein [Sports-club-specific aspects of personnel management]. In C. Breuer & A. Thiel (Eds.), *Handbuch Sportmanagement* (pp. 23–36). Schorndorf: Hofmann.

Vanberg, V. (1978). Kollektive Güter und Kollektives Handeln – Die Bedeutung neuerer ökonomischer Theorieentwicklungen für die Soziologie [Collective goods and collective action: The significance to sociology of recent trends in economic theory]. *Kölner Zeitschrift für Soziologie und Sozialpsychologie, 30,* 652–679.

Wicker, P., & Breuer, C. (2011). Scarcity of resources in German non-profit sport clubs. *Sport Management Review, 14,* 188–201.

Ziemek, S. (2006). Economic analysis of volunteers' motivations: A cross-country study. *The Journal of Socio-Economics, 35,* 532–555.

Changing roles: applying continuity theory to understanding the transition from playing to volunteering in community sport

Graham Cuskelly[a] and Wendy O'Brien[b]

[a]Griffith Business School, Griffith University, Southport, Queensland, Australia;
[b]Department of Tourism, Leisure, Hotel and Sport Management, Griffith University, Southport, Queensland, Australia

In many Western nations government policies are directed at increasing levels of participation in community sport. Recent research suggests that the sustainability of community sports system is under pressure due to declining volunteer numbers. Volunteers are often players transitioning from playing roles into non-playing roles such as administration and coaching. While a human resource management approach has been adopted to manage volunteers, little is understood in relation to the factors that contribute to players making the transition from playing to volunteering. Using Atchley's continuity theory, we propose a transition-extension framework that examines the psychological and social factors that provide the impetus for the transition to volunteering The framework also examines those factors that contribute to volunteers extending their involvement and may help community sport organisations provide an environment that will nurture volunteers in the transition phase to retain and extend their involvement to become long-term volunteers.

Introduction

In Australia (National Sport and Active Recreation Policy Framework), England (Active Communities) and Canada (Enhanced Participation) and some countries in Europe, government policies have been directed at increasing participation levels in community sport to capitalise on the espoused benefits of sport participation including social cohesion (Jarvie, 2003), educational attainment (Pfeifer & CorneliBen, 2010), reductions in youth crime (Nichols, 2004), drug use (Crabbe, 2000) and health costs (Galper, Trivedi, Barlow, Dunn, & Kampert, 2006; Manson, Skerrett, Greenland, & VanItallie, 2004). Increases in participation are reliant on a concomitant increase in the number of volunteers to continue to organise, direct and manage the community sport organisations (CSOs) which provide the vast bulk of participation opportunities in sport at a local level. Volunteers take on a range of roles including coaching, administration, training and committee membership and are frequently involved in multiple roles. The volunteer workforce is central to CSO's capacity to provide organised sport to both adults and children wishing to participate.

Australian Bureau of Statistics (ABS, 2010) indicate that while the rates of player participation have remained relatively static, volunteer participation rates had declined, from 10% in 2007 to 9% in 2010. While the volunteering rate in England has moved in the opposite direction (4.9–7.3%, Sport England, 2011), the increase is reflective more of the incorporation of a wider definition in volunteering, as previous statistics prior to the change indicate a decrease of 0.4% (Sport England, 2010). Sport volunteer rates in Canada have remained static at 11% from 2004 to 2007 (Statistics Canada, 2006; Statistics Canada, 2009). CSOs need volunteers to continue to deliver organised sport, yet as the preceding statistics indicate volunteer numbers are at best static if not declining. While the recruitment and retention of volunteers to service the needs of CSOs are an issue that has challenged researchers across a broad range of disciplines, our focus is somewhat different. We are seeking to explore how players transition from playing roles to extend their involvement in the organisation in which they have played by taking up non-playing volunteer roles.

Research on how the voluntary workforce can be managed through human resource management (HRM) approach has focused on how to maximise volunteers' potential and foster recruitment, retention, training and support. However, this approach has limitations as it fails to understand the complexity of volunteering. Two decades ago Pearce (1993) suggested that problems exist in relation to a management approach which neglects the meanings that volunteers attach to their involvement, a sentiment echoed by the Leisure Industries Research Centre (2003) and Schulz, Nichols, and Auld (2011). The factors that influence people to volunteer are often not the same factors that influence people to continue to volunteer (Chacon, Vecina, & Davila, 2007).

Similarly incomplete are understandings in relation to the factors that contribute to a volunteer becoming a 'stalwart' or 'career' volunteer. 'Stalwart' is used to describe volunteers as individuals who had extended their involvement in their CSO for more than 20 years beyond the cessation of their playing career (Cuskelly, 2004). Nichols (2005) and Cuskelly (2004) suggest that CSOs are increasingly relying on 'stalwart' volunteers to provide the core constituency of the voluntary workforce. Stalwarts are therefore critical to CSOs, as they maintain the club structure which enables sport to continue to be delivered (Nichols, 2005). Nichols (2005) suggested that further research is required to understand these key volunteers and the motivations that underpin their involvement. In Australia sport volunteers' involvement in their organisation exceeds that of other volunteers in non-sport sectors (e.g. welfare, religious and educational organisations), with almost 60% volunteering for 10 years or more (ABS, 2006b). While duration may be an indicator of retention it does not explain the intensity, the degree of involvement that characterises stalwart volunteers. Cuskelly (2004) suggested that such volunteers are often those who make the transition from playing to extend their involvement in the organisation, sometimes decades beyond the cessation of their playing career. Drawing on Atchley's (1989, 1999) continuity theory Cuskelly (2004) proposed a transition-extension proposition. The proposition seeks to explore the processes that occur as players transition from being a service user to extend their involvement with their sports organisation through changing roles to become a service provider such as a volunteer. He also suggested that the 'psychological factors and social pressures that predispose and motivate sport participants to make the transition from player to volunteer or to extend their volunteer participation need to be explored' (Cuskelly,

2004, p. 73). It was the purpose of this study to examine the factors that have influenced former players to make the transition to a non-playing role thereby extending their involvement and developing something akin to an identity as stalwart sport volunteer. While identity is clearly a significant component of continuity theory, identity theory is not the focus of this research. Rather as suggested by the concept of transition-extension, we examine the important connections that volunteers already had with the sport and their desire to maintain those connections which often precipitated the transition and then created the conditions in which they continued their involvement.

Theoretical background

Atchley (1989, 1993, 1999) argued that individuals use established social activities and patterns of behaviour as an adaptive strategy to transition across significant changes in the life course. Continuity theory therefore provided us with a general theory and framework or lens through which to explore the processes that people employ to create a sense of continuity in the face of change. While Atchley (1999) proposed measures through which to longitudinally capture continuity we were not seeking to measure these constructs, nor disprove them, but rather employ them to qualitatively explore how volunteers socially construct identity, and use past experiences, roles and relationships, to adapt to change. Adaptation and continuity are ongoing processes, drawing on past experience and internal and external constructs to create purpose in the present. Atchley (1989) suggests that disconti-nuity and continuity coexist, and while discontinuity may occur through loss of meaning, and a disparity between the current environment and the former environment, the focus of this article is on how people draw on past experiences to give continuity and meaning to current experiences. These current experiences in turn form the basis for continued involvement. As Atchley (1999) suggests, continuity theory is a 'conceptual way of organizing the search for coherent life stories and of understanding the dynamics that produce basic story lines' (p. 7). In this way continuity theory is providing a theory of adaptation and change through which to develop a way of thinking about and exploring the experiences of stalwart volunteers.

Atchley (1989, p. 183) suggested that individuals are 'both predisposed and motivated toward inner psychological continuity as well as outward continuity of social behaviour and circumstances'. Internal continuity is remembered structures of psychological characteristics, such as temperament, affect, attitudes, values and beliefs that shape notions of the self and identity (Atchley, 1993). The dimensions of internal continuity that are most relevant to the transition from playing to volunteering roles are self and identity. Identity refers to characteristics or traits of the self that individuals see as constant irrespective of the social situation. Continuity of self and identity tend to persist in the face of change, with new directions closely connected to and embellishing on already formed identity constructs (Atchley, 1993). Identity constructs are also supported by the activities within which individuals engage. Atchley (1993) argues that 'once people begin to stake their identities on activities, their motivation for continuity in activities is probably heightened' (p. 12). Certainly this consistency and linkage to a sense of personal history is essential for the maintenance of ego integrity that allows the individual to find inner stability amidst change. Through selective investments individuals focus their time and energy on activities in which they have some knowledge and competence and which will sustain their sense of identity (Atchley, 1993). As we illustrate in the results and discussion section, these dimensions of internal continuity, provide a way of understanding some of the processes of adaption and change that occur as players transition into non-playing roles.

Individuals also tend towards creating an external life that will support their inner psychological framework. For the purposes of this research the dimensions of external continuity involve the domain of activity, environments, roles and relationships that are cultivated and maintained across the life course for social support, affirmation of identity and creating a sense of belonging (Atchley, 1987). The dynamics of external continuity suggests that people tend towards 'using familiar skills to do familiar things in familiar places in the company of familiar people' (Atchley, 1989, p. 188). Individuals are more likely to look to a familiar domain of activity in which they feel proficient and competent and to selectively invest time and energy into that domain.

The transition-extension proposition draws on this concept of transitioning within a specified domain to maintain both internal and external continuity. In this way through the extension of involvement players are able to maintain the identity, relationships, environments and activity domain they had invested their time and energy into through their involvement in a particular CSO. For example a footballer or netballer, who is no longer willing or able to participate in their chosen sport as a player, may be able to maintain and further develop their sense of identity, relationships, familiar environments and domain of activity through transitioning into a volunteer role in order to extend their involvement. In addition to continuity theory, other theoretical literature, particularly a motivation perspective, supports the transition-extension proposition.

Volunteer motivation

Clary and Snyder (1999) argue that motivation plays a role in three key stages of the volunteer process: initiation of volunteer service (recruitment), satisfaction with the volunteer experience and sustained volunteer service (retention). Various models of volunteer motivation have been developed to explore the decision to commence volunteering (e.g. Clary, Snyder, & Ridge, 1992; Cnaan & Goldberg-Glen, 1991; Smith, 1981; Stebbins, 1996). Three models in particular contain constructs that support the transition-extension proposition: Knoke and Prensky (1984), Clary, Snyder and Stukas (1996) and Rochester (2006). Knoke and Prensky's (1984) model of three categories, utilitarian, affective and normative, seeks to explore the incentives that underpin volunteer's motivations. Utilitarian incentives comprise a range of personal benefits, such as enabling volunteers' children to participate in sport and joining community networks. Within the transition-extension proposition, volunteers are extending on the networks that they have already established over time (but often also extending their social networks through new relationships with other volunteers and players they coach). Affective incentives closely mirror the social and relationship aspects of the transition-extension proposition. Clary, Snyder and Stukas' (1996) volunteer function inventory contains socially motivated constructs, indicating that volunteers became involved to strengthen social relationships and meet the expectations of significant others. The key to transition-extension is that volunteers are seeking to extend and maintain the social relationships and connections that they had established through their playing career.

Role identification also falls under the affective incentive category, and has been used to explain volunteer motivation and retention in a number of studies (e.g., Chacon et al., 2007; Finkelstein, 2008; Finkelstein, Penner, & Brannick, 2005; Grube & Piliavin, 2000; Laverie & McDonald, 2007). Role identity suggests that high levels of participation in an organisation are dependent on the volunteer assimilating their volunteering identity into their self-concept. Role identity is therefore concerned with the development of a volunteer identity, whereas the transition-extension proposition enables the continuity of an already established identity. In line with role identity volunteers then do go on to develop their identity as volunteers. This identity then becomes an intrinsic part of defining who they are (Van Dyne & Farmer, 2005).

Knoke and Prensky's (1984) normative incentives are captured by the notion of suprapersonal, whereby volunteers are motived by altruistic concerns for the welfare of others. Clary, Snyder, and Stukas (1996) and Rochester (2006) also indicate that altruism, or activism, to act on the belief of the importance of helping others was a significant aspect in volunteer motivation. Rochester's (2006) model of volunteer motivation, in particular, links together activism with unpaid work and serious leisure. Altruistic and pro-social personalities and attitudes have been found to be associated with volunteering in a number of studies (e.g., Briggs, Petersen, & Gregory, 2010; Liao-Troth & Dunn, 1999; Penner, 2002; Tidwell, 2005). Volunteer motives have sometimes been conceptualised as the coexistence of altruism and self-interest (Stebbins, 1996; Smith, 1981). However, it is the link between altruism and serious leisure that are the most salient constructs that support the transition-extension proposition.

Cuskelly and Harrington (1997) drew on Stebbins' (1993) concept of serious leisure, which integrates altruism and self-interest, to examine the motivations of CSO members who had been elected or formally appointed to club administrating roles as volunteers. Serious leisure is the 'systematic pursuit of ... sufficiently substantial and interesting in nature for the participants to find a [non-work] career there in the acquisition and expression of a combination of its special skills, knowledge, and experience' (Stebbins, 1993, p. 18). Cuskelly and Harrington (1997) categorised volunteers based on their response to an open questions about their initial motivations for volunteering. It is the motivations underpinning the 'leisure careerists' and the sub-categories of 'altruistic leisure careerists' and 'self-interested leisure careerists' that are of particular interest to the present study. 'Altruists' were motivated by a desire to help others, had a love or attachment to the sport and wanted to develop the club or sport or both, or were motivated by an interest in the development of youth or young people. The 'self-interested leisure careerist' motivations were underpinned by personal development, including developing new skills, feeling they had something to offer, wanting to extend their participation and socialise with others in the sport, feeling an affinity with the club and wanting to continue to be involved.

Nichols (2005) extended this work in examining stalwart volunteers in sport and argued that the distinguishing characteristic of these volunteers is their current motivations and the rewards they gained from their involvement. Nichols' (2005) research found some overlaps with the work of Cuskelly and Harrington, indicating that the motivations for stalwarts initially becoming involved were children's involvement, altruism, a desire for continued involvement after playing and acquiring new skills. However, Nichols found that while there were some motivations that were common with 'leisure careerists' there were also overlaps with 'role-dependees'. Nichols also raised the point that the reasons volunteers gave for initially volunteering were often not what sustained their involvement to then become stalwarts. As we illustrate in the discussion of findings, within the transition-extension proposition, the reasons volunteers gave for initially volunteering fell into both the 'marginal' volunteers and 'leisure careerist' categories. This suggests that volunteer's motivations cannot be clearly demarcated into one category or another, but often form a unique and fluctuating combination of many aspects that may change over time; a consideration that the static nature of models does not take into account. The volunteers did not initially set out to become stalwarts but sought to extend their involvement; their already longstanding connection to the sport or club may be a key to identifying potential stalwarts.

Commitment

A key dimension of the theory of serious leisure is the notion of commitment. Cuskelly, Harrington and Stebbins (2002) drew together serious leisure and commitment to examine whether levels of organisational commitment changed from the initial decision to volunteer and the decision to continue volunteering. The research linked two points which support aspects of internal and external continuity. Within the commitment construct, Kelman's (1958) process of identification, where an individual wants to maintain and develop a satisfying relationship with a group or a person, mirrors external continuity. The notion of side-bets (Becker, 1960), which Cohen and Lowenburg (1990) define as 'the accumulation of investments valued by the individual which would be lost if he or she were to leave the organization' (p. 1016), reflects selective investments that help define internal and external continuities. Cuskelly et al. (2002) identified that for career volunteers, continuing their role was often prompted by the side-bets including the social world of the sports club which provided continuing attraction. The research also identified that the relationship volunteers had with the organisation also prompted volunteers to continue their involvement, with the volunteers willing to give of themselves to contribute to the well-being of the organisation (Mowday, Porter, & Steers, 1982). This form of affective commitment, or emotional attachment through identifying with an organisation (Sheldon, 1971), also reflects selective investments, investing time and energy into relationships which sustain self-concept. However, the significance of the transition-extension proposition is that it considers the important factor of continuity of identity through continued involvement. It also considers how the desire for familiar activities, environments, roles and relationships contribute to commitment.

Methods

Using a continuity theory (Atchley, 1999) framework, we examined the involvement of stalwart sport volunteers. The sampling frame was CSOs, located with the

Brisbane City Council local government area, which are representative of the male- and female-dominated sports of rugby and netball, respectively. Stalwart volunteers were defined as individuals who had played and volunteered for a particular sport or community sport club for more than 20 years (Cuskelly, 2004). Within the sample, years involved in the particular sport ranged from 20 to 64 with an average of 30 years. Interviewees were selected from 6 different CSOs for a total of 12 interviews (7 males and 5 females). All but two participants had held multiple volunteer roles in their CSO, ranging from referees to club presidents. The two other participants had held coaching only roles. After initial contact with the respective State Sporting Organisations, to identify potential interviewees, a snowball technique (Neuman, 2000) was used to make connections with subsequent interviewees.

A semi-structured interview technique was used to gather data. The semi-structured interview provides the interviewer with a clear guide, whilst allowing for flexibility in exploring ideas and understandings of the participants, allowing their voices to emerge. It provides structure in ensuring all interviews, covers the same topic and therefore provides reliable and comparable qualitative data (McCracken, 1988). The interview schedule (see Appendix 1) was developed within a continuity theory framework and pilot tested with two interviewees who were not included in the final study. The pilot interviews enabled the interview questions to be refined and worded more appropriately and to reflect the experiences and language used by interviewees rather than continuity theory. Interviews varied from 45 minutes to two hours and averaged approximately 70 minutes each. Interviews were digitally recorded after introducing the nature and purpose of the study and seeking informed and written consent consistent with the human research ethics committee approval.

Interviewees are identified in the reporting of results in this article as 'Px' for 'Person number' (e.g., P1) with the number reflecting the order in which respondents were interviewed for the study. The digital recordings of each interview were transcribed verbatim following each interview. The qualitative data were analysed using NVivo software and an illustrative method (Neuman, 2000), within the conceptual framework of continuity theory. This method uses empirical evidence to illustrate a theory and its application to a social setting (Neuman, 2000). Continuity theory provided the framework to consider the continuity of the volunteer's behaviour as they reflected on their experiences, rather than predicting intention to continue as is the purpose of theorists such as Ajzen and Fishbein (1980). Continuity theory therefore provided a framework for organising data as well as plotting the path of the journey through the transition from a playing role into a volunteering role. The purpose of the analysis was to examine the interview data to ascertain the relevance of and extent to which continuity theory and the transition-extension proposition was a useful heuristic for explaining the long-term involvement of stalwart volunteers within CSOs.

In developing the coding framework the two researchers used 'empty boxes' to fill with constructs from continuity theory (Neuman, 1997, p. 428, italics in original). The 'empty boxes' provided the nodes or coding framework for Nvivo and identified what participants discussed in relation to a particular construct. The researchers coded an interview to test the reliability of the codes. The remaining interviews were then coded using the tested interviews as a guide. Following the coding, the nodes were then used to generate the preliminary themes. These themes were summarised to gauge how they linked together and their links to continuity theory. A latent thematic analysis grounded in a constructionist approach (Burr, 1995) was used to develop a theorised interpretation of the data (Boyatzis, 1998). An iterative process was also employed, moving between the data, themes and literature to maintain the analytic focus and ensure reliability and validity (Morse, Barrett, Mayan, Olsen, & Spiers, 2002). In this way rather than simply relying on an audit or decision trail post hoc, the steps taken and decisions made were reviewed throughout the analysis process (Morse et al., 2002). The 'keyness' of a theme was not dependent on quantifiable measures, but rather on how it captured the important details of continuity theory (Braun & Clarke, 2006). The 'key' themes that participants spoke about were identified, and these then became the themes discussed in the results section. Through using participants' reflections, expressed in their own words, the validity of qualitative analysis is strengthened (Patton, 2002).

Results and discussion

In the following section we present the findings of the study and discuss the linkages to the transition-extension proposition. We therefore begin with the circumstances in which the players transitioned into their volunteering roles. The first theme captures the external continuity dimension of activity domain and reflects a transition into a domain of preference with which the individual was familiar. Under sub-themes of maintaining involvement and passing on the knowledge, we explore how players transitioned into volunteer roles. Maintaining involvement explores the reasons behind the transition from a playing role into a non-playing role. The sub-theme of passing on the knowledge is connected to a preference for a domain of activity; however, it also expresses altruistic motives which continuity theory does not discuss. We have included it in the discussion as it is a significant part of the transition process. We then move onto the second theme of volunteering and identity as this links in closely with transitioning from a playing role to taking up an identity as a volunteer. The third theme which is closely linked to identity discusses the relationships and sense of belonging that volunteers experience through the extension of their involvement. The final theme club/organisation environment, through the sub-themes of familiar things, familiar skills, familiar places and roles and activities, considers the external continuity dimensions of environments and roles that illustrate the multiple points of connection that were identified as significant factors in volunteer's decisions to extend their volunteering involvement.

Activity domain: circumstances of change and transition

The participants' initial decision to take on volunteer roles illustrates a transition and extension of involvement, as all participants had an existing connection, either as players ($n = 11$) or volunteer ($n = 1$), with their particular CSO. Many ($n = 8$) were still playing and had multiple volunteer roles. The majority ($n = 10$) of participants began volunteering when someone from their CSO asked them to take on a role as a coach or as an administrator. Being asked to volunteer is consistent with ABS (2006a) data, which indicate that sport volunteers first became involved because they were asked, or that they knew someone involved. For example, P7 said 'No, somebody just asked me and when you have that sporting background you think maybe I can do it'. Two other participants indicated that they were not approached, but had 'put their hand up' to volunteer.

Maintaining involvement

Rather than feeling obligated to take on a volunteering role, participants felt that it afforded them the opportunity to stay involved, thus maintaining continuity whilst extending their connection to their sport. As P5 indicated:

> I think I generally just want to do it and enjoy it. I don't think I have an obligation to do it. But I really feel, you know, I enjoy it. As long as I can be involved I will stay involved, you know.

It would also seem that once they had begun volunteering, participants were more likely to 'put their hand up' to volunteer for other roles, continuing their volunteer career and extending on the personal reward they gained as a result of their involvement. The complexity of the motives underpinning these decisions is captured in the following quote:

> I started the first year as a [team] manager, then I got involved on the executive of the [club name] and then I think it was the following year they were struggling for coaches. So I stepped in then and became a coach and never looked back. (P11)

Interestingly, six participants (P1, P2, P6, P9, P10 and P12) described creating their own opportunity to transition into a volunteering role through starting a club, setting up a competition, starting a programme and creating an administrative position within an existing organisation. For this group of volunteers, the desire to maintain their connection to their domain of preference, through transitioning into a volunteer role of their own making, adds another layer of complexity to extension of involvement.

Six participants, who volunteered because their child began playing the sport, had also played the sport; 'I really became involved in the volunteering part when the daughter started playing netball' (P11). In this way participants were again extending their previous involvement through their child's interests. Four participants specifically discussed how they took on volunteering roles because their playing career was ending, and as a consequence their transition to volunteering was gradual. The transition was nevertheless expressed as a desire to extend their involvement in a sport they had previously played.

> I came down here and I knew a lot of people playing and when they knew I was here and invited me along, so I played and enjoyed it. But I sort of knew that it was coming to an end and then the club knew that I coached here and so they got me involved. (P6)

The desire to maintain continuity of involvement with an organisation that the participants were already connected to, often as players, was a central motivating factor in transitioning into a volunteering role. Such was the strength of this desire that some participants had created their own role to ensure their continued involvement. Once volunteers had transitioned into a volunteering role they were more likely to 'put their hand up' for other roles.

Passing on the knowledge

Rather than feeling any pressure to put back into their sport, most participants described altruistic motives which drove their involvement. Cuskelly et al. (2002) also identified that 'career' volunteers persevered due to a desire to pass on their knowledge to others. For the volunteers in the present study this was primarily expressed as a desire to give to young players:

> I think the local community and community support and being able to put back into the community. Offering the opportunities for the children who live in the community is really important...I think if volunteers don't create things like the [club name] then there is going to be a whole host of kids that don't get that opportunity. (P8)

One participant captured the complexity of untangling the decision to initially become involved with the self-interested personal meanings that were attached to ongoing involvement:

> Not pressured because it just happened. Once I got involved I personally enjoyed it for many reasons. So therefore it was never a chore, whatever they wanted I would do. (P5)

Several participants thought they had acquired valuable knowledge about their sport which they wanted to pass on. As Atchley (1993) suggests 'people who see themselves as being good at one type of art, sports or scholarship tend to see themselves as having the capacity to be good in other specific areas within the same general domain' (p.13). Participant 5 expressed this sentiment succinctly:

> The reason I do it is primarily once it comes back to kids wanting something. If I've got the knowledge that is going to help the association [sport organisation] achieve something better for their kids then I'm more than willing to pass it on whether that be a paid or unpaid role.

Participants also indicated that providing the coaching so that children could play and then watching them enjoy and achieve in sport was a great source of satisfaction and a reason to continue. The interplay of altruism, activity domain, personal rewards and selective investments illustrates the fluctuating nature of these motivations:

> I had all this knowledge and to walk away from a sport that I have a lot of knowledge of, I should stay in it and pass it on. I did it the hard way of learning but I thought well I should pass it on and give it back to them. It's marvelous to see the things they are doing and that you tell them to do. (P4)

Two participants felt that they had been made guilty or 'conned' into taking on roles, although one participant diffused the negative overtones of 'conned' by then saying they were 'sweet talked' into coaching. These same participants also spoke about the desire to give or pass on knowledge to young players. The participant (P4), who spoke about being made feel guilty, was already coaching at the time and felt some pressure to take on another team when the club expanded.

These findings support Rochester's (2006) and Cuskelly and Harrington's (1997) research that indicate altruistic motives were an important aspect of volunteering.

As we have illustrated, altruistic motives often underpinned participants' decision to transition into a volunteering role. In this regard, the transition-extension proposition captures an important motivation in the decision to transition into volunteering that is not captured within the dimensions of continuity theory. Participants felt that their knowledge of the domain of activity was a valuable asset that they wanted to pass on to young players. The interplay of selective investments, altruism and personal rewards often then contributed to volunteers' motivations to extend their involvement.

Volunteering and identity

All participants indicated that they thought that volunteering was an important part of their identity and subsequently an important aspect of their life. Underpinning the transition in the volunteering identity was a strong sporting identity, with several referring to themselves as 'sports freaks'. Cuskelly et al. (2002) also found that 'career' volunteers had a love of sport. This elaboration on an existing sporting identity within the same domain had allowed volunteers to transition into taking up an identity as a volunteer (Atchley, 1993). One participant made some quite significant connections with how her role as a volunteer had assumed a defining aspect of her identity (Van Dyne & Farmer, 2005):

> I suppose it's who I am for the last bit. I don't know if it is necessarily important that it would make me any different a person, possibly not . . . it has never been number one. I think it is something that has been part of me and part of my life. (P7)

The manner in which volunteering assumed such a significant part of the volunteer's identity was often incidental, rather than planned. Participant 5 indicated that she began coaching netball because no-one else wanted the job. She had not played netball before, but had a sporting background. She undertook a coaching course, and within three years was asked by her peers to take on representative teams. She also developed a long-term affiliation with the one club (20+ years) and took on a range of administrative roles:

> Yes, but I had no idea at that stage that it was going to turn into a long-term commitment because the years just went by and I enjoyed it. It has to be enjoyment or you wouldn't be doing it for 20 odd years.

One participant, whose involvement with netball spanned more than 60 years, both as a player and volunteer was unsure how she would fill the gap in her life should she retire:

> Oh yeah 'cause my husband rings up and he says are you home tonight is it netball today . . . Oh yeah, I don't know what I'm going to do when it stops; I just enjoy it. (P1)

This sense of the identity was developed over the course of the volunteer's involvement, and had often transitioned from initially being driven by altruistic motives to maintaining a volunteer role identity, which Grube and Piliavin (2000) suggest predicts duration and sustains volunteerism:

> I've done it since the kids were in primary school and prior to that I was busy being a mum and taking them to playgroups…By that time, it was a part of me then. I started simply because there was need at the time for the kids, not just for my kids, but the rest of the kids for the parents to stand up and do some jobs, to allow them to play their Saturday sport. By the time they finished I was probably doing representative teams. (P7)

The knowledge that participants had acquired, both in their playing and volunteering roles, and the transference of knowledge and skills into the same domain had contributed significantly to the volunteer's identity to the extent that one participant referred to herself as a 'netball bible':

> I'm this netball bible. There are many like that too, but perhaps not quite as long as I've been round. I guess I sometimes look back and think this is all a big accident. Because I had an unwritten rule to myself that when my children went to school I was going to head to the golf course not the netball court. (P5)

Six participants made direct comments about a sense of ego integrity in relation to their involvement. One participant (P9) made some interesting connections between integrity and identity, which also illustrates the extent to which the participant had linked their past playing identity to sustain their current identity as a volunteer:

> Or who I am is an important part of volunteering, which comes first the chicken or the egg. I think the nature of the person determines whether they are going to be involved in the first place and probably also to a great extent of whether they will continue with it and how good they are going to be at it whatever they choose to do as a volunteer. I think people are volunteers by nature before they find something to volunteer for.

Another participant made a comment suggesting that the consistency and linkage to her previous sporting identity through her current role as coach afforded a sense of ego integrity that in turn reaffirmed her desire to continue the coaching role:

> You just coach…I think that is my love, coaching to me is almost like playing, not quite, but almost. (P7)

While the details of involvement had changed, the transition into the volunteering role had allowed continuity of commitment to sport as an aspect of the self and in turn identity (Atchley, 1999). As stalwart volunteers, the participants' sense of identity was deeply connected to their long-term involvement, their knowledge of the domain and the selective investments they had made. The extension of involvement often built on and sustained the identity they had constructed over the course of their association with the organisation.

Relationships and belonging

All participants spoke about the sense of belonging they experienced through volunteering, indicating they felt part of the team or club. The sense of belonging was fostered by the period of time, 'a huge amount of my life' (P3, 45 years as player and volunteer), that participants had been involved with a particular organisation both as players and now as volunteers:

> This is, well it is not mine, but I belong here . . . I think probably the fact that I am in the chair [wheelchair] gives me as more as, I think that I'm comfortable here. Because I am around people that have known me for years and years. Whereas if I went to do something else in another sport or in another association or something I probably wouldn't feel comfortable and I probably wouldn't have the confidence to go into it. (P11, 24 years as player and volunteer)

As the above quote illustrates the long-term involvement had allowed participants to foster relationships which were an integral part of external continuity and appeared to be key to the sense of belonging. This included being well known and being around people 'everybody, players, teams, parents, exec [executive committee] members' (P4) that have known the participant for 'years and years' (P11). As Kahn and Antonucci (1981) suggest these friends and family who travel across the life course form important social supports which also work to sustain individual identity. Importantly the affirmation of identity fostered through such social support also engendered a sense of belonging (Atchley, 1989). Participant 3, who had been involved with rugby union, discussed the meaning and sense of belonging he felt through the friendships he had established during his playing career and which had continued into his volunteering career:

> It's your friendship base, so you have to know everyone. If I didn't know most of them I probably wouldn't have hung around.

Another participant expressed the importance of these relationships in the following manner: 'Developing similar relationships is part of belonging and contributes to the sense of belonging' (P9). Interestingly the same participant indicated that he volunteered because he already felt a sense of belonging rather than volunteering to belong. This two-way-dynamic was also discussed by another participant:

> Yes. Definitely. It is in my blood . . . Yes. It is the only reason I'm there. It's about relationships, people respect you and it's amazing. (P8)

Other participants made similar comments such as: 'Belonging, what do I belong to, I think I belong to the sport but sometimes I think the sport thinks I belong to them' (P5). Participant 12 felt that a sense of belonging coupled with the investment of time and energy, allowed him to feel a sense of ownership of the club he belonged to:

> I probably have played football for so long, so I belong to the club. Yes I think about the gym area and torpedo bar and feel proud of it, but when you think about it's not yours but you work out the best way to do and the cheapest way. Rugby clubs are run on an oily rag. I suppose I feel a sense of ownership.

The sense of ownership and the enjoyment expressed through belonging to the club lends itself to suggest that the particular participant would continue to volunteer, not through a sense of obligation, but through selective investments which generated a sense of commitment to the organisation. This form of affective commitment, or emotional attachment results in a continued desire to remain connected to the organisation (Meyer & Allen, 1991; Mowday et al., 1982). The sense of commitment and emotional attachment also extended to the teams that volunteers coached and contributed to their sense of belonging as the following quote illustrates:

> just umm you know you sort it's a team sort of thing if you're part of that team you got to be there got to be part of that team continuously not just of every other Saturday or every other second week it is the same with training. (P1)

Being part of a team, through their coaching role, had allowed volunteers to develop relationships with the players they coached, providing an additional extension of their sense of belonging. Perhaps more importantly it also allowed a connection with the sport on another level:

> But within sport you tend to deal with a lot of people over a fairly long course of time and that can be years. There are girls still playing at [club name] that I coached when they were 6–7 years and now in their late 20s, there are people around that you have fairly long contact with. (P5)

The ongoing nature of this level of connection, the relationships fostered and the associated sense of belonging often underpinned volunteers' decisions to continue in their volunteering role. Belonging was also fostered by the familiarity participants felt through their sustained involvement with their CSO. Certainly transitioning into a volunteer role allowed the participants to maintain the relationships they had established over the course of their involvement both as players and also in their various volunteering roles. Many were also able to create new relationships with other volunteers and players they coached. The social relationships and affective commitment also affirmed the volunteers' sense of identity and their desire to extend their involvement.

Club/organisation environment

In a similar way that players expressed a desire to maintain involvement through transitioning into volunteering roles, the selective investments they had made within their organisation and the sense of competency they felt as a result created the conditions to continue in volunteering roles. Being in a familiar environment, with familiar things, as well as repetition of roles and activities also reaffirmed a sense of belonging as well as volunteering identity.

Familiar things, familiar skills and familiar places

Familiar things, skills and place were all identified as important to the participants, being well known at their club, and feeling trust and respect contributed to feelings of familiarity. Participant 7 discussed how important familiarity was to her involvement:

> Boring? Yes it is very ordinary I often think. I suppose I like it like that. I don't know I suppose if you are liking what you are doing, it's most unlikely that you go searching for something different ... Yes, that would be me, a grin from ear to ear. Being where I don't feel comfortable I would probably choose not to go.

Participant 9 expressed the sense of familiarity which also reinforced the volunteer identity he had taken up: 'Yes I have a comfortable jacket that slips on'. Eight participants (P2, P4, P5, P6, P8, P9, P11 and P12) indicated that the sense of familiarity they felt within their club and with their roles reaffirmed their commitment to volunteering. Atchley (1989, p. 188) suggests that this form of continuity is not a 'boring sameness, for most but rather a comforting routine and familiar sense of direction'. The most common reason behind the appeal was the relationships that were built through volunteering. Participant 9 discussed the appeal of familiarity:

> No. In some ways it's part of the attraction to keep on going. If it wasn't this I would have to do something else and build relationships and things like that and who wants to do work that hard. Although if you go into something as a volunteer and you are pretty good worker you do establish relationships a lot more quickly.

The majority of participants (*n* =9) thought that they would never leave the club or organisation they were currently involved with. Along with issues of loyalty, familiarity with their club and coaching skills developed in a particular sport were reasons cited for remaining in their volunteering role. Atchley (1993) argues that in maintaining external continuity, preference will be given towards a domain in which people feel competent and proficient. Through selective investments volunteers funnelled time and energy into their role in order to maintain their connection with their domain of preference. Participant 5 captured the complexity of these dynamics:

> I think I would find it very hard, because it's been my one and only sport that I have tackled at all different levels. It's been very fairly widespread and diverse as to what I've done within it. No, I can't see myself getting involved in sport other than maybe perhaps when I'm 80 and playing [lawn] bowls.

One participant indicated that he would never volunteer in any other sport because as he said 'rugby is in my blood. I would need to be completely drained' (P8), yet he also indicated that when he retired from volunteering in rugby he would like to continue volunteering in a welfare organisation. He also indicated that altruism, 'giving back to the community' was his primary motivation for wanting to do so. Three participants (P3, P5 and P6) indicated that they might volunteer elsewhere. Several were already involved, on an irregular basis, in another organisation, and several others indicated a willingness to move into volunteering in welfare.

The sense of continuity generated through extending involvement in familiar domain of activity also worked to reaffirm a sense of identity and sustain relationships. Like many aspects of the transition-extension proposition, ongoing involvement was a complex interweaving of motivations and behaviours that reflected continuity and adaption in the face of change.

Roles and activities: repetition of patterns

An interesting dynamic emerged in relation to the expectation that volunteers would continue in their role, affirmation of identity and competence through feedback from others that reaffirmed their desire to continue volunteering, and deriving satisfaction from the role. Atchley (1993) suggests that a significant factor in maintaining external continuity was the repetition of successful patterns of roles and activities which facilitated feelings of achievement, competence and satisfaction. Certainly several mentioned that they felt that there was pressure or an expectation they would continue their volunteering next year. Participant 11 discussed the expectation she felt to continue because it was something she had always done and also highlighted the volunteer shortage.

> Because this is something I have always done? Probably. At the moment they probably do because we are really short staffed...I will commit myself to whatever I can do anyhow. There is limits [*sic*]. I think a few of them expect me to stick around now as President to try to keep doing what we are doing here now.

Several volunteers expressed concern that there would be no one to take over the role if they stepped down. This situation is best captured by P5:

> Typical example, why come to me? Because everyone knows I've got it and everyone knows I could do it. We really need to see if somebody else can do it, because everyone knows that [person's name] can produce things like that, but I said no, we have got to start getting new adults and some are in their early twenties who we have managed talk into having some input.

However, this sense of obligation was often tempered by the 'pats on the back', and participants negotiated a fine line between feeling obligated to continue their volunteering, because of their commitment to the organisation, sport or team and perhaps feeling gratified that they were considered valuable enough to continue their roles:

> Yes. Every year the parents will say 'you are doing it next year aren't you'. Most of these guys have played top rugby before and would have the skills to do it. Some of them may not have the temperament to teach the kids. Some of them come and help out. Yes I do feel obligated. My boys do enjoy me being there, you do feel obligated. (P3)

Certainly receiving 'pats on the back' and the feedback from others that reaffirmed the volunteers' self-concept as a competent, provided the impetus to sign up next year.

> When you get kids and even parents that say I want you back next year to coach or something then the girls say can you come back and coach us again next year. I think that sort of gives you, you think you know I've done something right with them, and hopefully you have, and the parents are very supportive too so I think you realise then. (P11)

The preceding comment highlights the value attached to the sense of satisfaction volunteers felt from their achievements and the personal rewards they gained as a result. Atchley (1989) suggests that satisfaction was linked to the sense of mastery that people gained through their experiences. Ten (P1, P2, P4, P5, P6, P7, P8, P9, P11 and P12) participants felt that volunteering was still satisfying and had not lost its appeal. The rewards and appeal seemed to be more from coaching and revolved around satisfaction from giving to others, being recognised through sentimental gifts of appreciation, achieving success or watching a player put into practice a skill that the participant had taught them:

> Some little bit of wisdom that you have imparted and you can see is coming to fruition and it's just all the dominos falling. That is what volunteering is all about. That is the reward of imparting the wisdom and knowing that they have listened and learnt and practised it and it all happens. (P8)

One participant (P3) indicated that he would no longer be involved if his children were not playing. Participant 1 said that volunteering was still satisfying because as she says 'netball has become more or less my life'.

Repetition of roles and activities maintained external continuity in a similar fashion to familiar things, skills and places, both of which generated a sense of satisfaction through experiencing competence within a particular domain of activity over a sustained period of time. However, this same sense of competence and satisfaction also provided the motivation that underpinned volunteers' decisions to extend their involvement.

Conclusion

The results of this study support the view that continuity theory is a useful heuristic for understanding the multiple points of connection and behaviours that underpin stalwart volunteers' decisions to continue in their roles. The circumstances of the transition from a playing role into a non-playing role indicated that volunteers were indeed seeking to extend both their connection to and involvement in sport, and in most cases within a particular organisational setting. The sense of identity volunteers developed over the course of extending their involvement beyond playing their sport suggests that maintaining a sense identity was a significant aspect in their often revisited decisions to continue volunteering. The motivation to continue involvement was also fostered by the desire to maintain continuity of relationships built over the course of the volunteer's playing career and then extended into their involvement as a volunteer. These relationships contributed to a sense of belonging which in turn created a familiar environment in which to maintain a volunteering identity, maintain relationships which in turn, further deepened their sense of belonging. Feelings of competence through feedback from others and 'pats on the back' also proved to be significant motivators for continuing as a volunteer. The combination of these factors, as well as a complex interplay altruistic motivations and personal rewards, tempered the pressure volunteers sometimes felt to continue in their roles. We suggest that there is sufficient evidence to support the relevance of continuity theory for better understanding the ongoing involvement of volunteers in CSOs. The transition-extension proposition also appears to be well supported by the results of this study, and is a useful augmentation to continuity theory. More particularly it fostered an understanding of the factors that created the conditions for a transition into a volunteering role. Identifying players with longstanding connections to an organisation may be central to identifying potential stalwarts. As the participants in this study indicated, they were reluctant to leave a particular sport or club because of their substantial personal investment. Encouraging sports organisations to nurture players to transition into a volunteer role through highlighting the multiple points of connection identified within this research may assist them in maintaining a sufficient number of volunteers to effectively deliver the services offered by their organisation.

While continuity theory explains the ongoing involvement of individuals in familiar roles and settings it may have limited application in understanding a significant change in role, such as from player to volunteer, as it was in this study. The interviewees in this study were all volunteers who had been in their role for many years when they were interviewed. Further research is needed to more fully test both continuity theory and the notion of transition-extension in explaining the factors that influence ongoing involvement as a volunteer in sport and other settings. As suggested by Atchley (1993) longitudinal data captured at the point of transition and then at various points after transition would more fully explore the complexity of ongoing involvement and highlight the factors that contribute to both retention and decisions to cease involvement. Other theoretical perspectives such as identity theory, may offer important insights in research which explores the complex notions of identity within the context of transition and extension to a new role. Similarly engaging with broader debates over the changing nature of leisure in society and in turn leisure identities and roles might also uncover the complexity of the meanings and purpose of volunteer's leisure choices (e.g. Blackshaw, 2010; Roberts, 2011). Case studies of stalwart volunteers offer the possibility of shedding light on the complexity of the not uncommon circumstances where an individual has developed a particular identity, sense of belonging and familiarity with an organisation through long-term involvement. With the declining numbers of volunteers, nurturing stalwarts to maintain their involvement may provide CSOs with a much needed core voluntary workforce to continue to deliver sport. The insights provided through the use of the transition-extension proposition may go some way into providing CSOs with the tools to facilitate this extension of involvement.

References

Atchley, R.C. (1987). *Aging: Continuity and change* (2nd ed.). Belmont, CA: Wadsworth.

Atchley, R.C. (1989). A continuity theory of aging. *The Gerontologist, 29*, 183–190.

Atchley, R.C. (1993). Continuity theory and the evolution of activity in later life. In J. Kelly (Ed.), *Activity and ageing: Staying involved in later life* (pp. 5–16). Newbury Park, CA: Sage.

Atchley, R.C. (1999). *Continuity and adaptation in aging*. Baltimore, MD: The John Hopkins University Press.

Australian Bureau of Statistics. (2006a). *Volunteers in sport*, Cat. No. 4440.0.55.001. Canberra: Commonwealth of Australia.

Australian Bureau of Statistics. (2006b). *Voluntary work, Australia*, Cat. No. 4441.0. Canberra: Commonwealth of Australia.

Australian Bureau of Statistics. (2010). *Involvement in organised sport and physical activity*, Cat. No. 6285.0. Canberra: Commonwealth of Australia.

Ajzen, I., & Fishbein, M. (1980). *Understanding attitudes and predicting social behavior*. Englewood Cliffs, NJ: Prentice Hall.

Becker, H.R. (1960). Notes on the concept of commitment. *American Sociological Review, 66*, 32–42.

Blackshaw, T. (2010). *Leisure*. London: Routledge.

Boyatzis, R.E. (1998). *Transforming qualitative information: Thematic analysis and code development*. Thousand Oaks, CA: Sage.

Braun, V., & Clarke, V. (2006). Using thematic analysis in psychology. *Qualitative Research in Psychology, 3*, 77–101.

Briggs, E., Peterson, M., & Gregory, G. (2010). Toward a better understanding of volunteering for nonprofit organizations: Explaining volunteers prosocial attitude. *Journal of Macromarketing, 30*(1), 61–76.

Burr, V. (1995). *An introduction to social constructionism.* London: Routledge.

Chacon, F., Vecina, M.L., & Davila, M.C. (2007). The three-stage model of volunteers' duration of service. *Social Behaviour and Personality, 35*(5), 627–642.

Clary, E.G., & Snyder, M. (1999). The motivations to volunteer: Theoretical and practical considerations. *Current Directions in Psychological Science, 8*(5), 156–159.

Clary, E.G., Snyder, M., & Ridge, R. (1992). Volunteers' motivations: A functional strategy for the recruitment, placement and retention of volunteers. *Nonprofit Management and Leadership, 2*(4), 333–350.

Clary, E., Snyder, M., & Stukas, A. (1996). Volunteers' motivations: Findings from a national survey. *Nonprofit and Voluntary Sector Quarterly, 25*(4), 485–505.

Cohen, A., & Lowenburg, G. (1990). A re-examination of the side-bets theory as applied to organizational commitment: A meta-analysis. *Human Relations, 43*(10), 1015–1050.

Cnaan, R., & Goldberg-Glen, R.S. (1991). Measuring motivation to volunteer in human services. *Journal of Applied Behavioral Science, 27*(3), 269–284.

Crabbe, T. (2000). A sporting chance? Using sport to tackle crime and drug use. *Drugs: Education, Prevention and Policy, 7*, 381–391.

Cuskelly, G. (2004). Volunteer retention in community sport organisations. *European Sport Management Quarterly, 4*, 59–76.

Cuskelly, G., & Harrington, M. (1997). Volunteers and leisure: Evidence of marginal and career volunteers in sport. *World Leisure and Recreation, 39*(3), 11–18.

Cuskelly, G., Harrington, M., & Stebbins, R.A. (2002). Changing levels of organizational commitment amongst sport volunteers: A serious leisure approach. *Loisir/Leisure Special Issue: Volunteerism and Leisure, 27*(3–4), 191–212.

Finkelstein, M.A. (2008). Predictors of volunteer time: The changing contributions of motive fulfilment and role identity. *Social Behaviour and Personality, 36*(10), 1353–1564.

Finkelstein, M.A., Penner, L.A., & Brannick, M.T. (2005). Motive, role and identity and prosocial personality as predictors of volunteer activity. *Social Behavior and Personality, 33*(4), 403–418.

Galper, D., Trivedi, M., Barlow, C, Dunn, A., & Kampert, J.B. (2006). Inverse association between physical inactivity and mental health in men and women. *Medicine and Science in Sport & Exercise, 38*(1), 171–178.

Grube, J., & Piliavin, J.A. (2000). Role identity, organizational experience, and volunteer experiences. *Personality and Social Psychology Bulletin, 26*(9), 1108–1119.

Jarvie, G. (2003). Communtarianism, sport and social capital. *International Review for the Sociology of Sport, 38*(2), 139–153.

Kahn, R.L., & Antonucci, T. (1981). Convoys of social support: A life-course approach. In S.B. Keisler, J.N. Morgan, & V.K. Oppenheimer (Eds.), *Ageing: Social change* (pp. 383–405). New York, NY: Academic Press.

Kelman, H.C. (1958). Compliance, identification and internalization: Three processes of attitude change. *Journal of Conflict Resolution, 2*(1), 51–60.

Knoke, D., & Prensky, D. (1984). What relevance do organization theories have for voluntary associations? *Social Science Quarterly, 65*(1), 3–20.

Laverie, D., & McDonald, R.E. (2007). Volunteer identity: Understanding the role of identity importance on participation frequency. *Journal of Macromarketing, 27*(3), 274–288.

Liao-Troth, M.A., & Dunn, C.P. (1999). Social constructs and human service: Managerial sense making of volunteer motivation. *Voluntas: International Journal of Voluntary and Nonprofit Organizations, 10*(4), 345–361.

Leisure Industries Research Centre. (2003). *Sports volunteering in England 2002.* London: Sport England.

McCracken, G. (1988). *The long interview.* Newbury Park, CA: Sage Publications.

Manson, J.E., Skerrett, P., Greenland, P., & VanItallie, T.B. (2004). The escalating pandemics of obesity and sedentary lifestyle. *Archives of Internal Medicine, 164*, 249–258.

Meyer, J.P., & Allen, N.J. (1991). A three component conceptualization of organizational commitment. *Human Resource Management Review, 1*(1), 61–89.

Morse, J.M., Barnett, N., Mayan, M., Olson, K., & Spiers, J. (2002). Verification strategies for establishing reliability and validity in qualitative research. *International Journal of Qualitative Methods, 1*(2), 13–22.

Mowday, R.T., Porter, L.W., & Steers, R. (1982). *Organizational linkages: The psychology of commitment, absenteeism, and turnover.* San Diego, CA: Academic Press.

Neuman, W.L. (1997). *Social research methods: Qualitative and quantitative approaches* (3rd ed.). Boston: Allyn and Bacon.

Neuman, W.L. (2000). *Social research methods: Qualitative and quantitative approaches.* Boston, MA: Allyn and Bacon.

Nichols, G. (2004). Crime and punishment and sports development. *Leisure Studies, 23*(2), 177–194.

Nichols, G. (2005). Stalwarts in sport. *World Leisure Journal, 47*(2), 31–37.

Patton, M. (2002). *Qualitative research & evaluation methods* (3rd ed.). Thousand Oaks, CA: Sage.

Pearce, J.L. (1993). *The organizational behaviour of unpaid workers.* London: Routledge.

Penner, L.A. (2002). Dispositional and organizational influences on sustained volunteerism: An interactionist perspective. *Journal of Social Issues, 58*(32), 447–467.

Pfeifer, C., & CorneliBen, T. (2010). The impact of participation in sports on educational attainment—New evidence from Germany. *Economics of Education Review, 29*(1), 94–103.

Roberts, K. (2011). Leisure: The importance of being inconsequential. *Leisure Studies, 30*(1), 126–128.

Rochester, C. (2006). *Making sense of volunteering.* London: Volunteering England.

Schulz, J., Nichols, G., & Auld, C. (2011). Issues in the management of voluntary sport organizations and volunteers. In B. Houlihan & M. Green (Eds.), *Routledge handbook of sports development* (pp. 437–450). New York, NY: Routledge.

Sheldon, M.E. (1971). Investments and involvements as mechanisms producing commitment to the organization. *Administrative Science Quarterly, 16,* 143–150.

Smith, D.H. (1981). Altruism, volunteers and volunteerism. *Journal of Voluntary Action Research, 10*(1), 21–36.

Sport England. (2010). *Active people survey, 2009–2010.* Retrieved from http://www.sporteng-land.org/research/active_people_survey/active_people_survey_4.aspx

Sport England. (2011). *Active people survey, 2010–2011.* Retrieved from http://www.sporteng-land.org/research/active_people_survey/aps5.aspx

Statistics Canada. (2006). *Caring Canadians, giving Canadians: Highlights from the 2004 Canada survey of giving, volunteering and participating,* Cat. No. 71-542-XIE, Ottawa, ON: Ministry of Industry.

Statistics Canada. (2009). *Caring Canadians, giving Canadians: Highlights from the 2007 Canada survey of giving, volunteering and participating,* Cat. No. 71-542-X. Ottawa, ON: Ministry of Industry.

Stebbins, R.A. (1993). Social world, lifestyle, and serious leisure: Towards a mesostructural analysis. *World Leisure and Recreation, 35*(1), 23–26.

Stebbins, R.A. (1996). Volunteering: a serious leisure perspective. *Nonprofit and Voluntary Sector Quarterly, 25*(2), 211–224.

Tidwell, M. (2005). A social identity model of prosocial behaviors within nonprofit organizations. *Nonprofit Management & Leadership, 15*(4), 449–467.

Van Dyne, L., & Farmer, S.M. (2005). It's who I am: Role identity and organizational citizenship behavior of volunteers. In D.L. Turpinseed (Ed.), *Handbook of organizational behavior: A review of 'good soldier' activity in organizations* (pp. 177–203). New York, NY: Nova Science Publishers.

Appendix 1

Preliminary

- Complete ethics/informed consent including permission to record interview. Clarify any issues/concerns with the interviewee.

Ask interviewee to talk about their involvement in sport? Breadth and depth of involvement generally in sport (how many, what codes, typical roles) and in this sport (how long as a player, volunteer, official, general helper)? Life membership or other long or outstanding service awards? Involvement of parents, grandparents, children, grandchildren? Encourage interviewee to elaborate where necessary.

Internal continuity
- Start from the ways in which sport involvement, particularly as a long-time volunteer has met and is meeting important needs. What do you get out of this sport as a volunteer? Follow-up and probe where necessary.
- Does volunteer involvement offer you opportunities to develop and maintain friendships? Can you rely on your friends in sport for support in difficult times? What does your role as a sport volunteer say about you? Would you describe yourself as a predictable or reliable volunteer? Do you think others like to be around you as a volunteer?
- What knowledge, skills competencies have you developed as a volunteer? Have these skills helped with other aspects of your life?
- Do you feel as though being a long-term volunteer is an important part of who you are? Has volunteering given your life a sense of integrity? More so than other aspects of your life?
- What are your expectations of yourself as a volunteer? Have you been successful in meeting these expectations? Can you think of a situation where your expectations may have been too high or that you did not experience success when volunteering?

External continuity
- Do you think that other people expect you to continue in your role as a volunteer because it is something you 'have always done'?
- Do you think that volunteering has allowed you to have a sense of belonging? Do you enjoy this sense of belonging? Does this sense of belonging allow you to rely on others to provide support when you need it?
- Do comments you receive, either directly or indirectly, re-affirm your desire to keep volunteering?
- Has volunteering helped you to cope with the physical and mental changes that are frequently associated with ageing?
- Do you think volunteering has provided a sense of stability and purpose when other major changes have taken place in your life (e.g. if applicable – be especially sensitive here – empty nest, retirement or widowhood)?

Degree of continuity
- Ask about major changes in work/career, family and relationships, place of residence, sport generally and this sport, specifically. Were there any lengthy periods of non-participation? Try to get a feel for whether the interviewee feels as though their sport 'career' has too little, too much or about the right amount of continuity. Ask about friends, teams/clubs involved with, breadth of roles (volunteering only – different positions, other roles – playing, officiating, general helping). What about other continuity in other aspects of their lives?

Transition-extension
- When did you change roles, say from a player to official, player to volunteer, or official to volunteer? What were the circumstances of this change? Were you ever in a position

of holding down more than one position at a time – particularly as a player and volunteer or official? Was it your decision or do feel as though you were influenced by others (friends, family, in and outside sport)? In moving into your role as a volunteer did you feel pressured to put something back into sport? Obligated in any way? Was a way of keeping participation costs down? Did you get involved in volunteering because others were not doing a very good job?

Dynamics of internal and external continuity
- Doing familiar things, using familiar skills, in familiar places and in the company of familiar people. To what extent does this idea describe your role as a long-term volunteer?
- Has there been times (NOT between seasons) where you have dropped out of volunteering for an extended period?
- During your 'career' as a volunteer have you noticed then need for change, say to move into other more or less challenging roles? Has what is satisfying about volunteering changed for you?
- How important are knowing the community, being in familiar surrounds and in familiar relationships in volunteering?
- Does familiarity with being a long-term volunteer ever lose its appeal? Has it ever become too familiar?
- Could you ever see yourself moving on and volunteering in a different organisation with unfamiliar people, perhaps in a different neighbourhood?

Close interview and thank interviewee.
- Leave your contact details in case they think of other information that might be considered important or want further information about the study.

Front line insight: an autoethnography of the Vancouver 2010 volunteer experience

Erin Kodama, Alison Doherty and Megan Popovic

School of Kinesiology, Faculty of Health Sciences, Western University, London, ON, Canada

Building on a growing body of research regarding major sport event volunteerism, this paper shares the personal lived experience of the first author's involvement as a volunteer with the 2010 Winter Olympic Games held in Vancouver, Canada. Autoethnography was used to provide rich insight into the personal and cultural context of volunteering (Ellis & Bochner, 2000). The personal narrative is represented in six themes that reflect her most meaningful experiences leading up to, during and following the Games: (1) A figure skater's dream: making the cut, (2) Uncertainty: going with the flow, (3) The basics: training, (4) 'Blue team': volunteer culture, (5) An Olympic spirit is born: leisure time, and (6) Returning home: prestige. The narratives are compared and contrasted with the major sport event volunteer literature to understand their alignment with the existing body of research and to consider the further insights they provide. The paper concludes with recommendations for future research.

Volunteers are integral to many major sport events. There is little doubt that these events would not be so successful without the contribution of skills, time, and commitment of hundreds and sometimes thousands of volunteers. It is perhaps not surprising then that a growing body of research provides insight into their motivation, experience, satisfaction, and future intentions to be involved (Allen & Shaw, 2009; Bang & Chelladurai, 2009; Costa, Chalip, Green, & Simes, 2006; Coyne & Coyne, 2001; Doherty, 2003, 2009; Downward, Lumsdon, & Ralston, 2005; Downward & Ralston, 2006; Elstad, 1996; Fairley, Kellet, & Green, 2007; Farrell, Johnston, & Twynam, 1998; Green & Chalip, 2004; Kemp, 2002; Khoo & Englehorn, 2007; Kim, Kim, & Odio, 2010; Kim, Zhang, & Connaughton, 2010; Larocque, Gravelle, & Karlis, 2002; Love, Hardin, Koo, & Morse, 2011; Maclean & Hamm, 2007; Reeser, Berg, Rhea, & Willick, 2005; Shaw, 2009; Twynam, Farrell, & Johnston, 2002/2003; Williams, Dossa, & Tompkins, 1995). An understanding of why people volunteer, their satisfaction with various aspects of the event, and their likelihood of volunteering again is based largely on broad, quantitative field research incorporating survey design. There is a relative paucity of qualitative investigations that may provide richer insight that will further the existing body of knowledge.

Autoethnography is a qualitative method that provides rich insight into a phenomenon by exploring an individual's personal experience in depth (Ellis & Bochner, 2000). It allows for extraordinary and real-life aspects of personal experiences to be expressed. As a reflexive methodology, it offers a means of critically exploring social forces shaping the author's own involvement in leisure practices (Fleming & Fullagar, 2007). Rather than excluding personal insights and information, autoethnography embraces the researcher's subjective experience, putting the researcher back into the research. It has been used recently to examine individuals' sport and leisure practices in a variety of contexts (e.g., Douglas, 2009; Jones, 2009; Lashua & Fox, 2006; McCarville, 2007; Mobley, 2008; Popovic, 2010, 2012; Purdy, Potrac, & Jones, 2008), extending our understanding of the personal and social forces that shape one's experience. There has been a call for personal narrative and storytelling in sport management research as it may lead to new insights and different research questions regarding how the management of sport affects people (Rinehart, 2005). As Rinehart (2005, p. 500) notes, 'rather than solely trying, without much effect, to map the objective, value-free world, writers of personal narrative attempt to answer the questions related to what experience felt like, what understandings grew with the actual experience of being in the moment.'

Using an autoethnographic approach, this study explores my (first author) Olympic volunteer experience with the Vancouver 2010 Games. The purpose of this study is to generate a greater understanding of sport event volunteerism by illustrating that personal lived experience. Particularly meaningful aspects are represented and compared and contrasted with the sport event volunteer research in order to make sense of them, align them with existing knowledge, and identify new insights and directions for future research. In doing so, however, the presentation leaves space for the reader's personal reflection and interpretation of the story (cf. Jones, 2009).

Sport event volunteerism

The focus of sport event volunteer research in general has been major and 'mega' sport events, ranging from national multi- and single-sport championships, to international sport events, to the Olympic Games. Although the size, focus, and profile of these events vary, they are characterized by their relatively broad cultural significance and popular appeal (Baum & Lockstone, 2007). The impetus for this research is the desire to better understand, explain, predict, and ultimately manage or control the volunteer workforce in order to ensure a successful event and a legacy of volunteering in the host society. Research to date has focused on motives to volunteer for a major sport event, perceptions of the event volunteer experience itself, aspects of that experience that are particularly satisfying (and dissatisfying), and aspects that contribute to the likelihood that volunteers will become involved in the future. It paints a picture of major sport event volunteers that warrants a brief review here.

The reported primary motives for volunteering in various major sport events are consistently to make a difference to the event and/or community, do something different, and experience personal and social enrichment (Allen & Shaw, 2009; Bang & Chelladurai, 2009; Coyne & Coyne, 2001; Doherty, 2003; Downward et al., 2005; Farrell et al., 1998; Khoo & Engelhorn, 2007; Kim, Zhang, & Connaughtonor, 2010; Love et al., 2011; Maclean & Hamm, 2007; Reeser et al., 2005; Twynam et al., 2002/

2003). Additionally, love of the sport is a key motive for volunteers involved with single sport events (Coyne & Coyne, 2001; Love et al., 2011; Maclean & Hamm, 2007; Williams et al., 1995), while nostalgia for the excitement of the event and the connection with the Olympics and other volunteers there are fundamental to repeat Olympic volunteers (Fairley et al., 2007). Research further indicates that major sport event volunteers tend to realize social enrichment and community/event contribution to the greatest extent (Doherty, 2009; Kemp, 2002), while the greatest costs to volunteering are personal inconvenience (time, financial burden) and task underload (uninteresting tasks, too little to do) (Coyne & Coyne, 2001; Doherty, 2009; Larocque et al., 2002).

The extant research also indicates that sport event volunteers' satisfaction with their experience is particularly associated with their opportunity to connect with other volunteers in general (Allen & Shaw, 2009; Farrell et al., 1998), and to connect during training in particular (Costa et al., 2006; Green & Chalip, 2004). Elstad (1996) reports that most satisfying for student volunteers involved with the 1994 Lillehammer Winter Olympics were the opportunity for personal and social enrichment as well as the 'celebratory atmosphere' of the Games; most dissatisfying were the financial cost associated with volunteering and poor organization of volunteers. Similarly, Doherty (2003) found that social enrichment as well as community contribution significantly contribute to volunteers' overall satisfaction with their experience, while personal inconvenience and task underload that comes from poor organization significantly detract from their satisfaction. Furthermore, research indicates that volunteers are likely to get involved in another sport event to the extent that they experience personal and/or social enrichment (Doherty, 2009; Downward & Ralston, 2006), and feel a sense of contribution to the community (Doherty, 2009), and simply because of their satisfaction with their experience (Love et al., 2011). Doherty (2009) further reports that personal inconvenience is a deterrent to future sport event volunteering.

Despite this growing body of literature, Baum and Lockstone (2007) encourage continued research to expand our understanding of major sport event volunteering, research that might be addressed by pushing the boundaries of understanding the lived experience of volunteering (cf. Green & Chalip, 2004; Shaw, 2009).

Methodology

Autoethnography is gaining acceptance as a methodological approach that uses personal experience to move beyond passionless and objective voices in research (Ellis & Bochner, 2000). The 'insider's' perspective generated through autoethnography is purported to contribute to a fuller and, importantly, more balanced understanding of a particular phenomenon.

As a form of autobiographical narrative, autoethnography combines evocative writing and research that display multiple levels of consciousness, and is generally written in first person (Ellis, 2000, 2004). The representation of one's personal experience in written form should help readers to also experience so that they 'come away with not only knowledge of what has happened but a deeper underlying sense of empathy with [the author], an understanding of experience' (Rinehart, 2005, p. 503). According to Bochner (2000), narrative work must meet certain criteria: (1) abundant, concrete detail that capture the routines, emotions, and embodied experience; (2) structurally complex narratives whereby stories weave the past and present in a non-linear process of memory work; (3) quality of author's emotional credibility, vulnerability, and honesty in writing through the complexity, ambivalence, and contradictory nature of life; (4) a standard of ethical self-consciousness in which the writer shows concern for those in the story, and for oneself; and (5) a story that moves the reader, not simply by referring to subjective life, but by portraying it in a way that shows the reader what it feels like and what it means. The story must have the ability 'to evoke shared emotional experience and understanding' (Denzin, 2003, p. 13). The use of autoethnography can be insightful and scholarly if it makes readers believe an experience is genuine, credible, and possible (Ellis, 1995).

Alternate forms of qualitative inquiry like ethnography and autoethnography are increasingly being utilized in such disciplines as sport sociology and leisure studies (Amis & Silk, 2005); however, the value in these methods has generally not been realized in sport management (Edwards & Skinner, 2009; Rinehart, 2005; Skinner & Edwards, 2005). In particular, there are no known published autoethnographies of sport event volunteerism that might provide rich and new insight. The current study addresses these shortcomings through the representation of a highly personalized account of the volunteer experience at the Vancouver 2010 Olympic Games. In doing so, it provides readers with rich insight into this experience and advances the conceptualization of major sport event volunteerism.

Data collection and analysis

As a precursor to the autoethnographic account to follow, I provide a brief background on myself and the Vancouver 2010 Olympic Games. I am female, and at the time of the Vancouver 2010 Games I was a 22-year-old full-time sport management graduate student living in London, Ontario (in Eastern Canada). I had a past involvement as a competitive sport participant at the community, provincial, and national levels.

The 2010 Olympic Games were held in Vancouver, British Columbia, on the West Coast of Canada, February 12–28th. The main site of the Games was the City of Vancouver, with alpine and nordic ski and sledding (bobsleigh, luge, skeleton) events held in Whistler, BC, a two-hour drive northeast of Vancouver. The Vancouver Olympics Organizing Committee (VANOC) relied on a workforce of approximately 25,000 volunteers during the Games (Vancouver 2010 – A human legacy, 2010). Volunteer recruitment began in 2007 with selection and assignment in 2009. Games orientation and training began in late 2009 for local volunteers, while non-local volunteers (traveling from across the country and from abroad) participated in 'just in time' training focused on assigned venue(s) and task(s) as they arrived in Vancouver.

I was a 'Fleet Systems Driver' within the Transportation unit, based at the Burrard Bridge Compound in downtown Vancouver. As a T3-level driver, I was part of a general shuttle service that would drive VANOC personnel with T3-level accreditation or higher to and from venues in official Olympic vehicles. (A T1 driver – the highest level – provided exclusive service to one family throughout the Games; a T2 driver was assigned to two or more families.) T3 drivers would wait in sequence to pick up passengers, drive them to their desired destination, and then return to the initial staging area to line up again. I worked 14 ten-hour shifts (2:30 pm to 12:30 am or 6:00 am to 4:00 pm) from February 10th, just before the Games started, through March 2nd, just after the official closing, with a few days off in between.

As a Games volunteer I received a uniform prior to my training session, and a copious number of gifts and Olympic swag throughout the Games. My uniform included a winter jacket, two long sleeve shirts, a pair of pants, a vest, and a toque, all in the official blue of the 2010 Games, and bearing the logo of the Olympics and the Hudson's Bay Company, the volunteer uniform sponsor. Volunteers received a gift every three shifts, and the quality of the gifts increased the longer volunteers continued to fulfill their duties; we received Olympic pins and luggage tags at the outset, and over time received gifts of a notebook, sunglasses, an Olympic mascot stuffed animal, a 'Swatch' watch, and a silver medallion encrusted with the Olympic participation medal design. Volunteers like me who completed the hours to which they had committed received a 'thank you' pin from the International Olympic Committee (IOC) and a Birks silver-plated 'Team 2010' keychain. Our accreditation tag also gave us access to free public transportation throughout the Games, and a ten percent discount on lift passes at the Whistler-Blackcomb Mountain ski resort.

Consistent with the autoethnographic approach, I kept a personal journal throughout the three-week experience, including both objective (i.e., sight, sound, and action) and subjective (i.e., memories, thoughts and feelings) observations and experiences. All of my Games-related photographs, emails, newsletters, forms, schedules, training documents, and clothing were included as 'data.' At the outset of journaling, I recollected aspects of my personal background that seemed to relate to my Games volunteering, and I considered my experience leading up to departing for the Games.

Upon returning, I engaged in a reflective analytic process to consider the nature and personal meaning of my critical experiences (Ellis & Bochner, 2000; Fleming & Fullagar, 2007). Reflective techniques allow for specific experiences to be remembered, problematized, and written into narrative form (Fleming & Fullagar, 2007). I identified several themes that were indicative of my most meaningful moments as an Olympic volunteer: (1) A figure skater's dream: making the cut, (2) Uncertainty: going with the flow, (3) The basics: training, (4) 'Blue team': volunteer culture, (5) An Olympic spirit is born: leisure time, and (6) Returning home: prestige. Rather than presuming to provide a coherent account of identity, the autoethnography represented here is written through fragments of time that have been ordered chronologically to reflect my experience. The presentation critically links the narrative to the existing literature. This way, a contrast emerges between the thick descriptions of the personal experience (italics), and an academic detachment from those memories (cf. Trussell, 2010), while demonstrating 'how particular individual experiences fit into a more general understanding of the social world' (Jones, 2009, p. 382).

Front line insight

A figure skater's dream: making the cut

Going to the Olympics was a brief and naïve thought I had as a young figure skater. Growing up in Toronto, I trained in an elite program at a private club in the city. It was my 'home away from home,' as mom would call it. I wasn't the best skater but I loved it. My friends and coaches were a second family to me. We were all 'rink rats,' mom would say. Free skating was my favorite: jumping and spinning, mostly; the exciting stuff! I loved the crisp cool air on my skin, the smell of the rink, and seeing my breath in the middle of a stuffy Toronto summer – I still do.

The frozen white floor was my training ground. No boards. No circles or lines – a true figure skating rink. Off-ice activities were a regular part of our training as well. Fitness trainers in the gym helped us build our strength and endurance. Ballet teachers taught us how to be graceful, strong, and elegant – or at least they tried. Of the many talented skaters I trained with, it's no surprise to me that Patrick Chan represented Canada. Patrick was an extraordinary skater – his dedication surmounted anyone else we skated with. While others were late for practice sessions, eating greasy french fries or gossiping about who had a crush on whom, Patrick was focused. He was young and had an incredible work ethic on and off the ice. I always knew Patrick would go all the way. We carved edges on the same ice back then, but our journeys leading us to the Vancouver 2010 Winter Games, and our experiences there were nothing alike.

After giving my all at a synchronized skating audition toward the end of my career and not making the cut, I thought my one and only chance to make it to a senior national championship was gone. I was devastated and confused, and mad! 'I'm better than half the girls at that tryout!' I complained to my mom, upon hearing the bad news. 'Well, maybe the coach was looking for different skills, sweetie. You've never done synchronized skating before,' she had said, caringly. Mom is always so logical. The following week I received a phone call from the coach, informing me that a spot had opened up on the team and she wanted me to take it. I was thrilled and the rest, as they say, was history. The 6:00 am practices and tireless run-throughs resulted in us taking home the gold medal from Nationals.

My roots in and love for sport played a large part in my Olympic journey. The lure of rubbing shoulders with the best athletes in the world, and connecting with this incredible sport competition that captures the very essence of their sweat, tears, hard work, and dreams was irresistible. As noted earlier, wanting to be part of and contribute to a special event has been identified across the research as a primary yet quite broad motive for volunteers' involvement in major sport events. My experience revealed that, in particular, the opportunity to be connected to an elite sport environment again, and at a level I had only ever dreamed of, was a critical driving factor. This observation suggests that there are nuances of this broad motive that likely provide further insight into what it is about an event that people want to be a part of.

Indeed, Fairley et al. (2007) introduced the notion of nostalgia to the context of sport event volunteering when they determined that feelings elicited by volunteering at a previous Olympic Games are a key motive for returning volunteers. Nostalgia is 'a yearning to return to or relive a past period' (Fairley & Gammon, 2005, p. 183); it is, as Fairley and Gammon note, 'inextricably linked to one's identity' (p. 183). My drive to be involved with the Olympics stemmed, in particular, from my sport identity and a still lingering desire to experience the highest level of competition and performance possible, a nostalgia for the elite sport environment of which I was once a part. The determination of nostalgia in Fairley et al.'s (2007) work, and here, as a motive for major sport event volunteering, prompts the consideration of identity as a foundation for understanding individuals' personal motives. Identity theory has framed several investigations of long-term and repeat volunteering (e.g., Finkelstein, Penner, & Brannick, 2005; Laverie & McDonald, 2007), and has been considered in

81

the context of university sport events (Kim & Trail, 2007). It may be expected to have merit for understanding major sport event volunteering, with its presumption that individuals are attracted to activities that align with their self-identity (how they see themselves) and social identity (how they think others see them) (Erickson, 1980). So what particular aspects of identity (such as a connection with elite sport) drive major sport event volunteering? And what cohorts of (prospective) volunteers may be determined according to their shared identity? Gaining further insight into volunteer identity in this context has implications for segmenting and thus targeting the recruitment of those individuals (cf. Wood, Snelgrove, & Danylchuk, 2010). Identity theory also acknowledges that one's identity may be developed and transformed through involvement in chosen activities, which reflects my experience as my Olympic volunteering unfolded.

I fell in love with the West Coast of Canada during my early years in university. All of my vacation time and extra money was spent in the laid-back city of Vancouver and snowboarding the mountains. Midway through our undergraduate degrees, my jock Vancouverite boyfriend and I caught wind that VANOC began accepting volunteer applications. It was 2007; we knew we were sure to miss all the shots we didn't take. At least a year passed. I wasn't sure if they had even received my application. When VANOC volunteer recruitment finally did get in touch in early 2009, I missed the call. I thought, then, I had also missed my chance.

'Hello?' I whispered, sneaking out of my kinesiology class and around the corner. 'Hi, is this Erin Ko-da-ma?' a friendly voice greeted me on the other end. For some reason, people always have a hard time pronouncing my Japanese last name. 'Yes, it is,' I chuckled nervously as I paced back and forth in the hallway. 'Great, I'm so glad we could connect! I'm calling from the VANOC volunteer coordination centre. Is this a good time to answer a few questions about your application?' she asked excitedly. I began to break a sweat. I hate surprise interviews, but my excitement that they even called back negated a lot of my initial anxiety. 'It says here on your application that you have previous work experience in sport settings. Can you describe this?' the interviewer asked. I related my on-field part-time work experience with the Toronto Argonauts (of the Canadian Football League) and the Toronto Blue Jays (of Major League Baseball), as well as my volunteer work in figure skating. 'I've been an athlete all my life – it has carried over to my work and studies, and I really want to be a part of these Olympics!' I said, optimistically.

Random phone interviews continued sporadically throughout 2009. The recruiters asked an array of general questions as part of the screening process. VANOC seemed adamant about making sure that, since I was from out of the province, I would have accommodation during the Olympics, as it did not provide this service. Where I would be living appeared to be a key consideration, as well as my availability to volunteer for the entirety of the Games. I honestly wasn't sure about either at the time, but I convinced them I had it all sorted out. My application was finally approved in December, 2009. The process was long, sometimes inconvenient, and often frustrating. Was I in or not?! For example, my security forms had to be mailed in twice; I'm sure they got lost among the tens of thousands of others. I had volunteered for a few professional sport teams and events in the past, but getting to the Olympics was by far the most unique and drawn-out process. But I didn't give up, and I finally made the cut.

Even though I figured my chances of gaining a position on the VANOC volunteer workforce were low, I held onto the hope that I think most athletes feel when they may have a once-in-a-lifetime opportunity. It was that spirited optimism that enabled me to persist through the almost three-year application process. There appears to be little empirical understanding about the, perhaps extensive, time and effort required to become involved and difficulty even being chosen as a major sport event volunteer. As it happened, the process was not dissimilar to my somewhat unsettling experience trying out for the synchronized skating team (and my similar excitement in ultimately being chosen). The unexpected uncertainty and anxiety I felt during the volunteer selection process was heightened by the importance I attached to making the Vancouver 2010 volunteer 'team,' and contributed to the emotional roller coaster that culminated with the sense of accomplishment when I 'made the cut.' As it turns out, the selection process was the beginning of building a team of volunteers whose identities were shaped by the struggle just to make that team.

Uncertainty: going with the flow

With a backpack on my back, a massive duffle bag slung on my shoulder and a snowboard bag in hand, I waddle over to the red Pontiac Sunfire waiting for me outside Vancouver airport. 'Hey! How was your flight?' my brother David asks in his usual endearing tone. 'Good, thanks!' I reply, giving him a (probably unwelcomed) sisterly hug. 'Good to see you,' he says with a smile on his face. If he is worried about how the next few weeks will pan out, I can't tell. He has just finished the first year of his master's program at the University of British Columbia. His small one-bedroom apartment will be my temporary home until I figure out where I will be working exactly. 'So where are you going to get your accreditation and uniform tomorrow morning?' he asks, as we drive into the city. 'No idea. I have the address but I have to find out where that is and how to get there tonight,' I say yawning. It is late already and my watch is still three hours ahead of Pacific Standard Time. (Vancouver is three hours behind the time zone where I live.) 'Ok, and where's your work?' he asks. 'Don't know, have to look that up too,' I chuckle. 'It's in the city; I just need to get oriented.' He laughs too. The questions keep coming steadily. Both laughing together at my mysterious new job, I feel very grateful to have a brother willing to put me up on his couch and to make sure I find my way.

Having worked part-time for two professional sports teams in Toronto, I am used to being thrown into fast paced environments. I'm also fairly comfortable as a driver, so I'm not overly concerned about the chauffeur job that awaits me in VANOC's transportation department (as long as I have a city map). Not knowing where to go for accreditation and training, or where I may even be living in the weeks to come is a whole other mystery.

Although I knew some degree of uncertainty may be expected when working for an event like the Olympics, it was quite overwhelming at the outset. It was not my actual job that I was so uncertain of – I believed I could handle whatever task they asked of me during the Games – but rather the happenings outside my job. The short time frame between confirmation of my position (December 31, 2009) and my start date (February 10, 2010) meant last minute communication with VANOC regarding accreditation, training, and information that would help orient me to the city and the Games. I had little time to plan my travel and confirm my accommodation. This feeling of uncertainty may have been particular to my situation as a sport event volunteer tourist and a first time Games volunteer; for someone who was more familiar with the city and the volunteer process of the Olympic Games, or any major games, this may have been less stressful. The last minute and subsequently fast paced nature of planning and communication with regard to some of these logistical issues was unnerving and a critical factor in my volunteer experience.

This provides further insight into the limited research to date on volunteers' pre-event experience which notes little concern about the ability to handle assigned jobs and the volunteer working conditions (Doherty, 2003), yet particular concern about lack of communication regarding logistics such as training, transportation, and personal security (Ralston, Downward, & Lumsdon, 2004). Uncertainty appears to have more to do with the logistics of volunteering for the event, over which volunteers have no control – Where do I go? How do I get there? Whom do I report to, and when? – than the task itself, which pertains to one's perceived abilities. Uncertainty or ambiguity is an important, potentially detrimental, factor in individual attitudes and behavior in the workplace (Tubre & Collins, 2000), and appears to warrant further consideration in the sport event volunteer setting. Understanding volunteers' ambiguity with regard to various aspects of major sport events (including any variation among volunteers), and its consequences, may be expected to have implications for event managers to address those critical aspects (cf. Sakires, Doherty, & Misener, 2009). Perhaps not all volunteers are willing to 'go with the flow.'

The basics: training

Not being a morning person, and with little sleep from the time change, getting up for 8:00 am training is rough. Luckily, my brother is up and agrees to drive me the first day. I arrive to a massive white tent with security personnel checking accreditation, dressed in my blue uniform just like the other 250 volunteers on each shift. My volunteer barcode is scanned and I am cheerily directed toward the training session, where I may be the youngest person there by 20 years. A big, husky man informs the group of us about the features of the vehicles, signing them in and out, emergency procedures and, my favorite, two-way radio etiquette.

After the lessons in theory, we split up into groups and hit the road to explore the Olympic venues and routes in reality. The group of men I am teamed with decide that I should drive first. No pressure! I first double-check my route so that I have a good idea of where I am going. Fortunately, one of the fellow trainees in the car is a Vancouver local and assures me that he will steer me in the proper direction. The Olympic vehicles are sport utility vehicles, and much larger than the small car I am used to driving at home. Slow and steady does it, I tell myself – no need to rush. A few minutes into the ride, I start getting a feel for the vehicle, and am more comfortable driving it. Equipped with an official Games-time map and a radio, we take turns driving and navigating the city in a brand new Chevrolet Traverse.

The men in my car are very kind. Although I don't feel I have a lot in common with them, we have a fairly easy time connecting. We chat about where home is, what we do, and how we all became volunteers, while exploring different venues in and out of the vehicle. Our training outing is going well, until the last driver takes his turn. The rest of us in the car exchange a look of panic as he almost has an accident, twice! Nonetheless, we arrive back in one piece, and when noon rolls around training is over and we are (apparently) ready for our first day of work.

Back at the compound I get talking with Tony, one of the younger volunteer drivers. He's from Winnipeg (in Central Canada), and is apparently a top sales person at [a major sporting goods retail store]. I don't think he's too happy to be sharing a bed with his buddy for the next few weeks, but I can tell he's thrilled to be here. He also applied to volunteer for the Games over two years ago. We decide to meet for coffee tomorrow, before the start of our shift, to go through the maps and Olympic routes.

Although I had felt quite certain about my ability to do any assigned task, I was surprised to find that learning the job-specific basics during the short training period was vital to my performance at work, highlighting the importance of this aspect of event volunteer management. This aligns with Shaw's (2009) finding that registration volunteers, engaged in the critical role of moving event competitors through the registration and accreditation process efficiently and effectively, felt they were not properly trained for their role and had to figure it out as they went, resulting in considerable frustration and delays in many instances. The training gave me confidence in my tasks, and also helped my fellow volunteers and I understand the importance of our role within the larger event portfolio.

In addition, the in-class and on-road training sessions were important for orienting volunteers with each other. Costa et al. (2006) found that training can help create a sense of community among volunteers, particularly when individuals are given an opportunity to share and provide input to the group; a sense of community that can promote commitment to the event, and further satisfaction with the volunteer experience overall. From the outset of my job-specific training sessions, I began to feel a sense of shared purpose, identity, and support among my fellow volunteers. Even though it was quite a diverse group, we had all come through the rigorous selection process and now were all in this together. Thus, the 'team' I was selected to be a part of developed and continued to build through our job-specific training. This may have been particularly important for me, as a sport event volunteer tourist, and for us drivers as our actual task was quite solitary. My experience echoes Costa et al.'s (2006) claim that the impact of training for volunteers and the event may be multifaceted. It is important for sport event managers to recognize and facilitate job-specific training for establishing task clarity and confidence through volunteer learning (cf. Shaw, 2009), and for social interaction and team building, perhaps particularly among a diverse group of volunteers. Continued research may continue to unpack the nature and mechanisms of meaningful volunteer training.

'Blue team': volunteer culture

Lucky for me, the transportation department ends up being just a twenty-minute walk from my brother's apartment. Every workday I walk along the seawall to and from the Burrard Compound, the transportation hub that houses squads of drivers in a huge tent and holds hundreds of vehicles in a vast lot underneath Burrard Bridge.

As I peer around the tent full of people, it is a sea of aqua blue. Men, women, paid staff, volunteers, old and young, are all dressed the same: bright aqua blue jackets with silver Olympic rings on our backs, matching blue vests and long sleeve shirts. Some are wearing the matching hat too. The Hudson's Bay Company logo is plastered on every piece. We all carry big rectangular lunch bags and radios in case we are called out. Every shift, lines of people pass by the serving tables and fill their bags with prepackaged sandwiches, snacks and beverages, while others huddle around tables watching Olympic events on the big screen TV and cheering on our Canadian athletes.

This takes me back to my synchronized skating days. During competition, the whole team wore the same dresses, pants, shirts, jackets, and even underwear! Hair was slicked back into perfect buns and makeup was identical. Our coach decided what the team would eat, and a few dedicated moms would go to work prepackaging our meals for the competition. We operated as a unit, and cheered on our teammates.

Having spent many years as a singles skater, I was pleasantly surprised to make the connection between my volunteer team and synchronized skating team experiences. Once again, sport was the connecting theme, but this aspect of my Olympic volunteering resonated particularly with the recollection of my competitive sport group. In contrast to the body of research on sport team dynamics (cf. Carron, Hausenblas, & Eys, 2005), there has been little examination of the dynamics of sport event volunteer teams or workgroups, such as cohesion, sense of community, or shared culture. Yet, we were definitely a team, as we worked and rested, side by side, sharing the same daily routine, way of dress, and purpose for being there.

Volunteers from numerous departments can be found all over the city, at all times. We are everywhere. 'Smurfs,' they call us. Everyone is very friendly and it is difficult to tell the difference between a paid and unpaid worker.

I stop to fill up my gas tank before returning to the Compound for the end of my shift. Another 'Smurf' is filling up his tank at the pump next to mine. 'How are you enjoying your volunteer experience?' he asks, in a surprisingly concerned tone. 'It's been great so far! Our shifts are pretty long though,' I say, yawning. 'And I wish we were a little bit busier. I think the good weather has a lot of people walking and not using our service,' I reply, assuming he is also a volunteer driver. He walks over to me: 'Yes, I know. It's a bit of a trade-off isn't it? Are you having fun though? Is it all you expected it to be?' he asks genuinely. At this point, he is close enough that I can read the accreditation tag hanging from his neck. His title reads 'VP VANOC Volunteer Coordination,' whereas mine reads 'Driver.' We chat further before departing the gas station in our separate directions. I drive off with a smile on my face, feeling like a little more than just a blue jacket. I'm part of a really big team.

My experience in the volunteer culture that surrounds me, given that there is minimal time to become accustomed to it, is quite profound. The uniforms, message boards, shift gifts, mascots, and pin trading are just a few of the ways for us volunteers to identify, relate and talk to each other. I even (surprisingly) find myself getting excited over the Olympic pins. My accreditation tag lanyard becomes quite heavy over the weeks with pins running up both sides. I admit I even feel a bit jealous when others have more or better pins than me!

We look out for one another too. Certain venues are considered better to be at than others during our shifts. Canada Hockey Place is possibly the worst, and I make sure to warn anyone who is heading down to the underground staging area we refer to as 'the Dungeon.' 'Make sure you bring a book or a DVD to watch in your car, or something!' I preach to other volunteers on my team. 'It can get pretty boring down there waiting for the hockey games to finish.' As drivers, our accreditation does not give us access to most Olympic venues. We are confined to our cars, or to a drivers' lounge if we are really lucky.

'Watch out for the YVR Nazi,' I am told by a fellow volunteer driver. He is from Ireland; retired and taking part in the Games. 'She looks no more than twenty-five, and she's just right on her high horse.' 'Really? A volunteer?!' I ask. 'Oh yes, she's a loading zone attendant; in her mid-twenties, I'd say. She stands out on the side of the loading zone and just power trips all day,' he warns me. 'But don't mind her. She's in her own

world.' 'Good to know!' I laugh, wondering if I will be staged at the airport any time soon, and have a run-in with the 'YVR Nazi.'

VANOC worked actively to help develop a positive culture through such things as the volunteer uniforms, gifts, pin trading, and the volunteers' assembly tent with the provision of food and areas for taking in the Olympics on television. A general interest in and caring about each other continued to pull us together. Stories and humorous debriefs shared among drivers reinforced our common experiences. I felt like a part of the team, and identified with others easily; they became my friends, confidantes, and counselors.

Social enrichment has been identified in the research as both a primary motive for being involved and a particularly satisfying aspect of major sport event volunteers' experience. The opportunity to connect with others may be particularly important for sport event volunteer tourists who are from outside the host city (cf. Williams et al., 1995); the volunteer team may be their primary identification during the event. Research indicates that the social enrichment that comes from meeting, working, and developing relationships with different people is particularly mean-ingful for younger volunteers (Bang & Chelladurai, 2009; Doherty, 2003; Elstad, 1996; Kemp, 2002; Khoo & Engelhorn, 2007); it was certainly a critical part of my experience. However, it was not just the social interactions, but the culture which developed as a result of those relationships that framed my connection and thus identity with respect to the volunteer team and event. With the exception of Fairley et al. (2007) uncovering a subculture among a particular cohort of returning Olympic volunteers, again, group or even broader organizational dynamics such as culture has received little attention in the sport event volunteer research.

Culture has the potential to be a very strong force within an organization (Deal & Kennedy, 1999). As the 'learned, shared, compelling, interrelated set of symbols... [that] provide a set of orientations for members' (Terpstra & David, 1991, p. 6), culture represents 'how things are done around here' (MacIntosh & Doherty, 2005, p. 1). It provides an important guide for member behavior; a guide that continues to be shaped and reinforced through shared experiences (Schein, 1999). The volunteer culture that developed during the Games both reflected and reinforced my identity as an Olympic volunteer (cf. Parker, 2000). Volunteer culture may be a very powerful tool for major sport event managers, and warrants further consideration in this context. What is the volunteer culture, and how does it develop, particularly among individuals of diverse ages, backgrounds, and interests? Do the values and expectations that guide behavior align with what event managers intend? What impact does the culture have on individuals and the overall success of the event? At the 2010 Olympic Games, VANOC provided the mechanism and volunteers developed the culture through shared purpose, stories, experiences, problem solving, and support realized through social interactions during the event.

An Olympic spirit is born: leisure time

Days off are spent reacquainting myself with Vancouver, exploring the various attractions and pavilions, and meeting up with old and new friends. Exhausted at times, I force myself to go out and take part in the festivities, out of fear I will miss something. I feel surprisingly comfortable and 'at home.' I find a good five or six km route to jog along the seawall that I can definitely see myself getting used to. The ocean breeze and view of the mountains from the harbor are absolutely spectacular. Everything is 'Olympic,' and the city is buzzing with the excitement of hundreds of thousands of people visiting from all across the globe. It is no longer the laid-back destination I had known.

I wake up at 4:45 am on one of my days off to catch the shuttle up to Whistler. I am going to watch the men's giant slalom and combined event with fellow driver and new friend, Tony. He was given two tickets from the sporting goods store where he works and invited me along. It is a beautiful day at Whistler Creekside where the alpine ski events are held. The warm sun peaks over the mountains, shining on the timing flats stands where we spend the afternoon.

Hundreds of moving bodies, draped in their nation's colors, flood the stands and gather around the finish line behind media personnel and their heavy equipment. All day we follow each skier from the top of the mountain on a giant TV as they ski the first part of the course. As soon as an athlete skis into sight, no matter what country they represent, the whole crowd goes wild, every time without fail. Loud screams and 'woo-hoos,' cowbells and horns sound until each skier reaches the finish line.

While I appreciate all sports, I certainly do not consider myself a die-hard sports fan. Yet, at Olympic events I found myself getting as excited as if I was rooting for my favorite home team. My feelings of hype and exclusivity of being at such a historic event was incredible, regardless of any personal attachment to a sport or athlete. An Olympic spirit was born within me. While the student volunteers in Elstad's (1996) study also highlighted the celebratory atmosphere of the Olympics, it is not clear what this really meant to them. Notably, the 'Olympic Spirit' was developed to such an extent among the returning Olympic volunteers in Fairley et al.'s (2007) study that they were nostalgic for reliving it at a subsequent Games. Interestingly, for me, leisure time spent at the Games but away from my volunteer responsibilities was critical to experiencing the full breadth of what the event had to offer and generating that Olympic spirit.

Very little, if anything, has been examined or written about volunteers' leisure time during a major sport event. What do they do? And particularly sport event volunteer tourists? Do volunteers attend competitions, or the social and cultural happenings that are typically part of these events? What difference does leisure time make to their overall experience? The lack of scholarly attention may be due to leisure or non-work time not being considered a relevant part of the sport event volunteers' experience. In fact, my direct engagement in much of what the Vancouver 2010 Olympics had to offer, outside my volunteer involvement, was critical to enhancing my identification with the Games. For me, it also extended the social enrichment I experienced when on task.

Several studies note that relatedness and friendship are important aspects of the volunteer experience (Allen & Shaw, 2009; Fairley et al., 2007). My relationship with Tony, while relatively surface, was meaningful to my overall experience. He also came to Vancouver on his own as a volunteer tourist, and spending some leisure time together allowed us to share and reflect a lot about our own experiences getting to and being at the Games. I highly valued the closer and deeper connection I was able to make with another volunteer away from the task setting. These observations provide an even broader picture of volunteers' major sport event experience, suggesting that it should include consideration of leisure time away from the task. This may be particularly critical, and unique, to major sport events where volunteers sign on for the duration of the event. Instead, the focus of research and practice has typically been limited to the management of volunteers' on-task time.

My return: prestige

'So?' mom asks excitedly, as if I just arrived home from my very first date. 'How was it?' My mother has stated on multiple occasions that she lives vicariously through me, so I knew our frequent online chats and phone calls wouldn't be enough to suffice her interests. Glad to be back home, I open my suitcase to show my parents the vast amount of Olympic tokens I collected along my journey: trophies of my great expedition. 'It was incredible. I don't even know where to start,' I laugh, exhausted.

I can't help but pay attention to my father's reaction when I give him one of my official VANOC shirts. By the time I had arrived to claim my uniform, my size was mostly taken and so I was left with larger clothing. 'You're a Smurf now too, Dad,' I chuckle. 'A Smurf? What the heck is that?' he replies laughing. He puts the shirt on right there and then, and turns to me with a huge smile on his face. 'Now I can tell everyone my daughter brought this back for me from the Olympics!'

My return to school is exciting for others as well. Anyone and everyone I know wants to hear all about my time at the Games. 'How would you feel presenting your experience?' a professor in my faculty asks eagerly. 'Absolutely, I would be honored to!' I reply quickly, attempting to mask my nervousness. 'Great, I can't wait to hear all about it!' she says. In the following weeks, I put together a graphic presentation in hopes that others can share in my Games experience. I know a few other people who also went out to the Olympics, including the Dean of my faculty. I discover that he will also be presenting, about his volunteering at Canada Hockey Place. In a room full of both faculty members and familiar student faces, I have the privilege of sharing my experience alongside my Dean – yet another experience that presents me with a great feeling of accomplishment.

Upon returning home, everyone's curiosity and envy about my journey generated a feeling of prestige that was surprisingly satisfying for me. The constant recollection of my experiences and continued reflection, both socially and academically, created an incredible lasting impression of the Games for me, and seemingly for some of the people closest to me. Several studies have examined the volunteer legacy of major sport events (Doherty, 2009; Downward & Ralston, 2006; Love et al., 2011; Maclean & Hamm, 2007), with a particular focus on individuals' intent to volunteer again. Although I did not reflect on that particularly, focusing instead on returning to my graduate studies and what lies ahead professionally, I did realize an overwhelming sense of pride about my experience. Thus, similar to the Olympic volunteers in Fairley et al.'s (2007) study, an important legacy of the Games was the pride I continued to feel long after the event concluded. However, while Kim, Kim et al. (2010) found that volunteers' satisfaction with their involvement in a major sport event is a significant predictor of their pride in being a part of the event, my pride was particularly boosted by the interest, excitement, and prestige that others associated with my involvement. Perhaps a further legacy of my volunteering is the positive effect on others with whom I have shared my lived experience. It is not clear what that effect might be, but it suggests a broader conceptualization of volunteer legacy than simply intent to volunteer again. Researchers and practitioners should consider whether and how the legacy of major sport event volunteering reaches beyond the volunteers themselves.

Conclusion

The efforts of volunteers are critical to the success of Olympic Games and other major sport events. Learning about the lived experiences of these volunteers is likewise critical to understanding how the management of sport affects people (Rinehart, 2005). The lived experience represented here was further reflected upon with respect to various personal and cultural forces, advancing the conceptualization of major sport event volunteerism. Several directions for future research and implications for management have been suggested, and the reader's personal reflection and interpretation of the story may advance that further.

The study revealed insight into the process of 'making the cut' as a Vancouver 2010 volunteer, and my identity with and thus nostalgia for the elite sport environment as a personal driving force. Identity theory may thus be useful for uncovering a fuller range of more specific reasons for major sport event volunteering, with implications for targeting recruitment efforts. My identity with the volunteer team and the event also unfolded throughout my Olympic volunteering experience, and this phenomenon may be another topic for investigation. The study also revealed different aspects of volunteer uncertainty than have been identified in previous research, suggesting that major sport event managers should be aware of the potential detrimental impact of volunteer ambiguity regarding logistics and prompting research in this area. Continued research is also recommended to further understand the nature and mechanisms of job-specific volunteer training that I found to be not only critical to my role performance but also a foundation for developing camaraderie and positive group dynamics within the volunteer team. It is important for event managers to recognize and ensure the effective implementation of training that facilitates both role preparation and social connection.

The notion of my volunteer team, which resonated deeply in relation to my previous sport team experiences, was particularly manifested in the realization of the culture of that team. Our shared purpose, experiences, and support reflected, and reinforced, volunteers' identity and connection with others. Given that organizational culture has emerged as an important entity in a variety of institutions, and can be critical in bringing an organization together as a unified whole (MacIntosh & Doherty, 2010; Slack & Parent, 2006), its investigation in the context of major sport event volunteering provides another direction for future research. Meanwhile, event managers may draw on VANOC's success with providing the mechanism through which a positive volunteer culture developed at the Vancouver 2010 Games. Although not meaningful to my Olympic volunteer experience, subcultures may also be a strong force within an organization (MacIntosh & Doherty, 2005; Martin, 1992) and can be investigated in terms of whether they exist across or within various major sport event volunteer work units (e.g., transportation unit), and their role in the volunteer experience.

The study provided relatively novel insight into the volunteer leisure experience during a major sport event with several directions for future research. Leisure or non-task time was critical to my full Olympic experience and warrants further examination as to what volunteers do during their leisure time. Further insight may be expected to have implications for meaningful event volunteer management that attends to volunteers' particular leisure interests (e.g., passes to sports or cultural events, receptions, social opportunities). Finally, prestige and pride was an apparent legacy of my Olympic volunteer experience, and one that was enhanced by the opportunity to share my experience with others. While I did not reflect on whether that sense of prestige and pride would leverage into further volunteering for me personally, it does provide a direction for future research that would extend the understanding of volunteer legacy. I did observe that sharing my experience was seemingly very positive for others. That aspect of volunteer legacy warrants consideration, with possible implications for ensuring a positive volunteer experience that will be worth talking about and perhaps post-event initiatives to facilitate that sharing.

While traditional research continues to investigate the psychological, demographic, and organizational factors of sport event volunteers on a large scale, autoethnographic techniques allow for the extraordinary and real-life aspects of personal experiences to be realized. Beyond the directions for research emanating from the current study, sport event volunteer research may benefit still further from the use of autoethnography in the investigation of, for example, small-scale sport event volunteerism, or the experience of a planning volunteer or veteran volunteer, in contrast to the front line, first time volunteer experience illustrated here. Autoethnography may also be used, building on the work of Xing and Chalip (2009), to gain a richer understanding of the experience of major sport event employees who are also critical to event success.

Of course, the personal nature of autoethnography means generalizability is limited. The volunteer workforce at the Vancouver 2010 Olympics was extensive, and this study encompasses only one subjective view from within one department. However, these findings extend the major sport event volunteer literature by putting the researcher back into the study (Ellis & Bochner, 2000), and providing a new perspective on the front line experience of sport event volunteering.

References

Allen, J.B., & Shaw, S. (2009). "Everyone rolls up their sleeves and mucks in": Exploring volunteers' motivation and experiences of the motivational climate of a sporting event. *Sport Management Review, 12*, 79–90.

Amis, J., & Silk, M. (2005). Rupture: Promoting critical innovative approaches to the study of sport management. *Journal of Sport Management, 19*, 355–366.

Bang, H., & Chelladurai, P. (2009). Development and validation of the volunteer motivations scale for international sporting events (VMS-ISE). *International Journal of Sport Management and Marketing, 6*(4), 332–350.

Baum, T., & Lockstone, L. (2007). Volunteers and mega sporting events: Developing a research framework. *International Journal of Event Management Research, 3*, 29–41.

Bochner, A. (2000). Criteria against ourselves. *Qualitative Inquiry, 6*, 266–272.

Carron, A.V., Hausenblas, H.A., & Eys, M.A. (2005). *Group dynamics in sport* (3rd ed.). Morgantown, WV: Fitness Information Technology.

Costa, C.A., Chalip, L., Green, C., & Simes, C. (2006). Reconsidering the role of training in event volunteers' satisfaction. *Sport Management Review, 9*, 165–182.

Coyne, B.S., & Coyne, E.J.,Sr. (2001). Getting, keeping and caring for unpaid volunteers for professional golf tournament events. *Human Resource Development International, 4*, 199–214.

Deal, T.E., & Kennedy, A.A. (1999). *The new corporate cultures.* New York, NY: Perseus Books.

Denzin, N. (2003). *Performance ethnography: Critical pedagogy and the politics of culture.* London: Sage.

Doherty, A. (2009). The volunteer legacy of a major sporting event. *Journal of Policy Research in Tourism, Leisure and Events, 1*, 185–207.

Doherty, A. (2003). *A study of the volunteers of the 2001 Alliance London Jeux du Canada Games.* London, ON: The University of Western Ontario.

Douglas, K. (2009). Storying my self: Negotiating a relational identity in professional sport. *Qualitative Research in Sport & Exercise, 1*, 176–190.

Downward, P., Lumsdon, L., & Ralston, R. (2005). Gender differences in sports event volunteering: Insights from the Crew 2002 at the XVII Commonwealth Games. *Managing Leisure, 10*, 219–236.

Downward, P., & Ralston, R. (2006). The sports development potential of sports event volunteering: Insights from the XVII Manchester Commonwealth Games. *European Sport Management Quarterly, 6*, 333–351.

Edwards, A., & Skinner, J. (2009). *Qualitative research in sport management*. Oxford: Butterworth-Heinemann.

Ellis, C. (1995). *Final negotiations*. Philadelphia, PA: Temple University Press.

Ellis, C. (2000). Creating criteria: An ethnographic short story. *Qualitative Inquiry, 6*, 273–277.

Ellis, C. (2004). *The autoethnographic I: A methodological novel about autoethnography*. Walnut Creek, CA: AltaMira Press.

Ellis, C., & Bochner, A.P. (2000). Autoethnography, personal narrative, reflexivity. In N.K. Denzin & Y.S. Lincoln (Eds.), *Handbook of Qualitative Research* (2nd ed, pp. 733–779). Thousand Oaks, CA: Sage.

Elstad, B. (1996). Volunteers perceptions of learning and satisfaction in a mega-event: The case of the XVII Olympic Winter Games in Lillehammer. *Festival Management and Event Tourism, 4*, 75–86.

Erickson, E.H. (1980). *Identity and the life cycle*. New York, NY: W.W. Norton.

Fairley, S., & Gammon, S. (2005). Something lived, something learned: Nostalgia's expanding role in sport tourism. *Sport in Society, 8*, 182–197.

Fairley, S., Kellett, P., & Green, B.C. (2007). Volunteering abroad: Motives to travel to volunteer at the Athens Olympic Games. *Journal of Sport Management, 21*, 41–57.

Farrell, J.M., Johnston, M.E., & Twynam, G.D. (1998). Volunteer motivation, satisfaction, and management at an elite sporting competition. *Journal of Sport Management, 12*, 288–300.

Finkelstein, M.A., Penner, L.A., & Branick, M.T. (2005). Motive, role identity, and prosocial personality as predictors of volunteer activity. *Social Behavior and Personality, 33*, 403–418.

Fleming, C., & Fullagar, S. (2007). Reflexive methodologies: An autoethnography of the gendered performance of sport/management. *Annals of Leisure Research, 10*, 238–256.

Green, B.C., & Chalip, L. (2004). Paths to volunteer commitment: Lessons from the Sydney Olympic Games. In R.A. Stebbins & M. Graham (Eds.), *Volunteering as leisure/Leisure as volunteering: An international assessment* (pp. 49–67). Wallingford, UK: CABI.

Jones, R.L. (2009). Coaching as caring (the smiling gallery): Accessing hidden knowledge. *Physical Education & Sport Pedagogy, 14*, 377–390.

Kim, M., & Trail, G. (2007). Influence of role identities on volunteer intentions. *International Journal of Sport Management, 8*(3), 1–15.

Kemp, S. (2002). The hidden workforce: Volunteers' learning in the Olympics. *Journal of European Industrial Training, 26*, 109–116.

Khoo, S., & Engelhorn, R. (2007). Volunteer motivations for the Malaysian Paralympiad. *Tourism and Hospitality Planning & Development, 4*, 159–167.

Kim, M., Kim, M.K., & Odio, M.A. (2010). Are you proud? The influence of sport and community identity and job satisfaction on pride of mega-event volunteers. *Event Management, 14*, 127–136.

Kim, M., Zhang, J.J., & Connaughton, D.P. (2010). Comparison of volunteer motivations in different youth sport organizations. *European Sport Management Quarterly, 10*, 343–365.

Larocque, L., Gravelle, F., & Karlis, G. (2002). Volunteerism and serious leisure: The case of the Francophone Games. *Proceedings of the 2002 Canadian Congress on Leisure Research*, Edmonton, AB (pp. 181–183). Waterloo, ON: Canadian Association for Leisure Studies.

Lashua, B., & Fox, K. (2006). Rec needs a new rhythm cuz rap is where we're livin'. *Leisure Sciences, 28*, 267–283.

Laverie, D.A., & McDonald, R.E. (2007). Volunteer dedication: Understanding the role of identity importance on participation frequency. *Journal of Macromarketing, 27*, 274–288.

Love, A., Hardin, R.L., Koo, G.-Y., & Morse, A. (2011). Effects of motives on satisfaction and behavioral intentions of volunteers at a PGA event. *International Journal of Sport Management, 12*, 86–101.

MacIntosh, E., & Doherty, A. (2010). The influence of organizational culture on job satisfaction and intention to leave. *Sport Management Review, 13*(2), 106–117.

MacIntosh, E, & Doherty, A. (2005). Leader intentions and employee perceptions of organizational culture in a private fitness corporation. *European Sport Management Quarterly, 5*(1), 1–22.

Maclean, J., & Hamm, S. (2007). Motivation, commitment, and intentions of volunteers at a large Canadian sporting event. *Leisure/Loisir, 31*, 523–556.

Martin, J.J. (1992). *Cultures in organizations: Three perspectives.* New York: Oxford University Press.

McCarville, R. (2007). From a fall in the mall to a run in the sun: One journey to Ironman triathlon. *Leisure Sciences, 29*, 159–173.

Mobley, A.M. (2008). Sharing the dream: The opening ceremonies of Beijing. *Journal of Sport & Social Issues, 32*, 327–332.

Parker, M. (2000). *Organizational culture and identity.* Thousand Oaks, CA: Sage.

Popovic, M.L. (2012). Moksha rose from the heart: A prosaic and poetic embodiment of yoga autoethnography. Cultural Studies. *Critical Methodologies, 11*(6), 30–42.

Popovic, M.L. (2010). A Voice in the rink: Playing with our histories and evoking autoethnography. *Journal of Sport History, 37*, 235–255.

Purdy, L., Potrac, P., & Jones, R. (2008). Power, consent and resistance: An autoethnography of competitive rowing. Sport. *Education and Society, 13*, 319–336.

Ralston, R., Downward, P., & Lumsdon, L. (2004). The expectations of volunteers prior to the XVII Commonwealth Games, 2002: A qualitative study. *Event Management, 9*, 13–26.

Reeser, J.C., Berg, R.L., Rhea, D., & Willick, S. (2005). Motivation and satisfaction among polyclinic volunteers at the 2002 Winter Olympic and Paralympic Games. *British Journal of Sports Medicine, 39*, 20–25.

Rinehart, R.E. (2005). Experiencing sport management: The use of personal narrative in sport management studies. *Journal of Sport Management, 19*, 497–522.

Schein, E.H. (1999). *The corporate culture survival guide.* San Francisco, CA: Jossey Bass.

Sakires, J., Doherty, A., & Misener, K. (2009). Role ambiguity in voluntary sport organizations. *Journal of Sport Management, 23*, 615–643.

Shaw, S. (2009). "It was 'all smile for Dunedin!'": Event volunteer experiences at the 2006 New Zealand masters games. *Sport Management Review, 12*, 26–33.

Skinner, J., & Edwards, A. (2005). Inventive pathways: Fresh visions of sport management research. *Journal of Sport Management, 19*, 404–421.

Slack, T., & Parent, M.M. (2006). Managing organizational culture. In *Understanding sport organizations* (2nd ed.) (pp. 273–290). Champaign, IL: Human Kinetics.

Terpstra, V., & David, K. (1991). *The cultural environment of international business* (3rd ed.). Cincinatti, OH: South Western Publishing.

Tubre, T., & Collins, A. (2000). Jackson and Schuler (1985) revisited: A meta-analysis of the relationship between role ambiguity, role conflict and job performance. *Journal of Management, 26*, 155–169.

Trussell, D.E. (2010). Gazing from the inside out during ethically heightened moments. *Leisure Studies, 29*, 377–395.

Twynam, G.D., Farrell, J.M., & Johnston, M.E. (2002/2003). Leisure and volunteer motivation as a special sporting event. *Leisure/Loisir, 27*, 363–377.

Vancouver 2010 – A human legacy. (2010). *OIC latest news.* Retrieved from http://www.olympic.org/content/news/media-resources/manual-news/2010/02/22/vancouver-2010--a-human-legacy/.

Wood, L., Snelgrove, R., & Danylchuk, K. (2010). Segmenting volunteer fundraisers at a charity sport event. *Journal of Nonprofit & Public Sector Marketing, 22*, 38–54.

Xing, X., & Chalip, L. (2009). Marching in the glory: Experiences and meanings when working for a sport mega-event. *Journal of Sport Management, 23*, 210–237.

Williams, P.W., Dossa, K.A., & Tompkins, L. (1995). Volunteerism and special event management: A case study of Whistler's Men's World Cup of Skiing. *Festival Management and Event Tourism, 3*, 83–95.

Development of a hierarchical model of sport volunteers' organizational commitment

Se-Hyuk Park[a] and May Kim[b]

[a]Department of Sports Sciences, College of Energy and Bio Sciences, Seoul National University of Science & Technology, Seoul, Korea; [b]Department of Physical Education, College of Education, Korea University, Seoul, Korea

The present study was an attempt to understand sport volunteers' commitment to an organization from a developmental perspective and propose a hierarchical model of volunteer commitment based on Kohlberg's moral development model. The proposed model includes five stages of attitudinal commitment which are developmental and distinct in nature with the following hierarchical sequence: primitive commitment, continuance commitment, external commitment, normative commitment, and affective commitment. By comparing Kohlberg's moral development model with the three components of Allen and Meyer's organizational commitment, we contend that the external commitment and the primitive commitment need to be included to view sport volunteers' commitment from the developmental perspective. Along with these two new commitment concepts, the characteristics and theoretical reasoning related to each stage of sport volunteers' organizational commitment were addressed.

Introduction

In an era of financial constraints, governmental bodies have allocated static or even reduced budgets to public and nonprofit sport service organizations while at the same time demanding that organizations increase their service levels. Nonprofit sport service organizations depend heavily upon volunteers to provide direct leadership and supervision during times of fiscal constraint (Chelladurai, 2006). Kim, Chelladurai, and Trail (2007) argued that the involvement of citizens is essential to effectively and efficiently encounter fiscal stringency and raise levels of service. According to the Corporation for National Community Service (2011), about 26.3% of Americans volunteered 8.1 billion hours in 2010. In England and Australia, more than 25% of volunteers are involved in sport and recreation areas (Australian Bureau of Statistics, 2008; Institution for Volunteering Research, 1998).

Without the participation of volunteers, the provision and delivery of sport services might be degraded and reduced (Cuskelly, Hoye, & Auld, 2006; Cuskelly, Taylor, Hoye, & Darcy, 2006; Doherty & Carron, 2003). As volunteers have become increasingly important to sport service organizations, interest has grown in developing recruitment strategies, in-service training programs, and volunteer administrator programs. Recognizing the importance of effective volunteer management, Fairley, Kellett, and Green (2007) and Kim et al. (2007) noted that managerial efforts must be focused on existing volunteers first, before concentrating on recruiting new ones. The primary intent of sport organizations' volunteer programs may be effectively recruiting, retaining, and rewarding volunteers, resulting in a cohort of committed volunteers. More importantly, committed volunteers are essential for providing quality services (Kim, Patrice, & Rodríguez, 2008).

Thus, a better understanding of volunteers' organizational commitment may assist managers in attracting and retaining committed volunteers (Park, 2010). Based on previous commitment research (e.g., Cuskelly, McIntyre, & Boag, 1998; Meyer & Allen, 1997), Green and Chalip (2004) insisted that volunteer commitment is 'an evolving process that begins with expectations and that is carried forward by the nature of experiences that are obtained along the way' (p. 52). While explaining the phases of the volunteer socialization process, Haski-Leventhal and Bargal (2008) postulated that organizational commitment in volunteering not only changes over time but also is developmental in nature. Earlier, Kanter (1968) suggested that commitment be viewed in terms of a cognitive developmental process. Kanter proposed the different types of commitment binding a personality system to a social system, including cognitive orientation (the lowest level of commitment), socialization orientation (the middle level of commitment), and attachment to social norms and values (the highest level of commitment). These suggest that attitudinal organizational commitment can be viewed in terms of a cognitive developmental process from an external to an internal locus of control for internalizing a psychological state. However, despite researchers' continuous pondering on the possible development of volunteer commitment levels (e.g., Cuskelly, Harrington, & Stebbins, 2002/2003; Green & Chalip, 2004; Haski-Leventhal & Bargal, 2008), actual research or inquiry in the development process of volunteer commitment has been scant.

The purpose of this study is to understand sport volunteers' commitment to an organization from the developmental perspective and to propose a hierarchical model of sport volunteers' organizational commitment. The hierarchical model of sport volunteers' organizational commitment stemmed from Allen and Meyer's (1990) three-component model of organizational commitment but was expanded to five steps based on Kohlberg's (1969) model of moral development. Kohlberg's model was used as a guideline for three reasons. First, Kohlberg's model is known as one of well-described models to explain cognitive development processes that can relate volunteers' commitment development. In Kohlberg's model, the moral development processes of individuals include stages from external (lower stages) to internal (higher stages), as Ryan and Deci (2000) proposed in their social determination theory (i.e., extrinsic and intrinsic motives). These development processes and the subsequent theoretical reasoning in Kohlberg's model seem very relevant for developing the volunteers' organizational commitment model.

Second, many researchers in business ethics (Cullen, Parboteeah, & Victor, 2003; Schminke, Ambrose, & Neubaum, 2005; Street, 1995; Weeks, Loe, Chonko, & Wakefield, 2004; Weeks, Loe, Chonko, Martinez, & Wakefield, 2006) have shown the close relationship between ethics (i.e., moral development and ethical climate) and organizational commitment. Street (1995) insisted that individuals with high moral development were also likely to have high organizational commitment. Moreover, Weeks et al. (2004, 2006) found that moral development influenced the ethical climate which was related to organizational commitment. Based on previous research, it is assumed that volunteers' organizational commitment is closely related to their level of moral development (i.e., perception of what is good and what is bad). Hence, Kohlberg's moral development model may provide a relevant framework for expanding volunteers' organizational commitment to a hierarchical model.

Third, adopting Kohlberg's moral development model enables us to view volunteers' organizational commitment from the perspective of attitude change. Kelman (1958) proposed that individuals change their attitude and behaviors based on three types of social influence: compliance (i.e., accepting influence to receive a positive reaction from others), identification (i.e., accepting influence to build or maintain social relationships), and internalization (i.e., accepting influence because an individual truly believes it is right). Although Kohlberg's model was not developed based on social influence, each stage of the model includes social relations and reactions, which cannot be found in Allen and Meyer's organizational commitment model. Thus, by applying Kohlberg's model of moral development to Allen and Meyer's three-component model of organizational commitment, the hierarchical model of volunteer commitment can possibly embrace Kelman's three types of social influence. Thus, Kohlberg's moral development scheme provides a theoretical framework for understanding how the levels of sport volunteers' attitudinal organizational commitment develop.

Organizational commitment of volunteers

The concept of organizational commitment has received considerable attention in recent decades. Many researchers have studied organizational commitment by examining the antecedents and consequences of commitment (Lambert, Hogan, & Jiang, 2008; Lee & Peccei, 2007; Meyer, Allen, & Smith, 1993; Mowday, Porter, & Steers, 1982; Park, 2009). Researchers have found that volunteers' organizational commitment is associated with outcomes such as turnover intention (Cuskelly & Boag, 2001), job satisfaction (Costa, Chalip, Green, & Simes, 2006), job performance (Stephens, Dawley, & Stephens, 2004), willingness to be trained (Kim & Chelladurai, 2008), and intention for retention (Park, 2010).

Allen and Meyer (1990) developed a three-component model of organizational commitment, arguing that affective, continuance, and normative commitment be considered together as components of attitudinal commitment. Allen and Meyer defined affective commitment as an individual's emotional attachment to an organization. Continuance commitment refers to an individual's intention to be related to an organization because of the recognition of the costs of leaving or the rewards of staying, while normative commitment is defined as an individual's feeling of obligation to stay with an organization (Allen & Meyer, 1990). Although these three components of commitment together constitute organizational commitment, each component is regarded as conceptually distinct and is differently related to employees' organizational behaviors (Allen & Meyer, 1990; Lambert et al., 2008). Meyer, Paunonen, Gellatly, Goffin, and Jackson (1989) noted the differential effects of continuance and affective commitment on job performance, arguing that employees' affective commitment is positively associated with job performance, whereas their continuance commitment is associated with reduced turnover and is negatively related to job performance. Meyer, Stanley, Herscovitch, and Topolnytsky (2002) found in their meta-analysis on organizational commitment that both affective and normative commitment were correlated with various organizational outcomes (e.g., attendance, work performance, and organizational citizenship behavior), but the relationships of normative commitment with these outcomes were not as strong as those of affective commitment. In the volunteer context, Stephens et al. (2004) found that volunteer directors' levels of affective and normative commitment were positively associated with self-reported performance, emphasizing that affective commitment is most likely to exhibit a positive effect on job performance.

Kohlberg's model of moral development

Moral reasoning leading to ethical behavior has been viewed in terms of development processes. Piaget (1932) insisted that individuals' moral judgments were changed and developed through constructive stages over a lifetime. Following Piaget's work, Kohlberg (1969) asserted that an individual's decision making concerning what is right or wrong is strongly influenced by the individual's level and process of moral development principally in relation to justice. He further argued that morality is not linked to character but rather is defined by stages of moral reasoning. Kohlberg (1969) identified three levels of moral development, proclaiming that changes in moral judgment follow an unvarying developmental sequence of six irreversible stages (see Figure 1).

The first level of moral development is called the preconventional level, comprising stages 1 (obedience and punishment orientation) and 2 (naively egoistic and exchange orientation). At the preconventional level, individuals decide right and wrong mainly based on an egoistic perspective such as avoiding punishment or receiving rewards. The second level is the conventional level, comprising stages 3 (orientation to approval and pleasing others) and 4 (orientation to doing duty and regard for the earned expectations of others). At the conventional level, individuals' morally right actions refer to their social relationships or social context (e.g., peers, family, coworkers, and social cultures). The final level of moral development is the postconventional level, incorporating stages 5 (contractual legalistic orientation) and 6 (conscience or principle orientation). In stage 5, moral behaviors are what are

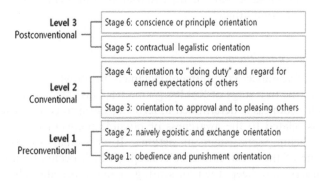

Figure 1.   Kohlberg's six stages of moral development. Source: Kohlberg (1986, pp. 57–58).

allowed by law and what are good for society in general, while in stage 6, moral reasoning is beyond personal benefits or legal systems and determines what is right based on abstract reasoning (Kohlberg, 1986).

Kohlberg (1986) posited that the stage sequence of his model would be identical in all cultures, because each stage is conceptually more advanced than the previous stage. Some scholars have criticized Kohlberg's model because it ignores gender and cultural differences. Kohlberg's model was originally developed based on an empirical study using a male-only sample; thus, Gilligan (1982) argued that the model ignored the female perspective. However, research using Kohlberg's model with both male and female samples did not show significant gender differences (Colby, Gibbs, Lieberman, & Kohlberg, 1983; Walker, 1989). Kohlberg's model has also been criticized as ignoring cultural differences (Crain, 1985). Kohlberg's model no doubt relies heavily on Western culture and philosophy; however, individuals in different cultures tend to move up through the stages proposed by Kohlberg, although the progress rates of individuals in different cultures are not identical (Harkness, Edwards, & Super, 1981).

Despite this criticism, Kohlberg's model has been utilized and cited by numerous researchers in many academic areas (Chesire & Karp, 2007; Chou, 1998; Cullen et al., 2003; Rest, Narvaez, Bebeau, & Thoma, 1999; Schminke et al., 2005; Schnodel & Kathryn, 2000; Street, 1995; Weeks et al., 2006). Beyond the academic fields of ethics and education, Kohlberg's model has often been cited in volunteer studies because the traditional view of volunteering includes altruism and morality (Chesire & Karp, 2007; Chou, 1998; Schnodel & Kathryn, 2000), and in business research associated with organizational commitment (Cullen et al., 2003; Schminke et al., 2005; Street, 1995; Weeks et al., 2006). However, no researcher has so far attempted to associate volunteer commitment with each stage of Kohlberg's model.

Developing the hierarchical model of volunteers' organizational commitment

As suggested by several researchers (Cuskelly et al., 2002/2003; Green & Chalip, 2004; Haski-Leventhal & Bargal, 2008), volunteer commitment can be viewed as an evolving and developing process. Thus, in this paper the hierarchical model of volunteer commitment is proposed by blending Kohlberg's (1969) model of moral development with Allen and Meyer's (1990) three-component model of organizational commitment; this hierarchical model comprises five stages: primitive commitment, continuous commitment, external commitment, normative commitment, and affective commitment.

Stage 1: primitive commitment

The first stage of volunteer commitment is named 'primitive commitment,' which is compatible with the first stage of Kohlberg's model. This stage of Kohlberg's scheme is one in which goodness is determined in terms of physical consequences. Primitive commitment is related to the awareness of possible punishment or the restriction derived from being inconsistent in actions. It is similar to Kelman's (1958) compliance, one of the social influence concepts, which occurs because individuals agree with others, but keep their dissenting opinion private. That is, primitive commitment occurs when individuals accept social influence to receive a favorable reward or avoid punishment. Primitive commitment, as proposed in this study, has not been identified or studied in the literature of organizational commitment thus far. Moreover, primitive commitment may not be commonly found among volunteers in a society where volunteerism is prevalent. Some might argue that volunteers with primitive commitment should not be called pure volunteers because their volunteering activities are not based on free will. However, many teenagers participate in mandatory community service as a graduation requirement (see Planty, Bozick, & Regnier, 2006), and some of them engage in sport volunteering. Those who participate in mandatory community service probably possess primitive commitment. Among adults, if employers ask their employees to volunteer for their own or sponsored sport events, some employees might volunteer unintentionally to avoid possible punishment. In addition, primitive commitment may possibly be applicable in some countries in which physical punishment is permitted or obedience to power is culturally required. For example, when South Korea hosted the 1988 Olympic Games, volunteering was not prevalent in Korean society; however, the Olympic Games required thousands of volunteers. Thus, the Korean government pressed government workers to volunteer during the Olympic Games (Kim, 2007). Although there was no apparent threat of physical punishment, it can be assumed that the government workers experienced some kind of pressure to obey the order to volunteer. In the competitive youth sport arena in some cultures where punishment is generally accepted and a coach can exert coercive power, the coach may force student-athletes to perform certain activities, for example, to volunteer for neighborhood sport programs. Thus, volunteers with primitive commitment would stop volunteering if the requirement or punishment were waived (Planty et al., 2006), and this may reduce their intention for future volunteering as well (Batson, Coke, Jasonski, & Hanson, 1978; Kunda & Schwartz, 1983). It is difficult to expect positive and direct outcomes related to volunteering at this level of commitment.

Stage 2: continuance commitment

The second stage of the volunteer commitment model is called 'continuance commitment,' which corresponds to the egoistic and exchange orientation of Kohlberg's model. At this stage in Kohlberg's model, an individual is concerned with external rewards and exchange. Hence, individuals make moral decisions based on their own interest and to obtain a fair deal. Continuance commitment relates to the awareness of the costs associated with leaving an organization. For instance, volunteers are reluctant to stop volunteering or change their volunteering organization to avoid the loss of benefits as their investment increases. Cuskelly et al. (2006) stressed the importance of well-designed compensation programs to increase volunteers' organizational commitment. This implies that when volunteers feel that the exchange is appropriate and that their investments are substantial, their commitment to an organization will be fostered. Indeed, several studies have revealed that instrumental factors (e.g., career-related motivation, education, and financial incentives) are significantly related to volunteers' intention to stay with or return to the respective organization (Kim, Won, & Harrolle, 2009; Mesch, Tschirhart, Perry, & Lee, 1998; Pearce, 1993; Strelow et al., 2002).

In addition, Stebbins (1996) indicated that some volunteers hope to gain experience as a job-finding strategy, which is labeled as marginal volunteering.

99

Marginal volunteers may be high on continuance commitment. College students volunteering in sport events or organizations for school credits or finding related job positions should be categorized as marginal volunteers who possess strong continuance commitment. It is clear that continuance commitment may not yield positive volunteering outcomes because of its calculative nature (see Meyer et al., 2002 for the case of paid employees). Thus, several scholars (Boezeman & Ellemers, 2008; Dawley, Stephens, & Stephens, 2005; Kim et al., 2008; Liao-Troth, 2001; Stephens et al., 2004) posited that continuance commitment may not be relevant to general volunteering contexts because of its instrumental ties between the volunteer and the organization.

However, volunteers with continuance commitment would be more willing to volunteer and, hence, be more favorable to the organization than volunteers with primitive commitment. Volunteers who are motivated because of exchange purposes may have a chance to be positively socialized into volunteerism, leading to a higher level of organizational commitment in the hierarchy. For example, many companies provide corporate volunteering programs that allow their employees to volunteer during their paid work hours. Employees who newly experience volunteering through such corporate volunteering programs and whose experiences are positive may develop a further interest in volunteering that is unrelated to any extrinsic benefits. This speculation can be supported by research in a sporting event. Although first-time volunteers at a particular event were less satisfied with their volunteering experiences than the returning volunteers, both types of volunteers showed a high intention to stay or return as long as their volunteering experiences remained satisfactory (Pauline, 2011).

Stage 3: external commitment

The third stage of the proposed model of volunteer commitment is called 'external commitment,' situated between continuance commitment and normative commitment. According to Kohlberg (1969), in the third stage (orientation to approval and to pleasing others) and the fourth stage (orientation to doing duty and regard for the earned expectations of others) of cognitive moral development, 'Moral value resides in performing good or right role in maintaining the conventional order and the expectancies of others' (p. 376). It means that goodness is defined as pleasing and seeking approval from significant others by conforming to their expectations. Kohlberg's third and fourth stages logically correspond to the external commitment phase proposed in this study. External commitment is defined as the recognition of social expectations and/or pressures on one's consistent line of actions from socially relevant or significant others.

It is logical to assume that some volunteers may develop a commitment to a particular sport organization because they feel pressured or expected to volunteer by socially relevant or significant others, not because of a personal moral standard or obligation to the organization. From the perspective of Kelman's (1958) social influence scheme, external commitment can be explained as an identification that involves accepting social influence to satisfy one's relationship with other individuals or groups. That is, volunteers are more likely to enact cooperative behaviors induced by external commitment (i.e., Kelman's identification) if they regard the social relationship as necessary or attractive. Moreover, external commitment relates to an individual's consistent line of action influenced by subcultural norms or the force of social expectations. According to Ajzen (1991), the major determinant of an individual's intention to perform a specific behavior is the subjective norm, defined as the perceived social pressure to perform or not to perform the behavior in question. An individual's participation in leisure activities (i.e., volunteering) is greatly influenced by social groups or subjective norms (Ajzen & Driver, 1991, 1992; Crandall, 1979; Young & Kent, 1985). Accordingly, some individuals may participate in volunteering, and continue to do so, to meet social expectations or after making public statements about engaging in such a good behavior (i.e., volunteering). Indeed, Hauser, Koontz, and Bruskotter (2012) found that subjective norms (i.e., others' expectations toward an individual's behavior) and personal requests were highly related to active volunteer participation.

In addition, the external commitment of volunteers, which is related to the perceived expectation of others, can also be understood from the perspective of role identity. The major source in developing volunteer role identity is known as perceived expectation of significant others (Grube & Piliavin, 2000). When the role-person merger (i.e., the degree to which the role reflects the self, Callero, Howard, & Piliavin, 1987, p. 250) occurs, individuals are more likely to engage in a particular act (Callero et al., 1987). According to Independent Sector (2001), 71% of volunteers initially engaged in volunteering after personal requests from others. Farrell, Johnston, and Twynam (1998) identified family tradition (i.e., external traditions) as an important motive for volunteering at a sporting event. Furthermore, supporting family and friends and favorable views of volunteering by significant others toward volunteering are listed as a common motive of volunteering in general (Clary et al., 1998) and specifically in the field of sport (Kim, Zhang, & Connaughton, 2010). In youth sport settings, many parents who sign up to coach may become committed because they perceive an expectation or pressure to volunteer from their children, family, or an organization's staff members. It is also logical to postulate that pressure to continue volunteering is determined by the perception of negative sanctions from significant others. Individuals with these volunteer motives might show strong external commitment.

Stage 4: normative commitment

The fourth stage of volunteer commitment is called 'normative commitment,' which is applicable to the fifth stage of Kohlberg's moral development, where good behavior is defined in terms of contractual and legalistic agreement. According to organizational behavior researchers (e.g., Allen & Meyer, 1990; Meyer & Allen, 1991; Prestholdt, Lane, & Mathews, 1987; Scholl, 1981; Wiener & Vardi, 1980), normative commitment derives from employees' sense of obligation to an organization. Wiener (1982) stressed that individuals deliver certain behaviors to meet organizational goals and interests 'not because they have figured that doing so is to their personal benefit, but because they believe that it is the "right" and moral thing to do,' based on 'totally internalized normative pressures' (p. 421). Thus, normative commitment in this study refers to a feeling of obligation to continue volunteering.

In the proposed model, the distinction between normative and external commitment depends on the degree of internalized obligation to a moral standard or normative pressure to be consistent. Whereas external commitment relates to an orientation toward pleasing others and meeting others' expectations without feeling indebted or obligated to the organization, normative commitment is associated with an internalized responsibility and obligation to a moral standard or right. It is contended that recognizing expectations from others does not necessarily incur an internal moral obligation to continue a certain action. Accordingly, the concept of normative commitment differs from the dimension of external commitment in this study.

Unlike paid employees, volunteers are not generally bound to the organization by any legal or written agreement. However, possible normative commitment of volunteers can be inferred based on the psychological contract theory. A psychological contract is a perceived mutual agreement between two parties. According to the psychological contract theory, an individual (i.e., a volunteer in the proposed model) and an organization act to fulfill the perceived mutual promises between the individual and the organization (Rousseau, 1995). In other words, sport volunteers possess sets of expectations and obligations and behave based on these perceived obligations (Taylor, Darcy, Hoye, & Cuskelly, 2006). Kim, Trail, Lim, and Kim (2009) also noted that a psychological contract indirectly impacts volunteers' adherence to volunteering. That is, volunteers perceiving strong obligations toward the organization probably possess high normative commitment. Volunteers with high normative commitment would be more beneficial for an organization and are more likely to stay longer than those who are committed based on external factors (i.e., primitive, continuance, or external commitment).

Stage 5: affective commitment

'Affective commitment' in the model is relevant to the sixth stage of Kohlberg's scheme (conscience or principal orientation) in which an individual follows self-selected ethical principles and becomes decreasingly egocentric. Affective commitment refers to an individual's identification and involvement with a particular organization as well as willingness to support it (Allen & Meyer, 1990). Meyer et al. (2002) found that affective commitment was more strongly related to several positive organizational outcomes (i.e., attendance, work performance, and organizational citizenship behavior) than normative and continuance commitment. Hence, affective commitment is regarded as the most crucial organizational commitment. Some researchers consider only affective commitment as true and genuine organizational commitment. Buchanan (1974) defined organizational commitment as 'a partisan, affective attachment to the goals and values of an organization, to one's role in relation to goals and values, and to the organization for its own sake, apart from its purely instrumental worth' (p. 533).

Affective commitment is very closely related to organizational identification (Gautam, Van Dick, & Wagner, 2004). Organizational identification refers to the degree to which an individual defines the self in terms of organizational membership (Ashforth & Mael, 1989). Thus, individuals with strong organizational identification tend to be intrinsically motivated (Ellemers, De Gilder, & Haslam, 2004) and perform cooperative, supportive, and group-oriented behaviors (Tyler & Blader, 2001, 2002, 2003). Knippenberg and Sleebos (2006) pointed out that the core difference between affective commitment and organizational identification is the degree of self-reference to the organization. However, affective commitment seems closer to organizational identification among volunteers than among paid employees because unlike most of paid employees, volunteers choose the organization based on its value and mission without expecting any financial reimbursement (see volunteer motivation, Clary et al., 1998). In other words, volunteers might more readily identify themselves with their respective organizations.

In the proposed model, the distinguishing characteristic of affective commitment is a volunteer's internalization of the organization's values and goals, which is closely related to Kelman's (1958) concept of the internalization of social influence. In this stage, volunteers look beyond contractual agreement, external pressure, or exchange orientation, and feel like a 'part of the family' in the organization. In this stage, volunteers might possess strong intrinsic motivation while those in the lower stages of commitment are more likely to behave based on extrinsic motivation (see the self-determination theory, Ryan & Deci, 2000). Moreover, intrinsically motivated pro-social behaviors tend to be sustained over time (Villacorta, Koestner, & Lekes, 2003). That is, volunteers with affective commitment might stay longer with their respective sport organizations. In fact, affective commitment was found to be positively associated with volunteers' feeling of pride and being respected (Boezeman & Ellemers, 2008). Furthermore, among sport volunteers, affective commitment is related to perceived organizational support (Bang, 2011; Pulis & Hoye, 2010), which leads to an intention to continue volunteering (Park, 2010). Volunteers with strong affective commitment might be ideal volunteers for sport organizations because they are the most favorable to organizational success and are willing to devote themselves to their organizations.

Conclusion

The present study extends previous research on organizational commitment by developing a theory-based model of sport volunteers' organizational commitment using Kohlberg's moral development scheme as a guiding framework. Although the stages in the proposed model are based on Kohlberg's stages of moral development, it should be noted that not all volunteerism can be conceived as a moral endeavor, and that moral commitment does not represent the zenith of the hierarchy. Thus, the ultimate goal of volunteer management is not just to make sport volunteers morally committed but to make them affectively committed to the respective organization. Kohlberg's stages of cognitive moral development describe a progression of ways of conceptualizing volunteers' organizational commitment from an external to an internal locus of control for internalizing a psychological state, which is also supported by the self-determination theory (Ryan & Deci, 2000) and Kelman's (1958) processes of social influence. Kohlberg's moral development scheme provides a theoretical framework to understand how the levels of sport volunteers' organizational commitment develop (see Figure 2), thus clarifying the differential influence of various factors along the vertical hierarchy. It is proposed that the construct of volunteers' attitudinal commitment is developmental in nature as suggested by many other researchers (Cuskelly et al., 2002/2003; Green & Chalip, 2004; Haski-Leventhal & Bargal, 2008; Kanter, 1968). In this present study, the five stages of volunteer commitment include primitive commitment, continuance commitment, external commitment, normative commitment, and affective commitment, which are organized sequentially and hierarchically.

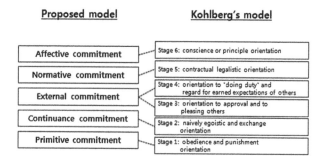

Figure 2.   Hierarchical model of sport volunteers' organizational commitment.

In proposing the hierarchical model of volunteer commitment, two new concepts of organizational commitment (primitive commitment and external commitment) were proposed in addition to Allen and Meyer's (1990) three components of organizational commitment. Primitive commitment might not be commonly observed among sport volunteers in Western countries; however, it was proposed because it could be the beginning of volunteer commitment where physical punishment is culturally accepted or obedience to authority is culturally prevalent. Moreover, the model incorporated external commitment because significant others and societal culture can influence an individual to engage in or continue with volunteering activities.

The transitions in sport volunteers' organizational commitment may not occur simply with the passage of time but rather result from processes that lead them from one stage to the next. In addition, the proposed hierarchical model of volunteer commitment does not imply that the commitment of every sport volunteer invariably develops from stages 1 to 5. It is important to note that the vertical hierarchy is not constrained exclusively to upward transition; nor do volunteers necessarily move from one extreme to the other. While adopting Kohlberg's framework, we assume that volunteers in sport contexts may not always operate from a single fixed stage of attitudinal commitment development. What is suggested here is that commitment in the higher stages is a more psychologically attached and internalized type of commitment and more favorable for sport organizations. Furthermore, it is necessary to analyze and apply the proposed hierarchical model of sport volunteers' organizational commitment to the management of sport volunteers after considering the specific characteristics of the sport organization as well as the sport volunteers.

Further empirical research is needed to finally confirm the proposed model. As the first step, in addition to Allen and Meyer's (1990) Organizational Commitment Scale, new instruments to measure primitive and external commitment should be developed. The newly developed scales will enable researchers to indicate whether or not the newly proposed concepts of volunteers' organizational commitment are constructed based upon the characteristics previously noted. Then, the proposed model should be empirically tested although testing the hierarchical model or relationships is known to be challenging. In order to develop a reliable and valid instrument for testing the proposed model, both quantitative and qualitative approaches should be used. As one way of testing the model, researchers may interview volunteers with different stages of commitment and search for different perceptions, attitudes, and behaviors associated with each stage of commitment.

After identifying the unique characteristics of each commitment stage, the quantitative approach may be applied to explore the empirical differences between the commitment stages.

Also, various organizational constructs should be tested with the proposed stages of volunteer commitment. Organizational commitment is known as a key construct related to many positive outcomes such as turnover intention (Cuskelly & Boag, 2001), job satisfaction (Costa et al., 2006), job performance (Stephens et al., 2004), willingness to be trained (Kim & Chelladurai, 2008), and intention to continue volunteering (Park, 2010). Thus, future research should focus on how these constructs are differently related to each stage of volunteers' organizational commitment. Furthermore, the proposed model might be strengthened by empirical research identifying the relationships of volunteer motivation and perceived organizational support at each organizational stage because these two constructs were used to explain the characteristics of the commitment stages of the proposed model.

Once it is empirically tested, the proposed model might suggest several managerial implications. The proposed model could help sport managers identify distinct motives for volunteers at each commitment stage and provide ideas for developing volunteer programs that appeal to volunteers at each commitment stage. Furthermore, the application of this model could serve as a diagnostic tool that allows sport managers to appropriately motivate volunteers based on their stages of organizational commitment. Research on the development of volunteer commitment might have a long way to go. However, the proposed study takes the first step of actually proposing the hierarchical model based on various theories and literature. The hierarchical model is important because it explains transitions between stages and details the processes and attitudes involved in each stage. The proposed model may serve as a guiding framework for further research on volunteers' organizational commitment, involving detailed stages and transitions.

References

Ajzen, I. (1991). The theory of planned behavior. *Organizational Behavior and Human Decision Processes, 50*, 179–211.

Ajzen, I., & Driver, B.L. (1991). Prediction of leisure participation from behavioral, normative, and control beliefs: An application of the theory of planned behavior. *Leisure Sciences, 13*, 185–204.

Ajzen, I., & Driver, B.L. (1992). Application of the theory of planned behavior to leisure choice. *Journal of Leisure Research, 24*, 207–224.

Allen, N.J., & Meyer, J.P. (1990). The measurement and antecedents of affective, continuance, and normative commitment to the organization. *Journal of Occupational Psychology, 63*, 1–8.

Ashforth, B.E., & Mael, F. (1989). Social identity theory and the organization. *Academy of Management Review, 14*, 20–39.

Australian Bureau of Statistics. (2008). *Australian social trends, 2008: Volunteer work.* Retrieved from http://www.abs.gov.au/AUSSTATS/abs@.nsf/Lookup/4102.0Chapter4102008

Bang, H. (2011). Leader-member exchange, perceived organizational support, and affective organizational commitment of volunteer members in non-profit sport organizations. *International Journal of Sport Management, 12*(1), 63–85.

Batson, C.D., Coke, J.S., Jasonski, M.L., & Hanson, M. (1978). Buying kindness: Effect of an extrinsic incentive for helping on perceived altruism. *Personality and Social Psychological Bulletin, 4*, 86–91.

Boezeman, E.J., & Ellemers, A.N. (2008). Pride and respect in volunteers' organizational commitment. *European Journal of Social Psychology, 38*, 159–172.

Buchanan, B. (1974). Building organizational commitment: The socialization of managers in work organizations. *Administrative Science Quarterly, 4*, 553–546.

Callero, P.L., Howard, J.A., & Piliavin, J.A. (1987). Helping behavior as role behavior: Disclosing social structure and history in the analysis of pro-social action. *Social Psychology Quarterly, 50*, 247–256.

Chelladurai, P. (2006). *Human resource management in sport and recreation* (2nd ed.). Champaign, IL: Human Kinetics.

Chesire, J.D., & Karp, D.R. (2007). Volunteer management in boards of probation: Perceptions of equality, efficiency, and reciprocity among Vermont volunteers. *Journal of Offender Rehabilitation, 44*(4), 65–99.

Chou, K. (1998). Effects of age, gender, and participation in volunteer activities on the altruistic behavior of Chinese adolescents. *Journal of Genetic Psychology, 159*(2), 195–201.

Clary, E.G., Snyder, M., Ridge, R.D., Copeland, J., Stukas, A.A., Haugen, J., & Miene, P. (1998). Understanding and assessing the motivations of volunteers: A functional approach. *Journal of Personality and Social Psychology, 74*(6), 1516–1530.

Colby, A., Gibbs, J., Lieberman, M., & Kohlberg, L. (1983). *A longitudinal study of moral judgment: A monograph for the society of research in child development.* Chicago, IL: University of Chicago Press.

Corporation for National Community Service. (2011). *Volunteering in America research highlight.* Retrieved from http://www.volunteeringinamerica.gov/assets/resources/FactSheet Final.pdf

Costa, C.A., Chalip, L., Green, B.C., & Simes, C. (2006). Reconsidering the role of training in event volunteers' satisfaction. *Sport Management Review, 9*, 165–182.

Crain, W.C. (1985). *Theories of development: Concept and applications* (2nd ed.). Englewood Cliffs, NJ: Prentice-Hall.

Crandall, R. (1979). Social interaction, affect and leisure. *Journal of Leisure Research, 11*, 165–181.

Cullen, J.B., Parboteeah, K.P., & Victor, B. (2003). The effects of ethical climates on organizational commitment: A two-study analysis. *Journal of Business Ethics, 46*, 127–141.

Cuskelly, G., & Boag, A. (2001). Organisational commitment as a predictor of committee member turnover among volunteer sport administrators: Results of a time-lagged study. *Sport Management Review, 4*, 65–86.

Cuskelly, G., Harrington, M., & Stebbins, R.A. (2002/2003). Changing levels of organizational commitment amongst sport volunteers: A serious leisure approach. *Leisure/Loisir, 27*(3/4), 191–212.

Cuskelly, G., Hoye, R., & Auld, C. (2006). *Working with volunteers in sport: Theory and practice.* New York, NY: Routledge.

Cuskelly, G., McIntyre, N., & Boag, A. (1998). A longitudinal study of the development of organizational commitment among volunteer sport administrators. *Journal of Sport Management, 12*, 181–202.

Cuskelly, G., Taylor, T., Hoye, R., & Darcy, S. (2006). Volunteer management practices and volunteer retention: A human resource management approach. *Sport Management Review, 9*, 141–163.

Dawley, D.D., Stephens, R.D., & Stephens, D.B. (2005). Dimensionality of organizational commitment in volunteer workers: Chamber of commerce board members and role fulfillment. *Journal of Vocational Behavior, 67*, 511–525.

Doherty, A.J., & Carron, A.V. (2003). Cohesion in volunteer sport executive committees. *Journal of Management, 12*, 181–202.

Ellemers, N., De Gilder, D., & Haslam, S.A. (2004). Motivating individuals and groups at work: A social identity perspective on leadership and group performance. *Academy of Management Review, 29*, 459–478.

Fairley, S., Kellett, P., & Green, B.C. (2007). Volunteering abroad: Motives for travel to volunteer at the Athens Olympic Games. *Journal of Sport Management, 21*, 41–57.

Farrell, J.M., Johnston, M.E., & Twynam, G.D. (1998). Volunteer motivation, satisfaction, and management at an elite sporting competition. *Journal of Sport Management, 12*, 288–300.

Gautam, T., Van Dick, R., & Wagner, U. (2004). Organizational identification and organizational commitment: Distinct aspects of two related concepts. *Asian Journal of Social Psychology, 7*(3), 301–315.

Gilligan, C. (1982). In a different voice: Women's conceptions of self and morality. *Harvard Educational Review, 47*(4), 481–517.

Green, B.C., & Chalip, L. (2004). Paths to volunteer commitment: Lessons from Sydney Olympic Games. In R.A. Stebbins & M. Graham (Eds.), *Volunteering as leisure/leisure as volunteering: An international assessment* (pp. 49–68). Wallingford: CAB International.

Grube, J.A., & Piliavin, J.A. (2000). Role identity, organizational experiences, and volunteer performance. *Personality and Social Psychology Bulletin, 26*, 1108–1120.

Harkness, S., Edwards, C.P., & Super, C.M. (1981). The claim to moral adequacy of a highest stage of moral judgment. *Developmental Psychology, 17*(5), 595–603.

Haski-Leventhal, D., & Bargal, D. (2008). The volunteer stages and transitions model: Organizational socialization of volunteers. *Human Relations, 61*, 67–102.

Hauser, B.K., Koontz, T.M., & Bruskotter, J.T. (2012). Volunteer participation in collaborative watershed partnerships: Insights from the theory of planned behaviour. *Journal of Environmental Planning and Management, 55*, 77–94.

Independent Sector. (2001). *Giving and volunteering in the United States.* Retrieved from http://www.angelfire.com/journal2/comunicarse7/GV01keyfind.pdf

Institution for Volunteering Research. (1998). *1997 national survey of volunteering.* Retrieved from www.ivr.org.uk/nationalsurvey.htm

Kanter, R.M. (1968). Commitment and social organization: A study of commitment mechanism in utopian communities. *American Sociological Review, 33*, 499–517.

Kelman, H.C. (1958). Compliance, identification, and internalization: Three processes of attitude change. *Journal of Conflict Resolution, 2*, 51–60.

Kim, M. (2007, November). *Spreading volunteerism through the Olympic Games.* Oral session presented at the 28th annual conference of North American Society of Sport Sociology, Pittsburgh, PA.

Kim, M., & Chelladurai, P. (2008). Volunteer preferences for training: Influences of individual difference factors. *International Journal of Sport Management, 9*, 233–249.

Kim, M., Chelladurai, P., & Trail, G.T. (2007). A model of volunteer retention in youth sport. *Journal of Sport Management, 21*, 151–171.

Kim, M., Patrice, J.N., & Rodríguez, A. (2008). Influence of work status on organizational commitment and sport identity of university athletic department workers. *Journal of Issues in Intercollegiate Athletics, 1*, 74–86.

Kim, M., Trail, G.T., Lim, J., & Kim, Y.K. (2009). The role of psychological contract in intention to continue volunteering. *Journal of Sport Management, 23*, 549–573.

Kim, M., Won, D., & Harrolle, M.G. (2009). The influences of gifts on perspective volunteers: A conjoint analysis. *International Journal of Sport Management, 10*, 1–17.

Kim, M., Zhang, J.J., & Connaughton, D.P. (2010). Modification of volunteer functions inventory for sport settings. *Sport Management Review, 13*, 25–38.

Knippenberg, D.V., & Sleebos, E. (2006). Organizational identification versus organizational commitment: Self-definition, social exchange, and job attitudes. *Journal of Organizational Behavior, 27*, 571–584.

Kohlberg, L. (1969). Stage and sequence: The cognitive-developmental approach to socialization. In D.A. Goslin (Ed.), *Handbook of socialization theory and research* (pp. 347–480). Chicago, IL: Rand McNally.

Kohlberg, L. (1986). *The philosophy of moral development.* San Francisco, CA: Harper and Row.

Kunda, Z., & Schwartz, S. (1983). Undermining intrinsic moral motivation: External reward and self-presentation. *Journal of Personality and Social Psychology, 45*, 763–771.

Lambert, E.G., Hogan, N.L., & Jiang, S. (2008). Exploring antecedents of five types of organizational commitment among correctional staff: It matters what you measure. *Criminal Justice Policy Review, 19*, 466–490.

Lee, J., & Peccei, R. (2007). Organizational-level gender dissimilarity and employee commitment. *British Journal of Industrial Relations, 45,* 687–712.

Liao-Troth, M.A. (2001). Attitude differences between paid workers and volunteers. *Nonprofit Management and Leadership, 11,* 423–442.

Mesch, D.J., Tschirhart, M., Perry, J.L., & Lee, G. (1998). Altruists or egoists: Retention in stipended service. *Nonprofit Management and Leadership, 9,* 3–21.

Meyer, J.P., & Allen, N.J. (1991). A three-component conceptualization of organizational commitment. *Human Resource Management Review, 1,* 61–89.

Meyer, J.P., & Allen, N.J. (1997). *Commitment in the workplace: Theory, research, and application.* Thousand Oaks, CA: Sage Publications.

Meyer, J.P., Allen, N.J., & Smith, C.A. (1993). Commitment to organizations and occupations: Extension and test of a three-component conceptualization. *Journal of Applied Psychology, 78,* 538–551.

Meyer, J.P., Paunonen, S.V., Gellatly, I.R., Goffin, R.D., & Jackson, D.N. (1989). Organizational commitment and job performance: It's the nature of the commitment that counts. *Journal of Applied Psychology, 74,* 152–156.

Meyer, J.P., Stanley, D.J., Herscovitch, L., & Topolnytsky, L. (2002). Affective, continuance, and normative commitment to the organization: A meta-analysis of antecedents, correlates, and consequences. *Journal of Vocational Behavior, 61*(1), 20–52.

Mowday, R.T., Porter, L.W., & Steers, R.M. (1982). *Employee-organization linkages: The psychology of commitment, absenteeism, and turnover.* New York, NY: Academic Press.

Park, S.H. (2009). The causal relationships among involvement, satisfaction, and organizational commitment for volunteers in recreational sport programs. *Journal of Leisure and Recreation Studies, 33*(3), 193–203.

Park, S.H. (2010). The influence of respect from the organization and affective organizational commitment among volunteers for leisure service. *Journal of Leisure and Recreation Studies, 34*(3), 141–148.

Pauline, G. (2011). Volunteer satisfaction and intent to remain: An analysis of contributing factors among professional golf event volunteers. *International Journal of Event Management Research, 6,* 10–32.

Pearce, J.L. (1993). *Volunteers: The organizational behavior of unpaid workers.* New York, NY: Routledge.

Piaget, J. (1932). *The moral judgment of the child.* London: Routledge and Kegan Paul.

Planty, M., Bozick, R., & Regnier, M. (2006). Helping because you have to or helping because you want to? Sustaining participation in service work from adolescence to young adulthood. *Youth and Society, 38,* 177–202.

Prestholdt, P.H., Lane, I.M., & Mathews, R.C. (1987). Nurse turnover as reasoned action: Development of a process model. *Journal of Applied Psychology, 72*(2), 221–227.

Pulis, L., & Hoye, R. (2010, September). *The relationship between sport event volunteers' commitment, satisfaction, and perceived organizational support.* Oral session presented at the 18th annual conference of European Association for Sport Management, Prague, Czech Republic.

Rest, J., Narvaez, D., Bebeau, M., & Thoma, S. (1999). DIT-2: Devising and testing a new instrument of moral judgment. *Journal of Educational Psychology, 91,* 644–659.

Rousseau, D.M. (1995). *Psychological contracts in organization: Understanding written and unwritten agreements.* Newbury Park, CA: Sage.

Ryan, R.M., & Deci, E.L. (2000). Self-determination theory and the facilitation of intrinsic motivation, social development, and well-being. *American Psychologist, 55,* 68–78.

Schminke, M., Ambrose, M.L., & Neubaum, D.O. (2005). The effect of leader moral development on ethical climate and employee attitudes. *Organizational Behavior and Human Decision Processes, 97,* 135–151.

Schnodel, C.K., & Kathryn, E. (2000). Motivational needs of adolescent volunteers. *Adolescence, 35*(138), 335–344.

Scholl, R.W. (1981). Differentiating organizational commitment from expectancy as a motivating force. *Academy of Management Review, 4,* 589–599.

Stebbins, R.A. (1996). Volunteering: A serious leisure perspective. *Nonprofit and Voluntary Sector Quarterly, 25*, 211–224.

Stephens, R.D., Dawley, D.D., & Stephens, D.B. (2004). Commitment on the board: A model of volunteer directors' levels of organizational commitment and self-reported performance. *Journal of Managerial Issues, 16*, 483–504.

Street, M.D. (1995). Cognitive moral development and organizational commitment: Two potential predictors of whistle-blowing. *Journal of Applied Business Research, 11*(4), 104–110.

Strelow, J.S., Larsen, J.S., Sallis, J.F., Conway, T.L., Powers, H.S., & Mckenzie, T.L. (2002). Factors influencing the performance of volunteers who provide physical activity in middle schools. *Journal of School Health, 72*(4), 147–151.

Taylor, T., Darcy, S., Hoye, R., & Cuskelly, G. (2006). Using psychological contract theory to explore issues in effective volunteer management. *European Sport Management Quarterly, 6*, 123–147.

Tyler, T.R., & Blader, S.L. (2001). Identity and cooperative behavior in groups. *Group Processes and Intergroup Relations, 4*, 207–226.

Tyler, T.R., & Blader, S.L. (2002). Autonomous vs. comparative status: Must we be better than others to feel good about ourselves? *Organizational Behavior and Human Decision Processes, 89*, 813–838.

Tyler, T.R., & Blader, S.L. (2003). The group engagement model: Procedural justice, social identity, and cooperative behavior. *Personality and Social Psychology Review, 7*(4), 349–361.

Villacorta, M., Koestner, R., & Lekes, N. (2003). Further validation of the motivation toward the environment scale. *Environment and Behavior, 35*, 486–505.

Walker, L.J. (1989). A longitudinal study of moral reasoning. *Child Development, 60*(1), 157–166.

Weeks, W.A., Loe, T.W., Chonko, L.B., Martinez, C.R., & Wakefield, K. (2006). Cognitive moral development and the impact of perceived organizational ethical climate on the search for sales force excellence: A cross-cultural study. *Journal of Personal Selling and Sales Management, 26*(2), 205–217.

Weeks, W.A., Loe, T.W., Chonko, L.B., & Wakefield, K. (2004). The effect of perceived ethical climate on the search for sales force excellence. *Journal of Personal Selling and Sales Management, 24*(3), 199–213.

Wiener, Y. (1982). Commitment in organizations: A normative view. *Academy of Management Review, 7*, 418–428.

Wiener, Y., & Vardi, Y. (1980). Relationships between job, organization, and career commitments and work outcomes – an integrative approach. *Organizational Behavior and Human Performance, 15*, 54–62.

Young, R.A., & Kent, A.T. (1985). Using the theory of reasoned action to improve the understanding of recreation behavior. *Journal of Leisure Research, 17*, 90–106.

A multi-level framework for investigating the engagement of sport volunteers

Pamela Wicker[a] and Kirstin Hallmann[b]

[a]Department of Tourism, Leisure, Hotel and Sport Management, Griffith University, Gold Coast Campus, Southport, Queensland, Australia; [b]Institute of Sport Economics and Sport Management, German Sport University Cologne, Cologne, Germany

Previous research has extensively investigated the drivers of the decision to volunteer on an individual level. As volunteering usually occurs within an institutional context (e.g., sport club and sport event), the characteristics of the institution must also be considered; however, they have been largely neglected in previous research. A review of the literature on both levels reveals both theoretical and methodological shortcomings which this paper attempts to address. The individual and institutional perspectives are combined resulting in a multi-level framework for the investigation of the drivers of volunteer engagement. Drawing on the heterodox approach and the concept of organizational capacity, the framework consists of an individual and an institutional level. Suggestions for indicators and statistical modeling (multi-level analysis) are provided. The suggested multi-level framework and the multi-level analysis can open new perspectives for research on volunteers in sport.

Introduction

Volunteers are a central part of today's societies in many countries as they make substantial contributions to communities at many levels (Cuskelly, Hoye, & Auld, 2006). Volunteers guarantee the functioning of many nonprofit sport clubs through their engagement and the operation of major and mega sport events (Adams & Deane, 2009; Fairley, Kellett,& Green, 2007; Lasby & Sperling, 2007; Vos, Breesch, & Késenne, 2012). In many countries, most sport clubs are run exclusively with volunteers as they have no paid staff (e.g., Gumulka, Barr, Lasby, & Brownlee, 2005; Lamprecht, Fischer, & Stamm, 2011). Moreover, many individuals opt to be part of a diverse range of sport events. Indeed, voluntary engagement is a key element for the production process and the staging of sport events (Getz, 1997). Through the engagement of individuals as volunteers, social capital on individual, organizational, and community levels can be accumulated. Onyx and Leonard (2000, p. 113) suggest that volunteering 'is at the heart of social capital.'

Both authors contributed equally to this article.

Generally speaking, volunteering is used as the umbrella term for nonsalaried services (Cnaan, Handy, & Wadsworth, 1996) and incorporates some form of altruistic benefit for the individual volunteer (Unger, 1991). In simple terms, volunteers are persons who work without coercion and without payment (Horch, 1994). Thus, a vital principle of volunteering is the exchange of work without direct remuneration. Nevertheless, volunteers make substantial contributions to communities and organizations. The monetary value of the hours volunteers spent in sport clubs amounted to, for example, €420 million in Flanders, Belgium (Vos et al., 2012), CHF2 billion in Switzerland (Lamprecht et al., 2011), and €6.7 billion in Germany (Breuer & Wicker, 2011). Although volunteers represent the main nonmonetary resource of sport organizations, many organizations experience difficulties in recruiting and retaining volunteers (Lamprecht et al., 2011; Lasby & Sperling, 2007; Sport and Recreation Alliance, 2011). A shortage of core volunteers (e.g., Seippel, 2004) or secondary volunteers (Sharpe, 2006) has been reported by the organizations. A comparison of volunteer numbers and workload per volunteer indicates that 'much comes from the few' (Lasby & Sperling, 2007, p. 33). The recruitment and retention of volunteers is also considered a challenge for major sport events like the Olympic Games (e.g., Fairley et al., 2007).

Considering the current situation, it is important to be aware of the various drivers of voluntary engagement, and adequate theoretical frameworks can help to further understand volunteers. In doing so, it must be considered that voluntary engagement is not only driven by individual factors, but usually happens in an institutional context (e.g., sport organization, sport event; Penner, 2002). It is therefore crucial that institutional circumstances are also considered. Hence, this paper suggests a multi-level framework that takes both individual factors (micro-level) and institutional factors (macro-level) into account. Along with the suggestion of a framework, another purpose of the paper is to create an application for the research. The multi-level framework advances the following research question: What individual and institutional factors drive the decision to engage as a volunteer in sport? A literature review indicates that several theories have been applied for investigating volunteers in sport; however, previous research has mainly focused on only one perspective (individual or institutional) and has not combined both perspectives. This paper contributes to the body of research on volunteers in sport by suggesting a theoretical multi-level framework to be applied by sport management scholars in future research on sport volunteerism.

Literature review

Individual level

Volunteering is associated with a range of positive outcomes such as socialization, well-being, and personal growth (e.g., Morrow-Howell, Hong, & Tang, 2009). Thus, there is a plethora of theories that have been used to describe voluntary engagement and working in the sport sector on an individual level (for an overview, see Table 1). Nonetheless, Cuskelly, Hoye et al. (2006) noted that the majority of studies on sport event volunteers are a theoretical and include only few implications for volunteer management (see also Skirstad & Hanstad, 2011). However, this is not the case for all studies in this research strand, and thus employed theories and their application are

Table 1. Overview of studies on the individual level (in a chronological order; without intending to be exhaustive).

Author(s)	Theory/concept	Method	Key findings
Skirstad and Hanstad (2011), Norway	No specific theory*	Quantitative survey; $n = 659$ event volunteers (FIS World Cup); t-test, factor analysis	Men volunteered more often because of their own interest in sport (intrinsic motivation), while women looked for events to strengthen their human and social capital to be used in the labor market. Young women were led by extrinsic motives
Brown et al. (2011), New Zealand	No specific theory*	Qualitative (case-study approach), document analysis, semi-structured interviews, focus groups; content analysis	Perceived creation of social capital was confirmed. Volunteers from within the community and paid crew share a common incentive for supporting events
Bang et al. (2010), USA	Social exchange theory	Quantitative survey; $n = 163$ event volunteers (triathlon); factor analysis, regression	Results confirmed the postulated seven dimensions of volunteer motivation, interpersonal contacts, love of sport, and personal growth as volunteer motivation factors had significant influence on volunteers' commitment to the sporting event
Kim et al. (2010), USA	Functional approach	Quantitative survey; $n = 1099$ volunteers working at international, national, local, and special-needs youth sport organizations/events; factor analysis, MANOVA	The Volunteer Functions Inventory which was modified for youth sport settings was identified as a valid and reliable scale. The six factors are value, understanding, social, career, protective, and enhancement
Allen and Shaw (2009), New Zealand	Self-determination theory	Qualitative; four focus groups, $n = 16$; content analysis	Three themes reflected the self-determination continuum: intrinsic motivation, self-determined 'mucking-in' extrinsic motivation, and lack of externally controlled extrinsic motivation
Bang and Ross (2009), USA	Self-determination theory	Quantitative survey; $n = 254$ event volunteers (marathon); factor analysis, regression	Results confirmed the postulated seven dimension of volunteer motivation. Expression of values, career orientation, and love of sport predicted best the level of volunteer satisfaction

Table 1 (*Continued*)

Author(s)	Theory/concept	Method	Key findings
Bang et al. (2009), USA/Greece	Social identity theory	Quantitative survey; $n = 206$ event volunteers (Olympic Games); factor analysis, MANOVA	Results confirmed the dimensions expression of values, patriotism, interpersonal contacts, personal growth, career orientation, extrinsic rewards, love for sport for motivation. Differences in motivations were found regarding marital status and gender
Doherty (2009), Canada	Social exchange theory	Quantitative survey; $n = 247$ planning volunteers and $n = 851$ on-site sport event volunteers (Canada Summer Games); factor analysis, MANOVA, ANOVA, regression	Planning volunteers' future volunteering was influenced by experienced costs of the event (task overload, personal inconvenience), and partly by contributing to the community and positive life experience. On-site volunteers' future volunteering was more influenced by experienced benefits of the event, including social enrichment, community contribution, and positive life experience
Hamm-Kerwin et al. (2009), Canada	Role theory	Qualitative interviews; $n = 20$; content analysis using open coding	A multi-dimensional framework was used and confirmed structural, cultural, cognitive, and situational dimensions of the volunteer experience. The majority of older volunteers had been involved previously in sports as athletes
Kim et al. (2009), USA	Theory of planned behavior, social contract theory, theory of work adjustment	Quantitative survey; $n = 224$ volunteers of the State Summer Games Special Olympics; SEM	Control beliefs of individuals are related to future behavior. Person–environment fit is related to empowerment which in turn mediates the relationship between person–environment fit and behavior. Relationship between person–environment fit and empowerment became weaker, as the psychological contract became fulfilled
Sakires et al. (2009), Canada	Concept of role ambiguity	Quantitative survey; $n = 79$ paid staff and $n = 143$ board members of voluntary sport organizations; CFA, correlation analyses, regression analyses	Role ambiguity consists of three dimensions: scope of responsibilities, means–ends knowledge, and performance outcome. Greater role clarity was associated with greater satisfaction, commitment, and effort. Scope of responsibilities has a positive impact on job satisfaction and organizational commitment, while means–ends knowledge and performance outcomes have a positive effect on effort

Table 1 (*Continued*)

Author(s)	Theory/concept	Method	Key findings
Bendle and Patterson (2008), Australia	Serious leisure	Qualitative survey using semi-structured interviews; $n = 41$; probably some sort of content analysis	Local voluntary groups are active in the local community and each artist group relies heavily on a small number of members who also undertake leadership duties and responsibilities to manage their group's activities and events. These members were identified as combining their creative amateur or hobbyist pursuits with a career volunteer role within their group
Boezemann and Ellemers (2007), The Netherlands	Social identity theory	Quantitative survey; $n = 172$ and $n = 164$ volunteers of a nonprofit organization; SEM	Volunteer organizations may do well to implement pride and respect in their volunteer policy, for instance, to address the reliability problem
Fairley et al. (2007), Australia	No specific theory	Qualitative survey (open ended questions), interviews, observations; $n = 22$; constant comparative method	Four key motives for repeated voluntary engagement: nostalgia, camaraderie and friendship, Olympic connection, and sharing and acknowledgment of expertise
Harvey et al. (2007), Canada	Social capital	Quantitative survey; $n = 271$ volunteers in sporting associations; regression analyses	Relationship between sport volunteerism and social capital which is stronger when controlled for gender, language, and age
MacLean and Hamm (2007), Canada	No specific theory	Quantitative survey and qualitative interviews; $n = 647$ event volunteers (golf); factor analysis, correlation, regression	Commitment was related to sport-specific factors of the event; motivation to volunteer was associated with being part of the community. Most of the volunteers intended to continue as golf volunteers (97.5%). Love for sport, golf pride, and volunteer role are predictors for remaining a volunteer
Costa et al. (2006), Australia	No specific theory	Quantitative survey; $n = 147$ event volunteers (Sunbelt IndyCarnival); SEM	The volunteer's sense of community had a positive impact on commitment to the event organization, and commitment to the organization had a positive impact on job satisfaction

Table 1 (*Continued*)

Author(s)	Theory/concept	Method	Key findings
Downward and Ralston (2006), UK	Economic theory of behavior (heterodox)	Quantitative survey; $n = 407$ event volunteers (Commonwealth Games); factor analysis, regression	Volunteering at a major event can raise interest, participation, and volunteering in sport generally; capitalizing upon this will require focusing efforts on particular triggers for change. There appears to be much stronger potential opportunity to generate wider social capital than necessarily produce changes associated with sport
Taylor et al. (2006), Australia	Psychological contract	Qualitative; focus groups with $n = 98$ sport club administrators thereafter interviews with $n = 48$ volunteers; comparative content analysis	Club administrators and volunteers perceive a range of components (e.g., assurance of good faith, intrinsic job characteristic, and transactional) of the psychological contract differently. Volunteers were in particular concerned with performing a rewarding activity
Burgham and Downward (2005), UK	Economic theory of behavior (heterodox)	Quantitative survey; $n = 126$ volunteers of swimming clubs; regression	Effects on decision to volunteer by age (+), children swimming (+), being a swimmer (+). Effects on the extent to volunteer: by gender (+), full-time work (+), salary (+), working time (−), having children (−), children swimming (+), being a swimmer (+)
Coyne and Coyne (2001), USA	No specific theory	Quantitative survey; $n = 478$ sport event volunteers (Golf); t-test	Veteran volunteer is revealed to be the lynchpin around which all recruiting effort should be focused. 'Love of golf' is the *sine qua non* for attracting volunteers. Both groups differ in motivation: first timers are more concerned about what impacts on them financially; the veterans more about relationships
Cuskelly et al. (2002), Australia	Organizational commitment, serious leisure	Quantitative survey; $n = 214$ volunteer sport administrators; Chi-square statistics, ANOVA, t-test	Volunteers reevaluate their commitment to an organization over time. Commitment is important in explaining career volunteering, since career volunteers are more committed than marginal volunteers. Volunteering is considered serious leisure by some volunteers; marginal volunteers rather consider it an obligation

Table 1 (*Continued*)

Author(s)	Theory/concept	Method	Key findings
Cuskelly and Boag (2001), Australia	Organizational commitment	Quantitative survey; $n = 262$ volunteer administrators; discriminant function analysis, ANOVA	Organizational commitment and perceptions about committee functioning were predictors of whether a volunteer stayed with or left the committee; organizational commitment was a stronger predictor of turnover than perceived committee functioning
Preuss and Kebernik (2000), Germany	Inducement contribution theory	Quantitative survey; $n = 202$ event volunteers (Olympic Games); descriptives, Chi-square statistics	Nonmaterial inducements were, for example, honor, Olympic prestige, and making contact with others, and contributions were vacation and work (8.7 h/day). Material inducements were, for example, clothing and access to venues, and contributions were travel and daily expenses (incl. accommodation in some cases)
Farrell et al. (1998), USA	No specific theory	Quantitative survey; $n = 137$ event volunteers (Scott Tournament of Hearts); factor analysis	Results confirmed factors for motivation: purposive, solidary, external traditions, and commitment. Solidary and purposive categories coincide with those described by Caldwell and Andereck (1994); categories of external traditions and commitments are new
Cuskelly et al. (1998), Australia/New Zealand	Organizational commitment	Quantitative survey; $n = 328$ volunteers in community-based sport organizations on three occasions; factor analysis, regression	Directional relationship between perceived committee functioning and organizational commitment. Organizational commitment was also predicted by age group, occupation, years of organizational membership, and time spent on administration
Clary et al. (1998), USA	Functional approach	Conceptual	Six dimensions of motivation to volunteer: values, understanding, career, social, esteem, and protective
Caldwell and Andereck (1994), USA	Incentives theory	Quantitative survey; $n = 371$ members of voluntary associations; factor analysis, t-test, ANOVA	Incentive typologies: Purposive, solidary, and material. Shift in importance of motives from joining to continuing membership; solidary benefits are especially important for members with a high level of participation

*Probably due to the shortness of being in conference proceedings.

synthesized in the following paragraphs. Studies on the individual level (or micro-level) dealt with (1) economic approaches such as the theory of human capital (Becker, 1962; Mincer, 1974) and the economic theory of behavior (Becker, 1976), (2) sociological perspectives including the theory of social capital (e.g., Coleman, 1988), role theory (Parsons, 1951), and social exchange theories (Homans, 1958; Thibault & Kelley, 1959), and (3) psychological standpoints such as motivation theories (Herzberg, 1968; Herzberg, Mausner, & Snyderman, 1959; Maslow, 1987) or psychological contract theory (Argyris, 1960; Levinson, 1962). Hamm-Kerwin, Misener, and Doherty (2009) refer to Peters-Davis, Burant, and Braunschweig (2001) and find support for their approach suggesting that a multidimensional framework is needed to explain voluntary engagement. Nonetheless, the majority of studies investigating voluntary engagement have utilized a one-dimensional framework as will be shown.

Economic approaches have not been used extensively in research on voluntary engagement, with some exceptions (Burgham & Downward, 2005; Downward & Ralston, 2006). One reason could be that the focus has for a long time been on motivations and commitment. The focus of the studies conducted was predominantly on the economic theory of behavior (Becker, 1976). Burgham and Downward (2005) emphasize two economic approaches being applied to decision making in sports, namely orthodox (or neo-classical) and heterodox approaches. While the orthodox approach focuses on the rational-choice framework and utility maximization, the heterodox approach includes a wider set of theoretical principles such as considering not only economic theory but also sociological and psychological approaches. However, Downward and Riordan (2007) also point out that the differences between those theories are quite subtle and that both approaches share the same predictions. Nonetheless, the heterodox approach might be better suited for a volunteering context, as it does not exclude other approaches, but rather integrates other perspectives, and utility maximization (focusing rather on resources than on choice) is not at the forefront. This is important, since psychological approaches highlight the importance of extrinsic and intrinsic motivations. Although utility can consist of both, extrinsic rewards are probably easier to detect. The concept of human capital has rarely been applied to voluntary engagement with a few exceptions (Wilson & Musick, 1997). Human capital and its accumulation are assumed to incur costs. These costs will be compensated by the market in earnings (Mincer, 1974), implying that individuals should invest in education. Thus, following the heterodox approach it is acknowledged that decisions taken are framed by a person's underlying socialization, experience, and motives. A general model of sport consumption acknowledges this approach and includes choice based on motives, tastes, preferences (e.g., relating to socialization and culture), and resources (time and income; Downward, Dawson, & Dejonghe, 2009). This model can easily be adopted for sport volunteering as the decision to volunteer is multidimensional and depends likewise on choice and resources.

Research applying economic approaches came to interesting conclusions. First, the accumulation of human capital proved to be more important than social capital in obtaining a job in sport management (Barros & Barros, 2005). Second, in modeling the decision to work as a volunteer and committing time to this activity, various determinants such as age, gender, income, and involvement with the sport were detected (Burgham & Downward, 2005). Thus, these findings can be related to the above-mentioned sport consumption model, while parallels can be found to research on the determinants of sport participation which detected the same drivers for taking part in sports (e.g., Downward & Riordan, 2007).

Social theories seem to dominate previous research on voluntary engagement (e.g., Allen & Shaw, 2009; Bang, Won, & Kim, 2010; Boezemann & Ellemers, 2007; Caldwell & Andereck, 1994; Doherty, 2009). First, the theory of social capital has been used to describe voluntary engagement. Though Haug (1997) criticizes the usefulness of the term 'social capital' since it has a double meaning, implying a function on the micro-level (as individual resource; Bourdieu, 1980) and a function on the macro-level (as collective good; Putnam, 1993). Following the micro-level perspective, the meaning of social capital for decision making of individuals is in the foreground (Coleman, 1988). Social relationships are regarded as resources for the individual, and social capital can be reduced, if it is not constantly renewed. Previous research confirmed the creation of social capital through a sport event (Brown, Tidey, & Ferkins, 2011): Volunteers from within the community and paid crew share a common incentive for supporting events. Surprisingly, individual club members considered themselves benefiting the club through volunteering rather than the paid crew benefiting events (Brown et al., 2011). Wilson and Musick (1997) documented that formal volunteering is among other factors determined by social capital. This implies that through voluntary engagement benefits are created that have added value for the individual. In this sense, this theory can be compared with economic theories where utility maximization is at the core. Nonetheless, resources (being part of the introduced sport consumption model of Downward et al., 2009) are not covered explicitly by this theory. Empirically, a strong relationship between sport volunteerism and social capital was found, but no indication about the direction of the relationship could be established (Harvey, Lévesque, & Donnelly, 2007).

Second, role theory implies that behavior (as expected in the role of a volunteer) is determined by cultural norms and values as well as socialization and restricted by situational factors (Parsons, 1951; Peters-Davis et al., 2001). However, this would only describe the choice part of the sport consumption model. Role ambiguity is a danger for organizations, while role clarity is associated with older age and greater job satisfaction (Sakires, Doherty, & Misener, 2009). These findings formulate a need for sport organizations to clarify the roles of volunteers.

Third, the social exchange theory postulates that social behavior is considered an exchange of goods; to be precise, it is based on the exchange between costs and rewards (Homans, 1958). Similar to the economic orthodox theory, it is acknowledged that individuals strive to maximize rewards, minimize costs, and form social relationships based on this notion. It is important to note that the reward must have a certain standard (a particular expectation must be fulfilled); otherwise, the exchange might come to a halt (Thibault & Kelley, 1959). The resources to be exchanged can be tangible and intangible (Cropanzano & Mitchell, 2005; Lawler, 2001). Thus, resources are at the core of this theory, whereas choice in the form of preferences (like in the general sport consumption model) seems to be neglected. Bang et al. (2010) emphasized that this theory is fundamental to understanding the volunteer's intention to continue volunteering. Individuals offer their time as cost to receive rewards such as personal growth, which in turn positively influences commitment. Moreover, extrinsic rewards positively impact the intention to continue volunteering (Bang et al., 2010). Doherty (2009) confirmed this notion in her study on the volunteer legacy of a major sport event: The intention of future volunteering was impacted by experienced benefits of the event (e.g., social enrichment, community contribution, and a positive life experience).

With regard to psychological approaches, a considerable body of research on volunteers and their working conditions exists (Clary et al., 1998; Farrell, Johnston, & Twynam, 1998; Kim, Zhang, & Connaughton, 2010; MacLean & Hamm, 2007; Strigas & Jackson, 2003). General motivation theories and particular motivation theories such as the self-determination theory (Deci & Ryan, 1985) and psychological contract theory (Argyris, 1960; Levinson, 1962) elaborate the understanding of why people take part in the voluntary experience. Important representatives for motivation theories are Herzberg and colleagues (Herzberg, 1968; Herzberg et al., 1959). Their two-factor theory is based on a study examining satisfaction and dissatisfaction at work. According to Herzberg et al. (1959), higher order needs have an impact on satisfaction (*motivators* or *satisfiers*) and lower order needs (*dissatisfiers* or *hygiene factors*) affect dissatisfaction in a working context. The hygiene factors must be fulfilled, otherwise dissatisfaction will result, and satisfaction can only be achieved if both are activated (Bowdin, Allen, O'Toole, Harris, & McDonnell, 2011). Maslow's approach (1987) is similar since he postulates that lower order needs must be fulfilled in order for people to satisfy higher order needs.

Interestingly, although several studies have studied motivation, reference to motivation theories is not made, but instead it is only referred to previous research in the field (e.g., Kim et al., 2010) with some exceptions (e.g., Allen & Shaw, 2009). Moreover, not all studies focusing on motivations have used motivation theories as their foundation; instead some studies have applied social exchange theory (e.g., Bang et al., 2010). Costa, Chalip, Green, and Simes (2006) as well as Cuskelly, Hoye et al.(2006) highlight that it is vital to examine psychosocial processes and thus acknowledge the interrelationship between sociological and psychological processes. This could also be a reason why, for instance, psychological processes such as motivations are explained with sociological theories like social exchange theory.

A range of motives have been identified in previous research, either as latent constructs or as simple indicators. For instance, Ralston, Downward, and Lumsdon (2004) documented that a major motive for event volunteers was to participate in something positive and to return something useful to their community and society. In contrast, Strigas and Jackson (2003) identified five factors, namely material, leisure, egoistic, purposive, and external influences as the main motivation for individuals to take up a voluntary engagement. Several scholars developed scales to measure volunteer motivation (Farrell et al., 1998; Kim, Trail, Kim, & Kim, 2009). This range of scales already hints at a major preoccupation of psychological approaches to volunteer research: scale development. Thus, the choice aspect of the sport consumption model seems to be predominant.

Further, expectations and obligations of volunteers were investigated using psychological contract theory (Taylor, Darcy, Hoye, & Cuskelly, 2006), and it was revealed that commonalities and differences between volunteers and sport club administrators exist. For instance, while the transactional component was highly important for sport club administrators, this component had less relevance for volunteers. In turn, volunteers appreciated more intrinsic volunteer characteristics than administrators referring to psychological contracts. These findings support differences in perceptions of both groups.

The role of gender also becomes evident when looking at motivations to volunteer. For instance, an important motive for women working as volunteers is the type of event, that is, women look for events that can strengthen their human and social capital to be used in the labor market (Skirstad & Hanstad, 2011). Women's motivation for volunteering was found to be more instrumental than that of men, which was more intrinsic based on their own interest in sport (Skirstad & Hanstad, 2011). Adams and Deane (2009) emphasize that the underlying motivations of individuals can also be related to different constructions of reality as a result of culture or political institutions. This notion was confirmed in a study about the underlying motives of potential repeat volunteers (Fairley et al., 2007), where volunteers explicitly stated their general interest in the host country's culture.

A central question that research is preoccupied with relates to the commitment of volunteers (e.g., Bang et al., 2010; Cuskelly, McIntyre, & Boag, 1998). Commitment can be related to the serious leisure concept developed by Stebbins (1996):

> Serious leisure is a systematic pursuit of an amateur, hobbyist, or a volunteer activity sufficiently substantial and interesting in nature for the participant to find a career there in the acquisition and expression of a combination of its special skills, knowledge, and experience. (p. 215)

Stebbins (1996) points out that altruism and self-interestedness are key motives of volunteers. The latter can again be related to the utility maximization concept of economic perspectives, while the former can be related to accruing social capital. Stebbins (1996) emphasizes that following the serious leisure approach, self-interestedness might be weighted higher than altruism. Satisfaction derived from the serious leisure activity emerges highest after completion of the activity. He also mentions that sometimes the distinction of a voluntary activity undertaken for occupational reasons between work and leisure is not easy to make. This can be applied to individuals who are paid by a sport club for coaching, while also volunteering at a particular event in a different role than being a coach. Thus, it depends upon the individual defining the activity as being voluntary engagement or work (Stebbins, 1996). Bendle and Patterson (2008) confirm empirically that several individuals actually combined their amateur or hobbyist pursuits with a career volunteer role within a particular group. This is further supported since commitment is an important construct in explaining career volunteering, since career volunteers are more committed than marginal volunteers (Cuskelly, Harrington, & Stebbins, 2002). Considering the inducement contribution theory (March & Simon, 1958), it becomes evident that the inducements offered must be at least as great as the contribution provided by the volunteers. This theory is somewhat related to motivations as applied in Preuss and Kebernik (2000).

To conclude, a range of theories stemming from several disciplines have been used to explain voluntary engagement on the individual level. Those theories proved to be useful in the respective studies in assessing the behavior of volunteers or psychographic issues related to volunteering. As those studies advance different objectives, the arguments for the use of the theory were mostly convincing and the results confirmed this. Thus, depending on the perspective that the researcher takes, some theories seem to be useful and others might be neglected. Nonetheless, it still must be mentioned that several studies were also a theoretical. Some studies attempted to explain psychological phenomena using sociological theories indicating attempts for multi-dimensional frameworks (e.g., Allen & Shaw, 2009; Bang et al., 2010; Hamm-Kerwin et al., 2009). However, those integrated frameworks are rather scant. Studies using those multi-dimensional frameworks emphasize the importance of utilizing such a perspective, in particular Hamm-Kerwin et al. (2009). Following a holistic approach, the heterodox economic theory of behavior (Burgham & Downward, 2005; Downward & Ralston, 2006) seems to be quite valuable as it integrates perspectives from several disciplines and does not advocate a strict economic standpoint (nor a sociological or psychological for that matter).

Group level

Several individuals can form groups within an institution, and therefore, character- istics of the group level can be relevant to explain the engagement of sport volunteers. For example, executive committees, boards, or various other teams of volunteers that work on specific projects can represent groups within an institution (e.g., Doherty & Carron, 2003; Hoye & Cuskelly, 2003). Several concepts have been applied to the group context such as group cohesion (Doherty & Carron, 2003), norms (Doherty, Patterson, & Bussel, 2004), performance (Hoye, 2007; Hoye & Cuskelly, 2003), psychological contracts (Farmer & Fedor, 1999), and commitment (Hoye, 2007). Although these concepts were theoretically explained in previous research, no specific theory has been used to frame the group level of these studies. In terms of measurement, a differentiation between group and individual level was not observed since an additional (group) level was not added to the analysis. Group characteristics such as size and gender structure (Doherty & Carron, 2003; Doherty et al., 2004) have rather been integrated into the individual level. This mixture of levels is also due to the fact that most group characteristics have been measured at the individual level (e.g., individuals have assessed group performance; Hoye & Cuskelly, 2003) and that the small sample sizes did not allow for differentiation among groups. To conclude, the group level has been considered in previous studies, but has neither theoretically nor statistically been modeled as a separate level.

Institutional level

A set of studies on the institutional level is summarized in Table 2 showing that several theories have been used to frame previous studies. Economic theories such as Weisbrod's (1986) theory of voluntary organizations, Hall et al.'s (2003) conceptual model of organizational capacity, Pfeffer and Salancik's (1978) resource dependence theory, as well as DiMaggio and Powell's (1983) institutional theory are examples of theories that have been applied. However, there are also several studies without a specific theoretical framework (e.g., Allison, 2001; Lamprecht et al., 2011; Seippel, 2004); this is likely because they were conducted as consultancies for national governing bodies and other contracting authorities. Moreover, it stands out that previous studies on the institutional level focused on sport organizations (e.g., sport clubs), whereas sport events have been largely neglected in previous research. One reason for this negligence could be that volunteers within one event had been investigated leading to insufficient variation on the event (institutional) level.

Table 2. Overview of studies on the institutional level (in a chronological order; without intending to be exhaustive).

Author(s)	Theory/concept	Method	Key findings
Breuer et al. (2012), Germany	Theory of voluntary organizations, resource dependence theory, theory of club goods	Quantitative survey; $n = 724$ sport clubs (longitudinal sample 2005–2007–2009); descriptive statistics, t-test	Sport clubs that have experienced a decrease in the number of core volunteers have different strategies for substitution. In the short term, they have more secondary volunteers and low-cost employees (people with jobs from the employment office). In the long term (2005–2009), paid staff is employed
Vos et al. (2012), Flanders, Belgium	Market price of equivalency model	Quantitative survey; $n = 651$ sport clubs; descriptive statistics, t-test, regression	The unit of human resource cost is significantly higher in sport clubs compared with fitness and health clubs. The unit cost is significantly determined by club size, owning sport facilities, and a number of extra-sportive activities
Wicker & Breuer (2012), Germany	Organizational capacity	Quantitative survey; $n = 19,345$ sport clubs; regression	Sport clubs with high annual per-capita revenues, no own facilities, a policy for formation and strategy, and that set value on conviviality experience smaller problems regarding the recruitment and retention of volunteers
Breuer and Wicker (2011), Germany	Concept of viable sport organizations	Quantitative survey; $n = 19,345$ sport clubs; descriptive statistics, t-test	Recruitment and retention of core volunteers is the biggest organizational problem; however, the perceived size of the problem has significantly decreased from 2007 to 2009
Lamprecht et al. (2011), Switzerland	No specific theory	Quantitative survey; $n = 6221$ sport clubs; descriptive statistics	85% of clubs rely only on volunteers (no paid staff). Many sport clubs experience serious problems regarding the recruitment/retention of voluntary coaches (15%), board members (16%), and judges/referees (18%)
Sport and Recreation Alliance (2011), UK	No specific theory	Quantitative survey; $n = 1942$ sport clubs; descriptive statistics	Sport clubs have on average 20 volunteers and 49% have a volunteer coordinator. For 53% of clubs, maintaining, recruiting, or retaining volunteers is identified as a challenge over the next 2 years
Wicker and Breuer (2011), Germany	Resource dependence theory, organizational capacity	Quantitative survey; $n = 13,068$ sport clubs; descriptive statistics, t-test	The number of core volunteers in German nonprofit sport clubs has significantly decreased between 2005 and 2007
Wicker and Breuer (2010), Germany	No specific theory	Quantitative survey; $n = 13,068$ sport clubs; explorative analysis with data mining	Sport clubs with fewer members and a high share of members participating in social events have smaller problems regarding the recruitment and retention of volunteers

Table 2 (*Continued*)

Author(s)	Theory/concept	Method	Key findings
Misener and Doherty (2009), Canada	Organizational capacity	Case study, qualitative; $n = 7$ interviews, active-member researcher observation	Human resources and planning and development capacity are of relatively greater importance for goal achievement. Need for more volunteers was an issue. Much work comes from a few volunteers
Taylor et al. (2009), UK	No specific theory	Quantitative survey; $n = 2991$ sport clubs; descriptive statistics	Clubs have on average 21 volunteers, 2 volunteers more than those in the previous year. 193 clubs identified the recruitment and retention of volunteers/staff as a challenge
CCPR (2007), UK	No specific theory	Quantitative survey; $n = 2022$ sport clubs; descriptive statistics	85% of clubs have part-time volunteers and 15% full-time volunteers. 93% of clubs make use of volunteers of either type
Lasby & Sperling (2007), Ontario, Canada	Organizational capacity* (only financial and human resources capacity)	Quantitative survey; $n \sim 2300$ sports and recreation organizations; descriptive statistics	75% of organizations operate without paid staff. 78% of the volunteer hours came from 25% of the volunteers. 18% of organizations have serious problems in recruiting the type of volunteer needed, 13% in retaining volunteers, and 11% in obtaining board members
Cuskelly, Taylor, et al. (2006), Australia	No specific theory (but refer to HRM)	Quantitative survey; $n = 375$ rugby clubs; CFA, correlation, regression	Planning, training, and support are associated with fewer problems regarding the retention of volunteers
Sharpe (2006), Ontario, Canada	Organizational capacity; economic, social, cultural, and symbolic capital	Case study (Appleton Minor Softball League); qualitative; $n = 32$ interviews, observations	Core volunteers have difficulties in fulfilling the professionalized demands due to increasing complexity, regulation, and bureaucracy. Shortage of secondary volunteers who help out with various supplementary tasks (e.g., coaching and officiating)
Taylor and McGraw (2006), Australia	No specific theory (but refer to HRM)	Quantitative survey; $n = 43$ state sport organizations; t-test, correlation, regression	26% of organizations have a formal human resource plan. Staff selection is priority for paid staff; extensive training is priority for volunteers
Gumulka et al. (2005), Canada	Organizational capacity* (only financial and human resources capacity)	Quantitative survey; $n = 13,000$ sports and recreation organizations; descriptive statistics	73% of organizations have no paid staff. Much work comes from only a few volunteers. 20% of organizations experience serious problems in recruiting the type of volunteer needed, 18% in obtaining board members, and 12% in retaining volunteers

Table 2 (Continued)

Author(s)	Theory/concept	Method	Key findings
Seippel (2004), Norway	No specific theory	Quantitative survey; $n = 534$ sport clubs; descriptive statistics, factor analysis, regression	For 15.1% of clubs, the lack of volunteers was an obstacle, for 12.6% it was the lack of leaders and coaches. Obstacle is higher in multi-sport clubs with a high share of under 13-year-olds
Enjolras (2002), Norway	Theory of voluntary Organizations, crowd-out effects	Quantitative survey; $n = 294$ sport clubs; descriptive statistics, regression	The level of commercialization was found to be already significant among clubs, but does not hinder voluntary work. Increasing commercial resources do not crowd out voluntary work
Papadimitriou (2002), Greece	Weberian theory of bureaucracy	Qualitative interviews; $n = 41$ sport clubs (board member); factor analysis, correlation	Tendency toward a loosely structured and less bureaucratic organization. Clubs are characterized by a high level of centralization, but low levels of formalization and specialization. Volunteers perform administrative tasks in most clubs
Allison (2001), Scotland	No specific theory	Quantitative survey; $n = 3485$ sport clubs; descriptive statistics	81% of clubs have volunteers. 50% of clubs stated a general shortage of volunteers, 33% a shortage of volunteers/staff with technical skills and 29% with management skills
Colyer (2000), Australia	Competing values framework	Quantitative survey; $n = 3$ sporting associations; descriptive statistics	Differences in values between volunteers and employees point to the existence of subcultures
Taks et al. (1999), Flanders, Belgium	Triadic model of homo movens, heuristic model	Quantitative survey; 1974: $n = 5361$ sport clubs, 1990: $n = 541$ sport clubs; descriptive statistics	Share of older persons and women on the club's board has increased from 1974 to 1990; 12% of clubs experience problems concerning board members
Amis and Slack (1996), Canada	Contingency theory	In-depth plans, reports, and interviews; $n = 36$ national sport organizations; correlation	Number of members and total income are used as measures of size. Bigger organizations had higher levels of specialization and standardization
Kikulis, Slack, and Hinings (1995), Canada	Design archetypes	Documents and interviews; $n = 36$ national sport organizations; ANOVA	No shift in decision making from volunteers to paid staff. Change in decision making rather associated with direction of change, decision-making dimension, and decision topic

*This conceptual model was not explicitly mentioned, but the two capacity dimensions belong to it; HRM = human resource management.

With regard to economic approaches, Weisbrod's (1986) theory of the voluntary nonprofit sector looks at the reasons why voluntary organizations exist in a three-sector economy. It has served as a theoretical basis in previous research (e.g., Breuer, Wicker, & von Hanau, 2012; Enjolras, 2002). Weisbrod (1986) relates the existence of the nonprofit sector to market and government failure because neither state (government) nor market (for-profit) organizations want to provide heterogeneous services to small-scale demand. Voluntary sport organizations produce such heterogeneous services since they provide various sport services (e.g., different types of sports, various sport programs, and health programs) and non-sport services (e.g., social events, conveying values like fair play, demonstrating tolerance of other people, and integration of minority groups; Breuer & Wicker, 2011; Lamprecht et al., 2011). Volunteers are needed for the provision of these services and thus the decision to volunteer can be influenced by the types of services provided by the institution; however, this relationship is not explicitly modeled in the theory.

The conceptual model of organizational capacity has often been used as a theoretical framework in previous research (e.g., Misener & Doherty, 2009; Sharpe, 2006; Wicker & Breuer, 2011, 2012). The main idea of this conceptual model is that an institution has five capacity dimensions to fulfill its mission and achieve its goals. These dimensions are human resources capacity, financial capacity, and structural capacity which is further divided into planning and development capacity, relationship and network capacity, and infrastructure and process capacity. Previous research has documented that human resources capacity (e.g., volunteers) as well as planning and development capacity was more important to the functioning of sport organizations than other capacity dimensions (Misener & Doherty, 2009; Wicker & Breuer, 2012). Nevertheless, all capacity dimensions influence the day-to-day work of volunteers who run the organization. For example, Sharpe (2006, p. 394) has noted that grassroots organizations tend to have low annual revenues and operate 'on a low economic scale.' Consequently, volunteers have to deal with financial capacity issues when they are working for an organization which can influence the decision to volunteer. The concept of organizational capacity does not explicitly model the decision to volunteer from an institutional perspective; it rather looks at volunteers within an organization and the areas that affect their work.

Without relying on specific organizational theories, previous research suggests that other institutional characteristics such as image, reputation, culture, and (sporting) success could have an impact on the decision to volunteer. For example, image 'has the power to influence the behavior of all those involved with a sporting organization' (Ferrand & Pages, 1999, p. 388) and consequently also the behavior of sport volunteers. The image of an organization can assist in decision making when various alternatives are available (Ferrand & Pages, 1999), that is, when volunteers have to decide to which institution they devote their work. The International Olympic Committee is an organization that specifically works on its image by emphasizing values like unity, solidarity, and friendship in its promotional campaigns. Previous research has documented that these values also mirror the drivers of the decision to volunteer at the Olympic Games (Fairley et al., 2007). Moreover, organizational culture influences volunteers (Warner, Newland, & Green, 2011), particularly when existing subcultures cause tensions between volunteers and paid employees (Colyer, 2000). Although not stated in previous studies, organizational culture and values can be attributed to infrastructure and process capacity within the concept of organizational capacity (Hall et al., 2003), highlighting the importance of this capacity dimension to the decision to volunteer. Consequently, some dimensions of the concept of organizational capacity have been applied in previous research without explicitly relying on that conceptual model.

The lifecycle of the organization can be a driver of the decision to volunteer. Organizations have their own lifecycles with different stages. These stages were summarized into four different stages labeled entrepreneurial stage, collectivity stage, formalization and control stage, and elaboration of structure stage (Quinn & Cameron, 1983). Particularly, the early two stages that are characterized by innovation, lots of ideas, and a low level of formalization might be attractive for volunteers who prefer unstructured positions and not being managed (Hoeber, 2010). The last two stages might be less attractive since they are characterized by a high level of formalization, institutionalization, control, and conservatism (Quinn & Cameron, 1983). During these stages, volunteers could be more likely to drop out because they do not have the time and skills to cope with increasing complexity and responsibility in the organization (Nichols et al., 2005; Sharpe, 2006). The presence of organizational lifecycles highlights that organizational characteristics are changing over time. For this reason, the timeframe has to be considered adding a longitudinal component to the decision to volunteer.

In addition to internal factors, external or environmental factors can influence the decision to volunteer in sport. Sport organizations are operating in an environment that has become increasingly complex and competitive (Ferrand & Pages, 1999). For example, sport organizations compete with other organizations for funds, resources, members, and volunteers (Breuer & Wicker, 2011). The resource dependence theory (Pfeffer & Salancik, 1978) looks at external factors that have an impact on organizational behavior and has served as a theoretical foundation in previous studies (e.g., Breuer et al., 2012; Wicker & Breuer, 2011). It is suggested that an organization tries to acquire resources from the environment when internal resources are scarce. The organization's inability to produce all the required resources internally leads to an increasing dependence on the environment. External resource providers can gain power and control over the organization, affecting the scope of decision making of the volunteers within the organization. This theory has helped to generally understand that sport organizations try do reduce their dependence on the environment. For example, organizations would only employ external (paid) staff when the internal (voluntary) resources are not sufficient (Breuer et al., 2012; Wicker & Breuer, 2011). The resource dependence theory does not explicitly explain the decision to volunteer; it has instead been used to explain the circumstances that affect voluntary work.

The pressure that external resource providers such as the government put on organizations has been investigated in previous research (e.g., Nichols et al., 2005). Institutional theory and in particular the concept of coercive isomorphism (DiMaggio & Powell, 1983) have been used to explain the response of sport organizations to such external pressures (Vos et al., 2011). Generally speaking, institutional isomorphism is the process of organizations becoming similar, whereas coercive isomorphism refers to the normative and regulative pressures that force organizations to meet expectations (DiMaggio & Powell, 1983). For example, the pressure on volunteers has increased because they have to write grant applications and implement government policies (Nichols et al., 2005; Vos et al., 2011). However, external factors must not necessarily relate to the government; they can also relate to the community. For example, the size of the community (number of inhabitants) is associated with the availability of potential substitutes for voluntary work and can thus influence the decision to volunteer for a specific institution (Wicker & Breuer, 2012). In summary, the influence of the environment has been related to organizational behavior in previous research, but it was not treated as a separate level of analysis. One explanation could be that most studies focused on only one country or only a few communities, and consequently, there was not sufficient variation in external factors. Similar to the resource dependence theory, this theory looks at external factors that impact on organizational behavior and as a result impact on the volunteers of the organization.

In summary, most previous studies have not explicitly looked at the institutional factors that drive the decision to volunteer; the links to volunteers were instead a side product of a study with another focus. Consequently, the applied theories do not really explain the decision to volunteer; they instead explain organizational behavior which then in turn determines the quality and quantity of voluntary work. Most of the above-mentioned organizational theories look at one specific aspect of the institution like the influence of external factors (resource dependence theory, Pfeffer & Salancik, 1978), whereas the conceptual model of organizational capacity represents a rather holistic model. This seems fruitful to the analysis of volunteers because the decision to volunteer is multi-dimensional (Hamm-Kerwin et al., 2009) and this multi-dimensionality should also apply to the institutional level (Doherty, 1998). Since some studies did not use any theoretical framework at all, theoretical shortcomings should be noted. These findings indicate the urgency of theoretical frameworks that also consider the institutional level.

In terms of methodological approaches, most previous studies have chosen quantitative research paradigms (e.g., Enjolras, 2002; Seippel, 2004; Taylor, Barrett, & Nichols, 2009) with a few exceptions (e.g., Misener & Doherty, 2009; Sharpe, 2006). The data analysis has often been restricted to descriptive statistics (e.g., Allison, 2001; Lamprecht et al., 2011; Taks, Renson, & Vanreusel, 1999), whereas other studies have used common inferential statistics like t-tests and regression (e.g., Enjolras, 2002; Papadimitriou, 2002; Seippel, 2004; Table 2). Thus, the portfolio of statistical tests has not yet been fully exploited. Another shortcoming – both from a theoretical and a methodological viewpoint – can be observed because the decision to volunteer has not yet been looked at from both levels (individual and institutional level), that is, both levels have not been linked in previous research.

Multi-level framework

Multi-level perspective

The multi-level perspective takes into account that different levels of analysis exist. For example, individuals are nested within organizations, school children within schools, players within teams (Todd, Crook, & Barilla, 2005), and in the current study volunteers are nested within sport institutions. Thus, individual behavior is not only determined by individual factors but also determined by organizational and socio-cultural factors (Dixon & Bruening, 2007). The levels are hierarchical levels, that is, there are higher levels (macro-level; e.g., institution) and lower levels (micro-level; e.g., volunteer). Previous research has recognized the fact that higher level factors can shape and constrain individual level factors taking a top-down perspective (Dixon & Bruening, 2007). Multi-level frameworks have already been applied in other areas of sport management like work/family conflict in coaching (Dixon & Bruening, 2007) and the role of sport supply in determining sport participation (Wicker, Hallmann, & Breuer, 2012).

The level of analysis and the choice of measures at each level matter. Previous research has pointed to the importance of the perspective (or frame) and has highlighted that different perspectives can lead to different findings (Allison, 1969; Bolman & Deal, 1991). Different levels of analysis illuminate different psycho-social phenomena. The levels of analysis are complementary to and inform one another. However, higher level factors do not result from the summation of lower level factors; they are separate measures (Allison, 1969; Bolman & Deal, 1991; Dixon & Breuning, 2007). Oberwittler (2003) has stressed that false conclusions can occur when macro-level effects are misleadingly ascribed to the individual level. Moreover, the differentiation of levels also means that several individuals can share the same characteristics at a higher level: For example, if several individuals volunteer for the same organization, the same organizational policies apply to them. In summary, the decision to volunteer in sport is a result of factors on different levels, and therefore, the suggested multi-level framework incorporates an individual and an institutional level (Figure 1).

Individual level (micro level)

In the literature review, it was shown that many theories stemming from economics, sociology, and psychology can be used to explain voluntary engagement. According to Burgham and Downward (2005), decision making in sports can be considered the

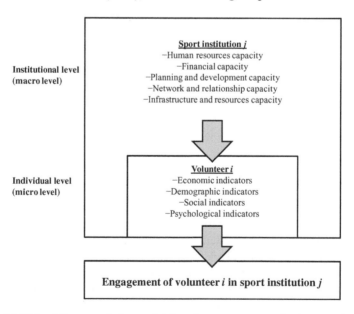

Figure 1.   Multi-level framework for explaining the engagement of volunteers in sport.

allocation of time toward an activity which is driven by the three above-mentioned theoretical approaches. Since the focus of this research lies on the decision-making process, economic theories seem to be adequate to answer the underlying research question. In doing so, a heterodox perspective is taken as it also encapsulates social and psychological approaches. Other theories focus oftentimes on a single approach (e.g., role theory and serious leisure) and are not deemed appropriate to study the phenomenon of voluntary engagement which is multi-dimensional. The advantage is that a rather holistic viewpoint can be taken. Moreover, the request of other researchers for a multi-dimensional framework (Hamm-Kerwin et al., 2009; Peters-Davis et al., 2001) is answered. Drawing upon Burgham and Downward (2005), Downward and Ralston (2006), and Bang et al. (2010), volunteering in sport should be determined by various demographic, economic, social, and psychological factors (Figure 1). Volunteering can be distinguished into the decision to volunteer and the time committed toward the voluntary engagement, and it is suggested that current voluntary engagement influences future voluntary engagement.

Demographic factors should influence the decision to volunteer: Gender plays a role in the decision to volunteer (Skirstad & Hanstad, 2011) and the time committed to volunteering (Burgham & Downward, 2005), since the underlying motivation varied between males and females (Skirstad & Hanstad, 2011). For instance, women have the aim to strengthen their social and human capital (Skirstad & Hanstad, 2011) which in turn points to the importance of a multi-dimensional framework. Thus, gender can be an indicator of the decision to volunteer. This decision is also assumed to be influenced by age since older people are more likely to volunteer (Burgham & Downward, 2005). Ethnicity has not been investigated as a determinant for volunteering except by Burgham and Downward (2005). This omission is quite surprising because ethnicity has been found to influence sport participation – that is, sport participation rates vary by ethnicity (e.g., Wicker, Breuer, & Pawlowski, 2009) and voluntary engagement might be valued differently in diverse cultures since different constructions of reality might exist (Adams & Deane, 2009).

Pertaining to economic indicators, human capital which can be described by an individual's experience and educational level (Mincer, 1974) is important for voluntary work (Wilson & Musick, 1997). It can be assumed that voluntary engagement contributes to the accumulation of human capital through the acquisition of new skills. Further economic determinants can be full-time employment, income, and working time (Burgham & Downward, 2005). These determinants are assumed to be essential since time can impose a restriction on voluntary engagement. Those having a high income might be more willing to engage as a volunteer since they already have income at their disposal. Notwithstanding, opportunity costs are higher for individuals with high income, since they could generate more income if they committed time to work instead of volunteering (Burgham & Downward, 2005).

It is more difficult to develop distinct social and psychological indicators as they are oftentimes interrelated and the difference is the underlying theoretical approach. For instance, in Burgham and Downward (2005), demographic variables are called social indicators, following an economic approach. Another example is the research by Doherty (2009), who used a social approach measuring experienced benefits and costs. Those could also be referred to as motivations (satisfiers and dissatisfiers) following a psychological perspective (Farrell et al., 1998). Based on the sociological approaches presented, the perceived creation of social capital can be relevant (Brown et al., 2011) and it is assumed that this fosters the decision to take up voluntary engagement.

In addition, psychological indicators should be important for voluntary engagement (e.g., Bang et al., 2010; Coyne & Coyne, 2001; Farrell et al., 1998; MacLean & Hamm, 2007; Strigas & Jackson, 2003). These factors stem mainly from motivation theories and include purposive, solidary, and external traditions (Farrell et al., 1998), or expression of values, patriotism/community involvement, interpersonal contacts, career orientation, personal growth, extrinsic rewards, and love of sport (Bang, Alexandris, & Ross, 2009; Bang et al., 2010; Bang & Ross, 2009). In particular, the factor love of sport should be emphasized, as its importance was also documented by several researchers (Coyne & Coyne, 2001; MacLean & Hamm, 2007). A scale including the peculiarities of sport and love for sport (as this dimension has oftentimes been neglected in the past; only few studies have actually included this latent factor) would be considered appropriate to be incorporated into psychological aspects of the voluntary engagement.

The group level is not considered in the current framework, because it should not influence the decision to volunteer. The main reason is the limited amount of information about group characteristics at the time when the potential volunteer makes his/her decision. A limited amount of information means that the information is unlikely to be known yet, simply because the group does not yet exist in many cases. For example, when a potential volunteer is in the process of deciding whether he/she should volunteer for a specific event (like the Olympic Games), any information about the group members (e.g., a group of volunteers that welcomes visitors and athletes at the airport) is not known yet, and therefore group characteristics such as size, gender structure, group cohesion (Doherty & Carron, 2003), and group performance (Hoye & Cuskelly, 2003) are not known either. Consequently, it is unlikely that the person can integrate any group characteristics in his/her decision-making process. A second example can be provided for the sport club context where a group comprising club members (or also non-members) is formed for a specific project like the organization of a sporting tournament or a social event. Also in this case, potential volunteers should not have information about the group characteristics at the time when they make their decision because the group does not yet exist. Although speculation about size and gender structure can be made, characteristics like group cohesion and performance are unlikely to be known. Therefore, the group level is not conceptualized in this framework.

Institutional level (macro level)

When investigating the engagement of sport volunteers, it is important to consider that volunteering usually occurs within an organizational context (Penner, 2002). Therefore, the respective characteristics of the institution (e.g., sport club and sport event) have to be taken into account as well. Moreover, the type of sport institution (club vs. event) or the type of sport can also play a role because some institutions or sports might be more attractive to volunteers than others. On the institutional level, the conceptual model of organizational capacity (Hall et al., 2003) serves as the theoretical framework. According to Hall et al. (2003, p. 4), 'the overall capacity of a nonprofit and voluntary organization to produce the outputs and outcomes it desires is a function of its ability to draw on or deploy a variety of types of organizational capital.' The concept of organizational capacity also consists of several components (i.e., capacity dimensions) like the heterodox approach on the individual level, and should therefore contribute to a more holistic model of the decision to volunteer in sport.

The first dimension is human resources capacity, which is referred to as the 'ability to deploy human capital (i.e., paid staff and volunteers) within the organization' (Hall et al., 2003, p. 5). It is considered the key capacity because it influences all other capacity dimensions (Hall et al., 2003). The definition already highlights the importance of volunteers and paid staff that can influence an individual's decision to volunteer. The number of volunteers in the institution can have an impact on an individual's decision to volunteer, because, for example, the more the volunteers, the less *visible* the contribution of each single volunteer. External pressures on organizations can lead to the employment of paid staff, which can impact on the decision to volunteer. Volunteers and paid staff can have different values and motivations for working in an organization, leading to potential conflicts (Colyer, 2000). Paid staff can have the tendency to take power and decision making away from volunteers and to manage them like minor employees of the organization (Auld, 1997). Therefore, the presence of paid staff can determine the decision to volunteer.

Financial capacity is the 'ability to develop and deploy financial capital' (Hall et al., 2003, p. 5) and can be described by expenses, revenues, assets, and liabilities. Given the low economic scale, the nonprofit context of many sport institutions, and relatively low accounting standards, many organizations only differentiate between revenues and expenses. Given that nonprofit organizations are not allowed to distribute profits among members, there are usually no substantial differences between annual revenues and expenses. The available financial resources (i.e., annual revenues) can influence the decision to volunteer because many sport organizations are notorious for having limited money (Sharpe, 2006), an issue volunteers have to deal with when they are working for the organization. Annual revenues or total income is a common indicator to describe the financial capacity of sport institutions (Amis & Slack, 1996; Wicker & Breuer, 2012). Moreover, the revenue composition can play a role in the decision to volunteer since the origin of income sources contributes to the reputation of the organization by its publics, including volunteers (Chang & Tuckman, 1994). Volunteers appreciate working for an institution that is highly recognized by its publics and has a good reputation (Fairley et al., 2007).

The third dimension relationship and network capacity is defined as the 'ability to draw on relationships' (Hall, et al., 2003, p. 6) with several people and institutions such as clients, funders, partners, and the government. The number of relationships with the sport institution can provide insight concerning the size of the network in which the institution is operating. The size of the institution's network can be an indicator for the complexity of volunteers' tasks if they have to collaborate with various stakeholders. This task complexity can be an issue for volunteers in sport institutions and it might be contrary to their expectations (Sharpe, 2006; Taylor et al., 2006). In addition to the mere quantity of relationships, the nature and quality of the existing relationships can play a role as they can also add to task complexity. For example, the relationships with some stakeholders can be associated with high levels of bureaucracy and regulations which might be an issue for volunteers (Sharpe,

2006; Taylor et al., 2006). Therefore, the relationships of the institution can influence the decision to volunteer.

Planning and development capacity represents the fourth dimension that refers to the institution's 'ability to develop and draw on organizational strategic plans, [. . .], policies, and proposals' (Hall et al., 2003, p. 6). Written and formal plans are not very common in sport institutions (Allison, 2001; Cuskelly, Taylor, Hoye, & Darcy, 2006), indicating that strategic planning is not a priority. Nevertheless, planning can be important for the overall functioning of the club and the reduction of problems related to the retention of volunteers (Cuskelly, Taylor et al., 2006; Wicker & Breuer, 2012), suggesting that this determines the decision to volunteer. Plans and policies can be useful to describe the roles of volunteers who appreciate role clarity and clear direction (Sakires et al., 2009; Warner et al., 2011). Therefore, strategic planning and policies should be considered in the framework, because they affect the volunteer workforce in the club. In this regard, a volunteer coordinator (Taylor et al., 2009) can help with the delegation and coordination of work and help explain how club strategies should be implemented. Such a coordinator can also ensure adequate communication with and recognition of volunteers, which can also determine their satisfaction (Farrell et al., 1998). As individuals invest in voluntary work to strengthen their human capital (Skirstad & Hanstad, 2011) and to learn new skills (Warner et al., 2011), a policy that ensures the training of volunteers in the institution can also be important for the decision to volunteer. Training of volunteers contributes to building a sense of community which in turn determines volunteer satisfaction (Costa et al., 2006). Moreover, training is positively associated with the retention of volunteers (Cuskelly, Taylor et al., 2006; Wicker & Breuer, 2012).

The fifth dimension infrastructure and process capacity is defined as the 'ability to deploy or rely on infrastructure, processes and culture' (Hall et al., 2003, p. 6). This capacity dimension covers all aspects that are relevant to the day-to-day operations of the institution. In this regard, it can be helpful for volunteers to have written job descriptions or manuals that explain critical procedures (Schulz & Auld, 2006; Warner et al., 2011). The formalization of daily operations makes the institution less dependent on the actual individuals who perform them. Moreover, the use of technology can have an influence on the decision to volunteer. Depending on the skills of the volunteer and the extent to which the institution uses technology, this influence can be positive or negative. Previous research points toward the latter as the board members of community sport organizations tend to have a limited understanding of technology (Hoeber & Hoeber, 2012). For example, a volunteer who is not used to managing databases and club statistics using specific computer software would perceive a task overload. Although the influence of technology on the decision to volunteer has not explicitly been investigated up to now, it can be suggested that this contributes to perceived task complexity (Sharpe, 2006) of volunteers when they have to work with new technologies and programs.

The timeframe of the investigation of the engagement of sport volunteers has to be taken into account as well. Both individual and institutional characteristics can change over time. For example, individuals get older, change jobs, earn more income, or become children, which can impact their decision to volunteer. Similarly, organizations have lifecycles, and consequently, institutional characteristics can also be subject to changes. For example, the degree of specialization and standardization changes when the organization gets bigger, that is, has more members and generates more revenues (Amis & Slack, 1996). These institutional changes can also affect the decision to volunteer. Therefore, it is important to note that longitudinal components that account for changes in individual and institutional factors over time are inherent to the framework.

Indicators related to the external environment of the sport institution are not considered in this framework for several reasons. The multi-level framework is already complex as it incorporates a wide range of indicators on both levels. Moreover, it is suggested that environmental factors first impact on the institution and are thus already inherent in many institutional factors. Several institutional policies exist because they are required by the government. For example, governments require written development plans for the provision of government subsidies (Allison, 2001). The focus of this framework is on the internal work environment (Doherty, 1998), which is influenced by the external environment. Furthermore, it is assumed that environmental factors do not contribute to the explanation of why one individual volunteers for one specific institution because these factors are similar for all institutions (within one community, state, or country). For example, all sport institutions within one community have to deal with the same government regulations leading to insufficient variation in these factors.

Multi-level analysis

The differentiation between individual and institutional levels leads to different levels of data, which are referred to as multi-level or hierarchical data. Although multi-level frameworks can be (and have been) analyzed using qualitative approaches (e.g., Dixon & Bruening, 2007), this paper suggests a statistical test that is able to deal with the hierarchical structure of data: the multi-level analysis (or hierarchical linear model (HLM)). While this method of analysis has already been applied to research on team sports (e.g., Todd et al., 2005) and sport participation (Wicker et al., 2012), it has been neglected in research on sport volunteers up to now. One study outside of the sporting context could be identified that applied multi-level analysis in volunteerism; however, only the state level and not the institutional level has been used in this research (Rotolo & Wilson, 2012). Given the fact that voluntary engagement usually occurs within an organizational context (Penner, 2002), the application of multi-level analyses allowing the statistical combination of the individual and institutional levels can open new perspectives for research on sport volunteers.

In the case of hierarchical data, it is important that the data is measured at the appropriate level (Bryk & Raudenbush, 1992). The difference in measurement becomes evident in the preparation of datasets for a multi-level analysis. In fact, two datasets are prepared, one for the individual and one for the institutional level. A key variable (in this study: institution j) has to be included in both datasets because it represents the connection between both levels. The dataset for the institutional level has fewer cases than the individual level dataset because several individuals belong o one institution. Biases would occur due to the nonindependence of observations in conventional regression analyses (Osborne, 2000), if the institutional level data were integrated into the individual level data (i.e., the number of cases is incorrect). Moreover, the multi-level analysis has to be preferred to the conventional regression since interdependent regression models are estimated (Todd et al., 2005) and a submodel is calculated for every level (Raudenbush, Bryk, Cheong, Congdon, & Du Toit 2004). The two different levels of data can also be seen in the equations which have two subindexes (*i* for micro-level and *j* for macro-level; Figure 1). On the contrary, there would be only one subindex (*i*) in a conventional regression analysis. For a multi-level model like in the current study, the equation would be of the following general form:

$$VOL\ ENG_{ij} = \beta_{0j} + \beta_{1j}AGE_{ij} + r_{ij} \tag{1}$$

Where *VOL ENG*$_{ij}$ is the outcome of interest (i.e., the dependent variable; in this study: voluntary engagement) for volunteer *i* in institution *j*; β_{0j} the intercept for each institution; β_{1j} the expected change in voluntary engagement with a 1-year change in *AGE*$_{ij}$; and r_{ij} the residual. Every micro-level estimate is modeled in separate macro-level equations of the following general form:

$$\beta_{0j} = \gamma_{00} + \gamma_{01}REV_j + u_{0j} \tag{2}$$

$$\beta_{1j} = \gamma_{10} + \gamma_{11}REV_j + u_{1j} \tag{3}$$

where β_{0j} is the intercept from the micro-level equation; β_{1j} is the slope; *REV*$_j$ is the macro-level variable (in this study: annual revenues); γ_{00} and γ_{10} are the macro-level intercepts; γ_{01} and γ_{11} are the macro-level slopes; and u_{0j} and u_{1j} are the macro-level residuals.

The application of multi-level analyses has some requirements. First, multi-level analyses cannot be run with SPSS, the standard software package in the social sciences. Specific software packages such as HLM (Raudenbush et al., 2004) are required. Second, multi-level analyses require large sample sizes, particularly for the institutional level. There should be at least 20 cases on this level (Tabachnick & Fidell, 2007). Adding longitudinal components to the framework is possible since multi-level models can also be estimated for panel data, for example, by controlling for the year of observation. In doing so, how changes in individual and institutional factors determine the decision to volunteer over time can be analyzed.

Conclusion

In this paper, a theoretical framework is presented, which explains the decision on voluntary engagement encapsulating a multi-level perspective. The voluntary sector consists of individuals who invest their time in the voluntary activity (micro-level) on the one hand and of institutions which need the hand of those individuals for their functioning (macro-level) on the other hand. Thus, a multi-level framework was needed to adequately capture these circumstances and allow a more holistic modeling of the decision to volunteer. One limitation of this framework might be its complexity, though without actually having tested it, this represents only an unproven notion. The proposed framework represents a suggestion for future empirical studies and can be subject to changes. As there should always be interplay between theory and empirics in applied research, individual and institutional indicators should be adjusted accordingly. If required by the research context, more levels like a group level or an environmental level can be added to the framework.

References

Adams, A., & Deane, J. (2009). Exploring formal and informal dimensions of sports volunteering in England. *European Sport Management Quarterly, 9*(2), 119–140.

Argyris, C. (1960). *Understanding organizational behavior.* Homewood, IL: Dorsey.

Allen, J.B., & Shaw, S. (2009). "Everyone rolls up their sleeves and mucks in": Exploring volunteers' motivation and experiences of the motivational climate of a sporting event. *Sport Management Review, 12*(2), 79–90.

Allison, G.T. (1969). Conceptual models and the Cuban missile crisis. *American Political Science Review, 63*(3), 689–718.

Allison, M. (2001). *Sports clubs in Scotland.* Edinburgh, UK: SportScotland.

Amis, J., & Slack, T. (1996). The size-structure relationship in voluntary sport organizations. *Journal of Sport Management, 10*(1), 76–86.

Auld, C. (1997). Professionalisation of Australian sport administration: The effects on organisational decision-making. *European Journal for Sport Management, 4*(2), 17–39.

Bang, H., Alexandris, K., & Ross, S.D. (2009). Validation of the revised volunteer motivations scale for international sporting events (VMS-ISE) at the Athens 2004 Olympic Games. *Event Management, 12*(3–4), 119–131.

Bang, H., & Ross, S.D. (2009). Volunteer motivation and satisfaction. *Journal of Venue and Event Management, 1*(1), 61–77.

Bang, H., Won, D., & Kim, Y. (2010). Motivations, commitment, and intentions to continue volunteering for sporting events. *Event Management, 13*(2), 69–81.

Barros, C.P., & Barros, C.D. (2005). The role of human and social capital in the earnings of sports administrators: A case study of Madeira Island. *European Sport Management Quarterly, 5*(1), 47–62.

Becker, G.S. (1962). Investment in human capital: A theoretical analysis. *Journal of Political Economy, 70*(5), 9–49.

Becker, G.S. (1976). *The economic approach to human behavior.* Chicago, IL: The University of Chicago Press.

Bendle, L., & Patterson, I. (2008). Serious leisure, career volunteers and the organisation of arts events in a regional Australian city. *International Journal of Event Management Research, 4*(1), 1–11.

Boezemann, E., & Ellemers, N. (2007). Volunteering for charity: Pride, respect, and the commitment of volunteers. *Journal of Applied Psychology, 92*(3), 771–785.

Bolman, L.G., & Deal, T.E. (1991). Leadership and management effeciveness: A multi-frame, multi-sector analysis. *Human Resource Management, 30*(4), 509–534.

Bourdieu, P. (1980). Le capital social, Note provisoires. *Actes de la Recherche Science Sociales, 31*, 2–3.

Bowdin, G., Allen, J., O'Toole, W., Harris, R., & McDonnell, I. (2011). *Events Management.* Oxford: Elsevier Butterworth-Heinemann.

Breuer, C., & Wicker, P. (2011). *Sport Development Report 2009/2010. Analysis of sport clubs' situation in Germany.* Abbreviated Version. Cologne: Sportverlag Strauß.

Breuer, C., Wicker, P., & von Hanau, T. (2012). Consequences of the decrease in volunteers among German sports clubs: Is there a substitute for voluntary work? *International Journal of Sport Policy and Politics* (in press). doi: 10.1080/19406940.2012.656681

Brown, A., Tidey, A., & Ferkins, L. (2011). Sport event volunteers or paid crew: Their impacts on social capital production. In H. Gammelsaeter & G. Bielons (Eds.), *Book of Abstracts of the 19th European Association for Sport Management Conference* (pp. 483–484). Barcelona, Spain: GB Creation & Advice Consulting.

Bryk, A.S., & Raudenbush, S.W. (1992). *Hierarchical linear models.* Newbury Park, CA: Sage.

Burgham, M., & Downward, P. (2005). Why volunteer, time to volunteer? A case study from swimming. *Managing Leisure, 10*(2), 79–93.

Caldwell, L.L., & Andereck, K.L. (1994). Motives for initiating and continuing membership in a recreation-related voluntary association. *Leisure Sciences: An Interdisciplinary Journal, 16*(1), 33–44.

CCPR. (2007). *Sports club survey 2007.* Retrieved from http://www.ccpr.org.uk/OneStopCMS/ Core/CrawlerResourceServer.aspx?resource=81979A80-E131-432A-A49D-3C1C2C064C81& mode=link&guid=cdc695da57e0418eb45f9 5641977338e.

Chang, C.F., & Tuckman, H.P. (1994). Revenue diversification among non-profits. *Voluntas: International Journal of Voluntary and Nonprofit Organizations, 5*(3), 273–290.

Clary, G.E., Snyder, M., Ridge, R.D., Copeland, J., Stukas, A.A., Haugen, J., & Miene, P. (1998). Understanding and assessing the motivations of volunteers: A functional approach. *Journal of Personality and Social Psychology, 74*(6), 1516–1530.

Cnaan, R.A., Handy, F., & Wadsworth, M. (1996). Defining who is a volunteer: Conceptual and empirical considerations. *Nonprofit and Voluntary Sector Quarterly, 25*(3), 364–383.

Coleman, J. (1988). Social capital in the creation of human capital. *American Journal of Sociology, 94*, 95–120.

Colyer, S. (2000). Organizational culture in selected Western Australian sport organizations. *Journal of Sport Management, 14*(4), 321–341.

Costa, C.A., Chalip, L., Green, B.C., & Simes, C. (2006). Reconsidering the role of training in event volunteers' satisfaction. *Sport Management Review, 9*(2), 165–182.

Coyne, B.S., & Coyne, E.J. (2001). Getting, keeping and caring for unpaid volunteers for professional golf tournament events. *Human Resource Development International, 4*(2), 199–214.

Cropanzano, R., & Mitchell, M.S. (2005). Social exchange theory: An interdisciplinary review. *Journal of Management, 31*(6), 874–900.

Cuskelly, G., & Boag, A. (2001). Organisational commitment as a predictor of committee member turnover among volunteer sport administrators: Results of a time-lagged study. *Sport Management Review, 4*(1), 65–86.

Cuskelly, G., Harrington, M., & Stebbins, R.A. (2002). Changing levels of organizational commitment amongst sport volunteers: A serious leisure approach. *Leisure/Loisir, 27*(3–4), 191–212.

Cuskelly, G., Hoye, R., & Auld, C. (2006). *Working with volunteers in sport. Theory and practice.* Abington: Routledge.

Cuskelly, G., McIntyre, N., & Boag, A. (1998). A longitudinal study of the development of organizational commitment amongst volunteer sport administrators. *Journal of Sport Management, 12*(3), 181–202.

Cuskelly, G., Taylor, T., Hoye, R., & Darcy, S. (2006). Volunteer management practices and volunteer retention: A human resource management approach. *Sport Management Review, 9*(2), 141–163.

Deci, E.L., & Ryan, R.M. (1985). *Intrinsic motivation and self-determination in human behavior.* New York, NY: Plenum.

DiMaggio, P.J., & Powell, W.W. (1983). The iron cage revisited: Institutional isomorphism and collective rationality in organizational fields. *American Sociological Review, 48*(2), 147–160.

Dixon, M.A., & Bruening, J. (2007). Work-family conflict in coaching I: A top-down perspective. *Journal of Sport Management, 21*(3), 377–406.

Doherty, A.J. (1998). Managing our human resources: A review of organisational behaviour in sport. *Sport Management Review, 1*(1), 1–24.

Doherty, A.J. (2009). The volunteer legacy of a major sport event. *Journal of Policy Research in Tourism, Leisure and Events, 1*(3), 185–207.

Doherty, A.J., & Carron, A.V. (2003). Cohesion in volunteer sport executive committees. *Journal of Sport Management, 17*(2), 116–141.

Doherty, A., Patterson, M., & van Bussel, M. (2004). What do we expect? An examination of perceived committee norms in non-profit sport organisations. *Sport Management Review, 7*(2), 109–132.

Downward, P., Dawson, A., & Dejonghe, T. (2009). *Sport economics. Theory, evidence and policy.* Oxford: Butterworth-Heinemann.

Downward, P., & Ralston, R. (2006). The sports development potential of sports event volunteering: Insights from the XVII Manchester Commonwealth Games. *European Sport Management Quarterly, 6*(4), 333–351.

Downward, P., & Riordan, J. (2007). Social interactions and the demand for sport: An economic analysis. *Contemporary Economic Policy, 25*(4), 518–537.

Enjolras, B. (2002). The commercialization of voluntary sport organizations in Norway. *Nonprofit and Voluntary Sector Quarterly, 31*(3), 352–376.

Fairley, S., Kellett, P., & Green, B.C. (2007). Volunteering abroad: Motives for travel to volunteer at the Athens Olympic Games. *Journal of Sport Management, 21*(1), 41–57.

Farmer, S.M., & Fedor, D.B. (1999). Volunteer participation and withdrawal. A psychological contract perspective on the role of expectations and organizational support. *Nonprofit Management and Leadership, 9*(4), 349–367.

Farrell, J.M., Johnston, M.E., & Twynam, D.G. (1998). Volunteer motivation, satisfaction, and management at an elite sporting competition. *Journal of Sport Management, 12*(4), 288–300.

Ferrand, A., & Pages, M. (1999). Image management in sport organisations: The creation of value. *European Journal of Marketing, 33*(3/4), 387–401.

Getz, D. (1997). *Event Management and Event Tourism.* New York, NY: Cognizant.

Gumulka, G., Barr, C., Lasby, D., & Brownlee, B. (2005). *Understanding the capacity of sports and recreation organizations.* Toronto, ON: Imagine Canada.

Hall, M.H., Andrukow, A., Barr, C., Brock, K., de Wit, M., & Embuldeniya, D. (2003). *The capacity to serve: A qualitative study of the challenges facing Canada's nonprofit and voluntary organizations.* Toronto, ON: Canadian Centre for Philanthropy.

Hamm-Kerwin, S., Misener, K., & Doherty, A. (2009). Getting in the game: An investigation of volunteering in sport among older adults. *Leisure/Loisir, 33*(2), 659–685.

Harvey, J., Lévesque, M., & Donnelly, P. (2007). Sport volunteerism and social capital. *Sociology of Sport Journal, 24*(2), 106–223.

Haug, S. (1997). *Soziales Kapital. Ein kritischer Überblick über den aktuellen Forschungsstand. Arbeitsbericht Nr. II/15* [Social capital: A critical overview over the present state of research. Working paper No. 11/15]. Mannheim: Mannheimer Zentrum für Europäische Sozialforschung.

Herzberg, F. (1968). One more time: How do you motivate employees? *Harvard Business Review, 46*(1), 53–62.

Herzberg, F., Mausner, B., & Snyderman, B. (1959). *The motivation to work* (2nd ed.). New York, NY: Chapman & Hall.

Hoeber, L. (2010). Experiences of volunteering in sport: Views from Aboriginal individuals. *Sport Management Review, 13*(4), 345–354.

Hoeber, L., & Hoeber, O. (2012). Determinants of an innovation process: A case study of technological innovation in a community sport organization. *Journal of Sport Management, 26*(3), 213–223.

Homans, G.C. (1958). Social behavior as exchange. *American Journal of Sociology, 63*(6), 597–606.

Horch, H.-D. (1994). On the socio-economics of voluntary associations. *Voluntas: International Journal of Voluntary and Nonprofit Organizations, 5*(2), 219–230.

Hoye, R. (2007). Commitment, involvement and performance of voluntary sport organization board members. *European Sport Management Quarterly, 7*(1), 109–121.

Hoye, R., & Cuskelly, G. (2003). Board power and performance within voluntary sport organisations. *European Sport Management Quarterly, 3*(2), 103–119.

Kikulis, L., Slack, T., & Hinings, B. (1995). Does decision making make a difference: Patterns of change within Canadian national sport organizations. *Journal of Sport Management, 9*(3), 273–299.

Kim, M., Trail, G.T., Kim, J., & Kim, Y.K. (2009). The role of psychological contract in intention to continue volunteering. *Journal of Sport Management, 23*(5), 549–573.

Kim, M., Zhang, J.J., & Connaughton, D. (2010). Modification of the volunteer functions inventory for application in youth sports. *Sport Management Review, 13*(1), 25–38.

Lamprecht, M., Fischer, A., & Stamm, H.P. (2011). *Sportvereine in der Schweiz* [Sports clubs in Switzerland]. Magglingen: Bundesamtfür Sport BASPO.

Lasby, D., & Sperling, J. (2007). *Understanding the capacity of Ontario sports and recreation organisations.* Toronto, ON: Imagine Canada.

Lawler, E.J. (2001). An affect theory of social exchange. *American Journal of Sociology, 107*(2), 321–352.

Levinson, H. (1962). *Men, management, and health.* Cambridge, MA: Harvard University Press.

MacLean, J., & Hamm, S. (2007). Motivation, commitment, and intentions to volunteers at a large Candian sporting event. *Leisure/Loisir, 31*(2), 523–556.

March, J.G., & Simon, H.A. (1958). *Organizations*. New York, NY: John Wiley.

Maslow, A.H. (1987). *Motivation and personality*. New York, NY: Harper & Row.

Mincer, J. (1974). *Schooling, experience, and earnings*. New York, NY: Columbia University Press.

Misener, K., & Doherty, A. J. (2009). A case study of organizational capacity in nonprofit community sport. *Journal of Sport Management, 23*(4), 457–482.

Morrow-Howell, N., Hong, S.-I., & Tang, F. (2009). Who benefits from volunteering? Variations in perceived benefits. *The Gerontologist, 49*(1), 91–102.

Nichols, G., Taylor, P., James, M., Holmes, K., King, L., & Garrett, R. (2005). Pressures on the UK voluntary sport sector. *Voluntas, 16*(1), 33–50.

Oberwittler, D. (2003). Die Messung und Qualitätskontrolle kontextbezogener Befragungsdaten mithilfe der Mehrebenenanalyse – am Beispiel des Sozialkapitals von Stadtvierteln [The measurement and quality control of context-specific survey data using multi-level analysis – The example of the social capital of suburbs]. *ZA-Information, 53*(1), 11–41.

Onyx, J., & Leonard, R. (2000). Women, volunteering and social capital. In J. Warburton & M. Oppenheimer (Eds.), *Volunteers and volunteering* (pp. 113–124). Sydney: The Federation Press.

Osborne, J.W. (2000). *Advantages of hierarchical linear modeling*. Retrieved from http://PAREonline.net/getvn.asp?v=2017&n=2011

Papadimitriou, D. (2002). Amateur structures and their effect on performance: The case of Greek voluntary sports clubs. *Managing Leisure, 7*(4), 205–219.

Parsons, T. (1951). *The social system*. New York, NY: Free Press.

Penner, L.A. (2002). Dispositional and organizational influences on sustained volunteerism: An interactionist perspective. *Journal of Social Issues, 58*(3), 447–467.

Peters-Davis, N.D., Burant, C.J., & Braunschweig, H.M. (2001). Factors associated with volunteering behavior among community dwelling individuals. *Activities, Adaptation, Aging, 26*(2), 29–44.

Pfeffer, J., & Salancik, G.R. (1978). *The external control of organizations: A Resource dependence perspective*. New York, NY: Harper & Row.

Preuss, H., & Kebernik, B. (2000). Social structure, inducements and opinions of volunteers from Nagano 1998. In M. Moragas, A. Bélen Moreno, & N. Puig (Eds.), *Proceedings of the Symposium on Volunteers, Global Society and the Olympic Movement* (pp. 315–324). Lausanne: International Olympic Committee.

Putnam, R. (1993). The prosperous community: Social capital and public life. *The American Prospect, 4*(13), 65–78.

Quinn, R.E., & Cameron, K. (1983). Organizational life cycles and shifting criteria of effectiveness: Some preliminary evidence. *Management Science, 29*(1), 33–51.

Ralston, R., Downward, P., & Lumsdon, L. (2004). The expectations of volunteers prior to the XVII Commonwealth Games, 2002: A qualitative study. *Event Management, 9*(1/2), 13–26.

Raudenbush, S., Bryk, A., Cheong, Y.-F., Congdon, R., & Du Toit, M. (2004). *HLM 6: Hierarchical linear and nonlinear modeling*. Lincolnwood, IL: International.

Rotolo, T., & Wilson, J. (2012). State-level differences in volunteerism in the United States: Research based on demographic, institutional, and cultural macrolevel theories. *Nonprofit and Voluntary Sector Quarterly, 41*(3), 452–473.

Sakires, J., Doherty, A., & Misener, K. (2009). Role ambiguity in voluntary sport organizations. *Journal of Sport Management, 23*(5), 615–643.

Schulz, J., & Auld, C. (2006). Perceptions of role ambiguity by chairpersons and executive directors in Queensland sporting organisations. *Sport Management Review, 9*(2), 183–201.

Seippel, A. (2004). The world according to voluntary sport organizations. *International Review for the Sociology of Sport, 39*(2), 223–232.

Sharpe, E.K. (2006). Resources at the grassroots of recreation: Organizational capacity and quality of experience in a community sport organization. *Leisure Sciences, 28*(4), 385–401.

Skirstad, B., & Hanstad, D.V. (2011). Understanding gender differences in sport event volunteering. In H. Gammelsaeter & G. Bielons (Eds.), *Book of Abstracts of the 19th European Association for Sport Management Conference* (pp. 491–492). Barcelona: GB Creation & Advice Consulting.

Sport and Recreation Alliance. (2011). *Survey of sports clubs 2011*. Retrieved from http://www.sportandrecreation.org.uk/sites/sportandrecreation.org.uk/files/web/Sports%20Club%20Survey%202011%20Final_lowres2.pdf

Stebbins, R.A. (1996). Volunteering: A serious leisure perspective. *Nonprofit and Voluntary Sector Quarterly, 25*(2), 211–224.

Strigas, A.D., & Jackson, E.N. (2003). Motivating volunteers to serve and succeed: Design and results of a pilot study that explores demographics and motivational factors in sport volunteerism. *International Sports Journal, 7*, 111–123.

Tabachnick, B.G., & Fidell, L.S. (2007). *Using multivariate statistics*. Boston, MA: Allyn & Bacon.

Taks, M., Renson, R., & Vanreusel, B. (1999). Organized sport in transition: Development, trends and structure of sport in Belgium. In K. Heinemann (Ed.), *Sport clubs in various European countries* (pp. 183–223). Schorndorf: Hofmann.

Taylor, P., Barrett, D., & Nichols, G. (2009). *Survey of sports clubs 2009*. London: CCPR.

Taylor, T., & McGraw, P. (2006). Exploring human resource management practices in nonprofit sport organisations. *Sport Management Review, 9*(3), 229–251.

Taylor, T., Darcy, S., Hoye, R., & Cuskelly, G. (2006). Using psychological contract theory to explore issues in effective volunteer management. *European Sport Management Quarterly, 6*(2), 123–147.

Thibault, J.W., & Kelley, H.H. (1959). *The social psychology of groups*. New York, NY: John Wiley & Sons.

Todd, S.Y., Crook, T.R., & Barilla, A.G. (2005). Hierarchical linear modeling of multilevel data. *Journal of Sport Management, 19*(4), 387–403.

Unger, L.S. (1991). Altruism as a motivation to volunteer. *Journal of Economic Psychology, 12*(1), 71–100.

Vos, S., Breesch, D., & Késenne, S. (2012). The value of human resources in non-public sports providers: The importance of volunteers in non-profit sports clubs versus professionals in for-profit fitness and health clubs. *International Journal of Sport Management and Marketing, 11*(1/2), 3–25.

Vos, S., Breesch, D., Késenne, S., Van Hoecke, J., Vanreusel, B., & Scheerder, J. (2011). Governmental subsidies and coercive isomorphism. Evidence from sports clubs and their resource dependencies. *European Journal for Sport and Society, 8*(4), 257–280.

Warner, S., Newland, B.L., & Green, B.C. (2011). More than motivation: Reconsidering volunteer management tools. *Journal of Sport Management, 25*(5), 391–407.

Weisbrod, B.A. (1986). Toward a theory of the voluntary nonprofit sector in a three-sector economy. In S. Rose-Ackerman (Ed.), *The economics of nonprofit institutions* (pp. 21–44). New York, NY: Oxford University Press.

Wicker, P., & Breuer, C. (2010). Analysis of problems using data mining techniques – Findings from sport clubs in Germany. *European Journal for Sport and Society, 7*(2), 131–140.

Wicker, P., & Breuer, C. (2011). Scarcity of resources in German non-profit sport clubs. *Sport Management Review, 14*(2), 188–201.

Wicker, P., & Breuer, C. (2012). Understanding the importance of organizational resources to explain organizational problems: Evidence from non-profit sport clubs in Germany. *Voluntas* (in press). doi: 10.1007/s11266-012-9272-2.

Wicker, P., Breuer, C., & Pawlowski, T. (2009). Promoting sport for all to age-specific target groups – The impact of sport infrastructure. *European Sport Management Quarterly, 9*(2), 103–118.

Wicker, P., Hallmann, K., & Breuer, C. (2012). Micro and macro level determinants of sport participation. *Sport, Business, Management: An International Journal, 2*(1), 51–68.

Wilson, J., & Musick, M. (1997). Who cares? Toward an integrated theory of volunteer work. *American Sociological Review, 62*(5), 694–713.

Index

Note: Page numbers in **bold** type refer to figures
Page numbers in *italic* type refer to tables

For Product Safety Concerns and Information please contact our
EU representative GPSR@taylorandfrancis.com Taylor & Francis
Verlag GmbH, Kaufingerstraße 24, 80331 München, Germany